PROPHECY OF WRATH

(BOOK I)

Spin Off of the novel
Journey to the Great White Throne Judgment

To Casco Senior Card Group
In Loving Memory
of our dear friend and founder
Ellen Applehans

JUDY KAY SCOTT

Judy Kay Scott

1st Edition with editorial changes

ISBN 978-1-63525-327-6 (Paperback)
ISBN 978-1-63525-328-3 (Digital)

Christian Faith Publishing, Inc.
296 Chestnut Street
Meadville, PA 16335
www.christianfaithpublishing.com

Printed in the United States of America

INTRODUCTION

For the Lord Himself shall descend from heaven
with a shout, with the voice of the archangel,
and with the trump of God. And the dead in
Christ shall rise first. Then we who are alive and
remain shalt be caught up together with them
in the clouds to meet the Lord in the air. And so
shall we ever be with the Lord. (1 Thessalonians
4:16-17, KJV)

There is no doubt that the Bible verse you just read describes the rapture, but as to when this glorious event will take place is left opened to interpretation. The pre-tribulation theory is the most widely accepted position; however, it has only been around since the 1800s. This view teaches that the rapture will take place before the seven-year tribulation. Like most Christians, I was taught and believed that position most of my Christian life. But what if this interpretation of the rapture is actually incorrect?

In Christian eschatology, there are five main positions dealing with the timing of the biblical rapture. Views 2–5 are all pre-millennialists interpretations. These four views state that Jesus Christ will return to the earth prior to His literal reign on the earth for one thousand years.

1. Amillennialists believe that God's promises regarding the end-times are figurative and will not be literally fulfilled, particularly the one-thousand-year reign of Jesus Christ on the earth.

2. Pre-tribulationist believe that the rapture will occur prior to the seven-year tribulation but not necessarily immediately before it.

3. Mid-tribulationist believe that the rapture will occur at the midpoint, three and a half years into the seven-year tribulation.

4. Pre-wrath tribulationist believe that the rapture will occur beyond the midpoint of the seven-year tribulation. Their theory is that the rapture will occur right after the sixth seal. However, they believe it will occur before the trumpet and vial judgments (God's wrath). This is a newer view and made popular by the late author Robert Van Kampen when he wrote his bestseller *The Sign*.

5. Post-tribulationists believe that the rapture will not occur until the end of the seven-year tribulation just prior to Armageddon.

God reinsures us in the Bible that Christians will not go through His wrath. However, He never promised us that He would keep us out of Satan's wrath. The pre-tribulation theory was popularized in the 1830s by John Darby and the Plymouth Brethren Church in England. It was further popularized in the United States in the early twentieth century by the circulation of the Scofield Reference Bible. Do we really know what the early churches were teaching before 1830? How about the apostles; what were their views on this subject? What if our modern-day interpretation is wrong? What if the rapture doesn't take place until sometime into the last half of the tribulation?

Can you imagine the confusion and chaos, which would happen if the rapture didn't occur by the time we thought it should? What if there is a seven-year peace treaty with Israel and the rapture hadn't happen yet? The Bible tells us that the contract with death between Israel and the Antichrist will usher in the tribulation. Imagine how overwhelmed and unprepared Christians would be if they had accepted the pre-tribulation theory! Would they be able to survive Satan's wrath? How easy will it be for the world's leader to convince weak Christians to take the mark? The Bible tells us that no one will be able to buy or sell without this mark. People will need food on the table and a roof over their heads. Can you envision parents watching their children starving and not being able to feed them? They must choose between eternal salvation or survival. To survive, they would have to receive a mark on their forehead or hand. This mark would prove their allegiance to the world leader (which in reality is the Antichrist). Without their allegiance, people will be put to death. Jews and Christians alike will be beheaded for Christ's sake.

And the third angel followed them, saying with a loud voice, If any man worship the beast and his image, and receive his mark in his forehead, or in his hand, The same shall drink of the wine of the wrath of God, which is poured out without mixture into the cup of his indignation; and he shall be tormented with fire and brimstone in the presence of the holy angels, and in the presence of the Lamb: And the smoke of their torment ascendeth up for ever and ever: and they have no rest day nor night, who worship the beast and his image, and whosoever receiveth the mark of this name. Revelation 14: 9 – 11.

If you weren't prepared, would you be able to hold out? Would you give in to these pressures, or would you become a martyr for Jesus Christ? There is only one unpardonable sin, and that is the rejection of God! The Bible states clearly that when someone takes the mark of the beast or worships him, they are accepting Satan and rejecting God, which is the unpardonable sin.

The signs are all here. In fact, most Bible scholars agree that the tribulation will be in our generation, in our lifetime! I would love to believe that God is giving us an easy way out. If I had my choice, I would rather the rapture be before the tribulation! However, it is not my decision to make; it is God's. Have we been lulled into a complacent state of mind, given false hope? If not physically, I at least want to be mentally prepared for the possibility that the rapture could take place after the tribulation is well underway.

There is absolutely no doubt in my mind that the rapture will occur. However, years of research and study have given me some uncertainly as to when the rapture will take place. In spite of my uncertainty, I will still keep watching each day for Christ's imminent glorious appearing. Nevertheless, my inquisitive mind, asks, "What if?" The following story, *Prophecy of Wrath,* addresses that possibility. This novel is based on the post-tribulation theory.

1

Bowling Green, Ohio, June 23

Lorraine slowly closed her Bible. She laid her head back against the couch and blinked to fight back the tears threatening to spill out. Her hand caressed the soft leather cover, and she let out a sigh that turned into a sob. Why did the joy and happiness David described with such beauty in the Psalms always escape her?

As the hot tears spilled down her cheeks, the pain she carried in her heart poured out in prayer. *Dear Lord, why am I still hurting so much? You promised that if I gave my burdens to you, you would take them all away.*

Unable to put words to her aching heart, silence filled her mind. She remained motionless for several long minutes before she swiped at the tears, set the Bible on the coffee table, and headed to the bathroom. Maybe the hot water of a massaging shower would relax her.

A half an hour later, she ran a brush through her hair. Her heart felt as black as her hair as she pulled it up into a ponytail. Twenty-six years of a wonderful marriage and she'd ruined it. She bit her lip to keep the tears from returning. *Lord, if it's your will that Thomas never comes back, please give me the strength to carry on without him.*

She shuffled down the hallway, back to the couch. At least, the plaid purple flannel of her favorite old pajamas offered soft comfort. A few punched buttons on the remote brought up the menu of programs showing. Just in time for the news.

She tucked her feet under her and navigated to her favorite local news station. The camera zoomed in on an anchorman with salt-and-pepper hair. An icon of the raging war glowed beyond his shoulders. She was tired of hearing about all the devastation that World War III was pouring out throughout the world. When would it end? During the last few years, the war had been a huge threat to the whole world, especially Israel.

World War III was becoming very intense as of late; however, the war had been going on for decades. It had only been declared a world war three years prior. Most high-ranking officials believed that World War III was triggered by the events of September 11, 2004. It was the attack on the United States soil by the Islamic terrorist group, al-Qaeda. A suicide mission was used to target symbolic United States landmarks. Four passenger airlines were hijacked by nineteen al-Qaeda terrorist to be flown into buildings. The attacks were a series of four coordinated attacks. Two of the planes, America Flight 11 and United Airline Flight 175 were crashed into the north and south towers of the World Trade Center complex in New York. American Airline Flight 77 was crashed into the Pentagon (headquarters of the United States Department of Defense). The fourth plane, United Airline Flight 93 was headed for Washington, D. C. but was crashed in Pennsylvania after its brave passengers tried to overcome the hijackers. Thus, the war that started by al-Qaeda that day killed 2,996 people, launching a war against Islamic terrorists. Since the 9/11 bombings Islamic terrorism has continued to get increasingly more aggressive throughout the whole world.

Lorraine turned the volume up as she heard the anchorman say, "The European Union, United Nations, and NATO together are working on a solution to end all bloodshed in the world. They are drastically looking for a solution to end World War III and bring peace to the world. Prior to the twentieth century, there has never been a war with over one million fatalities. World War I had 8.2 million killed. In World War II, 52 million perished. Since this war was declared a little over three years ago, nearly one billion have lost their lives to the war."

The anchor paused for a moment of reverence. He then continued, "President Omidi strongly believes that peace needs to start where it began—in the Middle East. Earlier today, President Omidi spent hours with several members of the United Nations in Manhattan. They were discussing a solution for decades of fighting between Israel and the Islamic world. Omidi was seeking a long sought-after peace treaty with Israel and the Muslims. President Omidi says that he is convinced that a two-state solution for Israel and Palestine would be crucial to world peace.

The news reporter went on to say, "In other world news, throughout major cities in the United States, Great Britain, Germany, and France, there are demonstrations and rioting in the streets. With war raging in all parts of the world, the economics throughout the world has collapsed. There is widespread hunger and homelessness! Businesses are closing, and unemployment is at an all-time high! Scores of banks and lending institutions have been crashing, leaving their depositors broke! Economists are predicting that this will lead to the one-world money that has been proposed by the European Union. What's next? A one-world government? Could this be the beginning of the end of the world as we know it?"

Lorraine stood, stretched, and then turned to go to the bedroom. She was stopped dead in her tracks when she heard the doorbell ring. Who in the world could that be? She hadn't formed any close friendships since moving to Bowling Green. Both her children lived hours away. Fear gripped her as she slowly stepped up to the door and looked through the peephole. Her mind raced, *It's Thomas!* She was stunned and a bit apprehensive when she saw her estranged husband on the other side of the door! She hadn't seen him since he walked out on her six months earlier. Her smile quickly changed to fear as she looked at her watch. *It's so late, God, please, let the kids be all right! What is so important that he's here at this hour? Oh dear God, please, let him be here to forgive me. Please, let that be the reason he is here!*

Lorraine opened the door and just stood there a moment looking at her handsome husband who she had been missing so terribly. Thomas felt awkward as he stood in the doorway. Then he couldn't hold back a silly grin that spread across his face. He broke out in a nervous laugh.

Lorraine quickly tucked the loose ends of her hair behind her ear as she said, "What's so funny? You've seen me like this before."

"No, no, Lorraine." He laughed. "I'm sorry, I didn't mean to laugh. It's just that you look so darn cute. After six months of not seeing you, I forgot how cute you are!"

"Cute! I remember when you used to tell me I was beautiful." *Oops,* she thought. *Why did I say that?*

"And you are! But right now, cute is what comes to mind. Are you going to ask me in?"

"Oh, I'm sorry. Please, come in. I still have your favorite chair. I really don't know why I didn't throw the old thing out when I moved."

"Okay, thanks. I thought for a minute you were going to leave me out in the hallway," he said with a small nervous laugh as he sat down in the old recliner. "Kind of miss this old chair."

"At least you miss something from our past," she said while looking him straight in the eye. "It's good to see you, even if it is after ten o'clock. You do remember that I'm a teacher, and I have to be up bright and early, don't you?"

"I'm so sorry, Lorraine. I didn't realize the time. I had something on my mind, and it couldn't wait."

"You came all the way from Detroit just to talk? You could have called. What's up?"

"Well, there are a couple of things on my mind that I need to talk to you about. First of all, how have you been?"

She gave him a funny look and replied, "Good as can be expected, I guess. I'm fine, just a little confused and lonely. Other than that, I'm okay. I've been kind of lonely without the kids around." Then she smiled and said, "I even miss you a little. How about you? How have you been?"

"I've been okay. I was fortunate to get into the wind turbine industry, which seems to be the only thing moving these days." When Lorraine didn't laugh at his attempt at humor, Thomas said, "Just a little windmill satire. You know, moving...windmill. Anyway, the business world is very different. It's vicious out there!"

"I know! I really don't see how you can survive in it. You have such a gentle, caring nature. The business world is a dog-eat-dog world. It's not in your nature. That's not you, Thomas."

"It is not easy to deal with, believe me. I have to do a lot of traveling for the job. It can get real lonely out on the road."

"Well, it was your decision to leave the ministry."

"Yes, I know, but I couldn't continue feeling the way I did. I just couldn't do my job as a pastor. And there was our breakup." Thomas nervously changed the subject. "How about your job? I hear in the news that there are many schools closing. Are you still working?"

"Yes, Thomas. I have been one of the lucky ones, thanks to God. However, there are days when I question the lucky part."

"What do you mean? I thought you loved teaching."

"Yes, I still enjoy teaching, but there is so much decay in the student's moral behavior nowadays."

"I don't doubt that! The entire world's morals have gotten worse."

"The morals of students have been going downhill ever since they took God and prayer out of the schools several years ago."

"Yeah, remember I told you then that without God in the schools, it would be all downhill from there?"

"I sure do."

"Heck, I remember my dad telling me about when he was back in school, the teachers could discipline children in the classroom."

"That's the truth! Now you can't even look cross-eyed at them, or you will be terminated. Most teachers don't even have control over their classrooms. I have been lucky. I still can maintain some respect from my students. Once in a while, I throw a little something in about God, but I have to be careful because it's a public school."

"That's a big risk, but I'm proud of you!"

"Thanks."

After a couple awkward long minutes of silence, Lorraine spoke up, "Have you heard anything from the kids lately?"

"Yes, every now and then, but they know how disappointed I am with them. It broke my heart that Linda dropped out of Bible college and married Harold."

"Yeah, I know what you mean. I'm afraid Harold has not been a very good influence on our daughter. It sounds like all they do is party. She was never like that before he came along."

"No, she wasn't. Linda was always a good kid...and Scott! I can't believe that he would take a job bartending, especially after just graduating from the seminary."

Lorraine gave Thomas a sympathetic smile and said, "I know how disappointed you must be. You were so proud when he wanted to follow in your footsteps and become a pastor."

"Yes, of course, but I guess I'm not a very good role model anymore."

"You're not the only one. So a...do you see the kids much?"

"No, not like I would like to, but I call them periodically. I'll always be there for my kids no matter what."

"What if they disappoint you as I did. Will you abandon them too?"

"Come on, Lorraine, that's different."

"If you say so. You still haven't told me the real reason why after six months, you show up at my doorstep."

"Like I said, I wanted to make sure you were okay. And, yes, there is something important that we need to talk about."

"Are you trying to say that you missed me?"

"Yes, of course, I miss you, but I'm still having a problem with you being unfaithful."

"I never meant for that to happen, Thomas!"

"Maybe not, but the devil finds a weak spot and hits people where they are the most vulnerable. Of all the women in the world, I never would have believed that I couldn't trust you!"

"It was only a lunch date."

"Lunch date? You drank wine with the jerk, and he kissed you! Then the two of you made plans to meet again when I was out of town. After what happened on the first lunch date, I shudder to think what would have happened on the second."

"But it didn't happen! Thank God he stopped me by allowing that car accident!"

"So you're saying that without God's intervention, you probably would have committed adultery?"

"No, I don't know! What about you? We've been apart for a while. Have you been faithful to me?"

"Well, at least we're separated. That's what I need to talk to you about."

Lorraine's heart skipped a beat. With a big frown on her face, she said, "I was afraid of that."

"There is this one coworker that I have gotten close to. We go out to dinner occasionally, mostly business dinners. We talk a lot. Mostly, we share stories about our broken marriages. Lorraine, I don't want to hurt you, but you need to know. Our feelings go beyond friendship."

Lorraine felt as if she was being swallowed up in some big dark hole. She didn't want to hear anymore, but she couldn't help but ask. "Thomas, are you telling me that you are having an affair with this woman? Are you about to ask me for a divorce?" she cried out.

"A divorce has certainly crossed my mind. I'm confused. To tell you the truth, I don't know what I want. That is why I needed to let you know before my relationship with Diane goes any further. I owe you that much."

"Thomas, please, stop! Don't you remember how you counseled couples that were having marital problems? You told them that unless there was adultery or abuse, divorce should be out of the question. I didn't commit adultery!"

"No, but adultery was undoubtedly on your mind."

"No, I don't think so. But even if it was, after the accident, I was a new person in Jesus Christ. He awakened me to the sin in my life. You know that I changed. You could see for yourself the changed attitude that I showed the church members. I was there for you when our marriage began to crumble. I understood why you were having such a hard time accepting what I did. I don't mean to make excuses, but my unjustifiable jealousy was part of the reason that I did what I did. I hated when you counseled single women or the ones on the brink of divorce."

"The stupid thing about that, Lorraine, is that you had no reason to be jealous! You knew that I always had a third party with me when I counseled any woman. Heck, you were with me most of those times!"

"I know, I know! I don't know what I was thinking. I guess, I just let my imagination run wild."

Thomas hesitated for a moment and then asked, "What about you? Have you been seeing anyone since I left?"

"Absolutely not! I told you that I am a new person in the Lord. We are still married in God's eyes! As long as there is hope for us, I will stay true to you."

Then tears began running down Lorraine's cheeks as she said, "It sounds like you are saying that there's no chance for us. Thomas, are you in love with this woman?"

"To tell you the truth, I'm not sure what my feelings are for her. I know I enjoy her company a lot. I've just been so lonely."

"Maybe you have been lonely for me! Have you ever thought about that?"

"Yes! Of course, I have missed you. I have tried desperately to forget you. Maybe that is why I became interested in Diane. Her situation was similar to mine. Diane's husband left her for another woman. That was his second affair that she knew of."

A loud clap of thunder rumbled and turned the intense conversation to the weather at hand.

"Looks like we're in for a big storm," Thomas said.

"I guess so. I've never seen such radical weather in all my life," Lorraine said as she began to shiver.

"Not only here but all over the planet. The amount of earthquakes, floods, hurricanes, and tornadoes are astronomical! Each year has been worse than the last."

"I know! There was no warning this was coming tonight! That's just how crazy the weather has been."

Then the heavens let loose as a deluge of rain came down. Next, the lights flickered a couple times, and then the electricity went out. Lorraine scrambled around the coffee table and found a lighter that she had left there because of all the recent outages. She lit the candles that were on the coffee table. The glowing candles seemed to soften the edgy mood between the estranged couple.

"Thomas, I really think the accident was part of God's plan. He made me come to my senses! It was His way of teaching me how my choices would affect my whole life, that every sin has a consequence."

"You are absolutely right about that! We are both experiencing consequences from the sins that we have committed. You betrayed me with another man, and I couldn't find it in my heart to forgive you."

"Yes, it has ruined our marriage."

"Not only that, but look at what happened to our kids! Scott lost his desire to go into the ministry. Linda dropped out of Bible college and married a nonbeliever."

"Oh, Thomas, if what we have done in the past has hurt our kids so much, what do you think it will do to them when they find out you are involved with another woman? That you want a divorce?"

"It shouldn't come as a shock to them. We've been separated for a long time now. I'm not sure how they will take it. That's why I have made plans to go with Scott on a fishing trip. I'm going to tell him then."

"Oh really! I would think that we would be telling the kids together."

"No. I need a good man-to-man talk with my son. I told you I am not sure what I want. Maybe he will have some insight. Besides, I just need to have some time alone with him. We aren't as close as we used to be."

"What about Linda?"

"I'll wait until after my trip to talk to Linda. Maybe, we can talk to her together when I get home from the trip. I plan to do a lot of soul searching while I am gone. I'm not taking this decision lightly, Lorraine."

Feeling a bit of relief, she asked, "Where are you going?"

"You know our sportsman son, he has some place all picked out. One of his friends was telling him about some area in Upper Michigan where the fishing is great! Scott says where we are going will be remote and desolate."

"Sounds rugged but fun."

"It will be good getting away with just my son. Good thing he was an Eagle Scout, at least one of us will know what to do. I never had the time to go camping or fishing that much."

"Will you let me know your decision when you get back?"

"Yes, of course, I will. I hope to have answers when I return, and I promise to share them with you."

The electricity finally came back on, along with the reality of what Thomas had told her. Trying to hold back tears, Lorraine sadly said, "Well, maybe you ought to go. I need to get up early for school in the morning."

"Yeah, you're probably right. I need to be up early in the morning too. I've got quite a ride ahead of me."

Lorraine slowly walked her estranged husband to the door and opened it for him. Thomas kissed her lightly on the forehead and told her good-bye. She turned away quickly and shut the door behind him. With her back tightly pressed against the door, she sluggishly slid to the floor in a heap of tears.

2

Detroit, Michigan, June 30

Thomas silenced the annoying alarm clock. It was five thirty in the morning, and he was thoroughly enjoying his comfortable bed. This would be the last time to enjoy the comforts of home before he left on his primitive camping trip with his son. Thomas had never been that interested in camping or fishing, but perhaps, that was because he never had time for it. On the other hand, Scott was an avid outdoorsman. He was excited about spending a week roughing it in the wilds. They would be exploring ghost towns of the Keweenaw Peninsula, in the Upper Peninsula of Michigan's world famous "copper country."

He hit the snooze a couple of times and then thought he'd better get up. He rolled out of bed and rubbed his eyes. He was suddenly wide awake as he thought about the day ahead of him. This was the day he was leaving to go on a camping trip with his son!

He kneeled down beside his bed and prayed. *My dear precious Lord and Savior, thank you for all your blessings. I thank you for my comfortable bed that I am about to give up for a bed of dirt and sticks. Thank you, God, that I am able to have this special week with my son.*

I pray that we won't get too lost in the wilderness. Please, keep us safe from all harm, including the black bears, which the UP is so well known for. Above all, Lord, please, bless the time that Scott and I have together. Please, let us bond again and get back the closeness that we once had. Please, help me get answers to the questions that are burdening my heart. Help me make the right decisions. Should I forgive Lorraine? Or should I start a new life with Diane? May your will be done. Amen.

Thomas took a quick shower, towel dried his muscular large physic, and then blow dried his graying dark-blond hair. After shaving and brushing his teeth, he threw on a pair of shorts and a tee shirt that he had laid out the night before. He grabbed a couple packed suitcases and was out the door. The directions were simple. Go west on highway ninety-four for about one hundred and thirty-eight miles. Get off at the Kalamazoo exit toward South Haven. Thomas was eager as he turned into the mobile home park where his son lived. From the visor, he pulled down a map that he got off Google with directions to where Scott lived. On the bottom of the page, he had scribbled some drawings. The crude drawings showed several rows of rectangles, which represented mobile homes. From Scott's directions, he had put a big red *X* on one of the rectangles, with Lot #48 written underneath it.

It was 9:15 when Thomas pulled up to his son's mobile home. In the driveway was a fully packed jeep waiting for the adventure ahead. Before Thomas could get out of his car, Scott came rushing out of the trailer, yelling, "Hey, Dad, I thought you would have been here an hour ago. What kept you?"

Scott got his striking good looks from his mother. He had the same black hair and sapphire-colored eyes that his mother had. He even had her big dimples. His tall, muscular build was from his dad.

Thomas was out of the car and halfway up the deck when the two clinched in an embrace. After a big hug, Thomas joked back,

"What do you think, I hot rod like my son? I thought I made good time."

"What time did you leave?"

"I was in the car and rolling by six."

"Did you have any breakfast?"

"No! I didn't take the time. Besides, you said that you were treating me to breakfast when I got here."

"Jump in the jeep. I'll take you on a tour of South Haven. There is a nice restaurant downtown. If it was later, I could have taken you out to the eatery that I bartend at."

"My son, a bartender?"

"Come on, Dad, let's not start this trip with an argument. It's a real nice place. A lot of class. The tips are terrific, and the food is delicious. They have excellent perch!"

"Well, maybe another time. Do you need any help packing?"

"Heck no! I was packed and ready to go last night. Now we just need to take off!"

Thomas settled into Scott's jeep, and they were on their way. As they drove through the town, Thomas asked, "So, son, what possessed you to move to this little spot on the map?"

"Just wait until my tour is over and you'll understand."

Scott was right; his dad was very mesmerized by the quaint little town of South Haven with its scenic sandy shores and its thrashing Lake Michigan waves.

The two men enjoyed the magnificent view as the waves hit upon the red lighthouse. The town had everything in it that Scott wanted. It had fishing excursions and plenty of boating. In addition to all of the outdoor fun, the town had unique stores and eateries. There also was a lot of history in the town. There was the hundred-year-old lighthouse, a one-of-a-kind maritime museum, art center, and numerous galleries. Scott promised his dad that the sunsets over Lake Michigan were the most beautiful sunsets he'd ever seen.

"Why do we need to go any farther? This would be a great place to vacation."

"No way, Dad, I live here! I want to get away! You can save that vacation for another time. Right now, you and I are on our way to a rustic wilderness adventure."

Scott drove them to one of his favorite restaurants, where they enjoyed a hardy breakfast. With stomachs full, father and son were off on their great quest to the Upper Peninsula of Michigan.

By six thirty that evening, the two men spotted the huge bridge off in the distance. Scott had been across it a few times, but this would be Thomas's first time. He was overwhelmed at the majesty of the great Mackinaw Bridge.

"Wow, Scott! I am impressed. I had no idea that this bridge was so long."

"Yeah, it's the longest suspension bridge, with two towers between anchorages, in the world."

"How long is it?"

"It's 8,614 feet."

It was a busy time of day. The bridge's lanes were all packed with traffic. Scott was quiet as he started to drive across. Halfway through the ride, he looked at his dad. He could see the fear in his dad's face.

"You aren't afraid of this little old bridge, are you, Dad?" Scott teased.

Not wanting his junior to think he was frightened, he answered, "No, of course not. You said 'old.' How old is this bridge?"

"Well, if I remember my history lesson right, the construction started May 7, 1954. It took three and a half years and the cost of five men's lives that worked on the bridge. It opened November 1, 1957."

"Man, that's quite old."

"You really don't have to worry. The bridge is well maintained. I've heard that as soon as they get done painting it, they turn around and start all over again."

"It just seems with all these vehicles that the weight would be too much for the bridge to hold up."

"Dad, trust me, it is perfectly safe. However, if you feel better, you're not the only one who gets scared crossing it. They have this service where bridge employees actually drive people across in their own cars just so they can take a trip over it."

After a long pause, Thomas broke the silence, "Where are you planning on us camping tonight?"

"Here by the bridge! Just the other side of the bridge there is a beautiful, primitive campsite. I have stayed there before. You'll love it!"

Soon after crossing the bridge, Scott turned left on highway two. After going a short distance, he turned onto a narrow road, which led to the campground. They drove past many campsites until Scott stopped to the perfect spot. From there, they could see the fabulous Mackinaw Bridge with all its glory. It was getting dark, and the bridge was lit up like a city. It was breathtaking.

That evening, they relaxed by the campfire, watching the lights from the bridge and an occasional boat sailing past. It was the most peaceful evening Thomas could remember.

Scott leaned back in his lawn chair and said, "This has to be the most gorgeous view I've ever seen."

"I agree, son. I believe with all those lights on the bridge, it has to be the most gorgeous site that I've ever seen. It is man's workmanship at its best, combined with God's beauty all around it."

A few hours later, they let the campfire burn itself down. Left were only the hot coals of the burned out logs that gave off its amberoid glow. It had served its purpose. The campfire took the chill out of the night air and had produced a delicious meal of steak and potatoes. Scott could put most camp cooks to shame with his tasty camp culinary skills. With full stomachs, the two men sat around the fire pit watching the hot ambers glow. After a period of serene quietness, Scott spoke up, "Penny for your thoughts, Dad."

"Son, you really don't want to know," Thomas said with a slight chuckle in his voice.

"Sure I do! What's on your mind?"

"I've just been mesmerized by watching the coals of the campfire. When I look down into the fire pit, I see an ancient city. A city that is full of fire and hot coals. Son, it makes me fantasize about what hell might be like."

"That's kind of out there, Dad. Are we having a guilt trip or something?"

"Maybe," he said as he laughed a little.

"Come on, if there was ever anyone who didn't have to worry about hell, it's you."

"Scott, you know that I have always been sure of my salvation. I have preached to the congregation more times than I can count how they can be sure of their salvation. God tells us that once we are saved, we are sealed with Him forever. After we accept His Gospel message that he died, was buried, and arose for our sins, we are purchased by God. He guarantees to bring us to Himself. I know that! However, I feel so unworthy. God called me to be in the ministry. Now look at me. I'm so out of fellowship with God right now. Lately, I have felt that God turned His back on me, but in reality, I have turned my back on Him. I have always preached that God wants us to forgive others as He has forgiven us. I believe that with all my heart, so why can't I forgive your mother?"

"Dad don't be so hard on yourself. At first, I blamed you for the breakup, but then Mom told me what happened. I have to admit, I am disappointed in both of you. In fact, that's why I don't want anything more to do with being a pastor of a church."

"Oh no, son, you don't mean that! You worked so hard to go through Bible college. You are now an ordained minister. Surely, you wouldn't give up your calling?"

"You did, didn't you?"

"Yes, but I had a reason to."

"So do I. The father that I admired and wanted to be just like since I was a boy has given up on serving God. You have always been my hero, so why should I continue doing something that you don't care enough about?"

"Scott, you are your own man. You have to answer for yourself, regardless of what I have done. You need the Lord, son!"

"Dad, I've grown away from Him, don't you understand? I work in a bar, for Pete's sake! I date a lot of hot ladies. I kinda like my new lifestyle."

"I'm so sorry that my actions have affected you so much."

"No, it's okay. I'm just growing up. I need to explore life a little."

"It's called backsliding."

"I'm sorry, Dad, but aren't you doing the same?"

The two men sat there silently, pondering about what the other had said. It was the last thing they said to each other until they put out the embers and said good night.

3

Upper Michigan, July 1ˢᵗ

The UP's crisp, cold morning air woke Thomas and Scott up early. In spite of a few aches and pains, Thomas was feeling exhilarated. Scott made a fire, and soon, the aroma of fresh coffee filled their campsite. After breakfast, Scott spread the map out as he and his dad planned the next leg of their journey. They decided that they were going to take highway two to Manistique. Then north on ninety-four until they got to highway twenty-eight toward Munising. From Munising, they would continue on twenty-eight until they came to highway forty-one north, which would lead to Hancock where they would be seeing their first ghost town. It was the remains of the Quincy Smelter mine, which sits on the shores of Portage Lake.

Scott studied the map and then said, "We've got another long day's drive ahead of us. Looks like approximately two hundred and sixty-five miles."

"Okay, so if we stop for lunch and have a couple of breaks to stretch our legs, we should be at Hancock by three or four o'clock this afternoon?"

"Yeah, I'd say so, Dad."

All packed up and ready to roll again, Thomas and Scott left the bridge behind and started out once more on their big journey. It proved to be a very fun and interesting ride. Shortly after noon, they spotted a large sign, which read, FEED THE BEARS.

"What do you say, Dad, shall we stop and check out the bears?"

"Absolutely! Sounds like fun to me."

Scott pulled into a restaurant parking lot next to the sign. "Looks like a good place to eat. Besides, we can get some information about feeding the bears," Scott said anxiously.

The two men jumped out of the jeep and went into the restaurant. Scott asked the waitress about feeding the bears. The waitress told them that all they needed to do was to buy a six-pack of soda and feed it to the bears.

The bears were caged in a large facility behind the restaurant. When the men walked up, three bears came running to their feeding tubes in the fence. Scott and Thomas got a kick out of the way the bears guzzled down the sodas. Within a half hour, all the pop was gone, but they couldn't believe all the fun they just had feeding the bears.

The next attractions they came upon were the beautiful waterfalls along the way. These were excellent spots to stop and stretch their legs while admiring the waterfall's beauty.

Around seven-thirty that afternoon, they finally got to their destination. They pulled up next to a small river about twenty miles from Hancock and started setting up their campsite.

"Man, I'm sure glad we decided to stop and eat dinner at that restaurant earlier today," Thomas said as he and Scott finished putting the tent up.

"You got that right! What did they call those things we ate?"

"Pasties. The waitress said that the Upper Michigan Yoopers are famous for making them. They sell them at most of their restaurants up here."

"Yeah, they are really good. Kinda like a big potpie but not so moist. It tastes really good smothered in ketchup."

Tired out, the men barely said another word as they got their camp set up. Supper that evening was a cold sandwich. Scott set the alarm for five, and then they both snuggled down in their sleeping bags for the night.

The next morning came early, but after another hardy camp breakfast, they were ready to hit the road again. Today would be another long ride, with a lot of exploring and hopefully a little fishing thrown in. Their first stop would be in Hancock where they wanted to find the Quincy Mine Smelter. It was an easy task; there were signs all over. It was quite the tourist attraction; however, at this time, it was closed due to hazardous material warnings. It was owned by Franklin Township and was undergoing treatment to remove the hazardous materials.

Thomas and Scott stopped into a small diner near the site. The locals were happy to share their town's rich historical past, and soon, the stories began to fly. A few were related to some of the original miners. An old-timer told them, "My granddad worked in that mine. It was built back in 1898. Quincy Mine is the only copper smelter site remaining in the Lake Superior region."

A man across the table spoke up, "Our township is hoping to restore it soon. It is an important historical site."

A third man joined the conversation, "The smelter used heat chemical processes to turn copper ore into ingots, that's metal castings. The ingots were then sold and shipped to factories where they were turned them into products such as copper wire or tubing."

Anxiously, Scott asked, "Are there any other old mining towns that you would recommend for us to see?"

The elderly gent laughed and said to him, "You just go north of here, and you'll see more than you could visit in a lifetime, eh."

"You got to be kidding?" Thomas said.

"Well, George likes to exaggerate a bit, but there are a lot of them," the man from across the table commented. "I don't think they all have been discovered either. I wouldn't doubt if there are some of their ruins in desolate places, and they are forgotten about. Some of the well-known ones are straight up on highway twenty-six. There's Cliff, Phoenix, Central, Delaware, and Mandan."

From across the room, a different man chimed in, "Don't forget the one on the other side of the peninsula called Gay."

"Okay, sounds good," Thomas said to the man. He then turned to his son and said, "Looks like a great trip ahead of us."

"Yeah, it sure does. What about the fishing, guys?"

"Best fishing in the world, eh." The old man chuckled.

"Where are you fellows from?" one of the younger Yoopers asked.

"We're originally from New York City, but now, we live in Lower Michigan. My son lives in South Haven, and I live in the Detroit area."

"That's farther than a crow can fly," the old Yooper said.

"Yes, you could say that, but we are having the time of our lives, right, son?"

"Absolutely!" Scott agreed.

The waitress served them their meals, which were pasties again. They thanked her, had a short prayer, and then began enjoying their hardy meal.

There were big grins on the Yoopers' faces as they noticed how much the "trolls" (lower Michiganders) were enjoying their famous pasties.

"You know, there's a lot of history behind those good-tasting pasties," the elderly gent explained. "They were brought over by the copper and iron miners from Cornwall, England, in the early 1850s. They were made for holding in the hand. They didn't have time to eat them off a plate in the mines. The miners reheated their pasties underground. Some kept them at body warmth in a chest pocket. Others set them on shovels and held them up to the light of a lantern, eh!"

Thomas and Scott thanked the Yoopers for all their information and stories and then set out for more exploration. Twenty miles later, they were pulling up to a village called Cliff. It sprang up from the fabulous Cliff Mine established in 1844. The mine closed in 1873. The two men walked around, looking at some old foundations and rock piles, but little remained.

The next stop was Phoenix, located about four miles north of Cliff. At the site of the old mine, there was only a few old buildings and a church standing. There was a plaque in front of the church that read that the church was built in Cliff in 1858. It was dismantled in 1899 and reassembled in Phoenix, where it is to this day, and is called Church of the Assumption. The Keweenaw County Historical Society purchased it and restored the church to what it was like over one hundred years ago.

Thomas and Scott walked inside the unlocked church in reverence and awe. It was simple, but at the same time, it had a spiritual beauty. Thomas could imagine the old copper miners and their families singing in the wooden pews. The old gospel song, "He Leadeth Me" popped into his head, and it lingered for some time.

Thomas walked up to the altar and fell on his knees in prayer. With tears filling up in his eyes, he prayed out loud, "Dear Lord Jesus, please, forgive me. You have led my path to the ministry, and I have let you down. God, give me the strength I need to pick up your cross and follow you again. I have backslid so far. Please, help me get back to You. I have hurt my family so much by not being able to forgive. You have been a perfect example of forgiveness, but I haven't been able to forgive my wife. Please, let me learn from your examples."

Hearing his prayer, Scott came up behind his dad and put his hands on his shoulders. The tears were trickling down both father and son's checks. When Thomas' prayer was over, he stood to face Scott. Then the father and son gave each other a big hug.

Later that afternoon, when they were through exploring the historical town of Phoenix, they decided that they would drive toward the next stop, the ruins of the Central Mine. It was only four miles from Phoenix. When they got there, they were overwhelmed again by the historical enchantment of an era gone by. There were several buildings still standing. Most of them looked like they were occupied, but they were all locked up. Scott had guessed that they were vacation homes. It was awesome to see some of the old mine's buildings and rock piles. It definitely had the look of an old ghost town. An old Methodist Episcopal Church had a sign on it. It had been built in 1868 and had recently been restored. The area had a beautiful river, the Eagle River, and a waterfall. The guys thought they were in heaven. This would be the ideal place for them to camp that night. There also was the Eagle River lighthouse to explore in the morning.

By six thirty, the campsite was set up, and their fishing lines were in the water. That evening, Thomas and Scott stuffed their stomachs with as much fresh fish as they could hold.

"Nothing tastes better than fresh caught fish in the UP!"

"You've got that right, Dad," Scott said as he lay down on the ground, staring up at the stars, holding his stomach and moaning.

"Unfortunately, fish are becoming scarce all over the planet," Thomas said as he looked out over the river.

"Yeah, Dad, with all the massive oil spills in the last few years, I can understand why."

"Then there's the increasing dead zones in our seas and major rivers."

"Yeah, I heard about it on the news. They said that at least half of the fish in the seas have been depleted."

"That's right, son. I also heard that it is caused from agriculture. The fertilizer they spray on the crops is toxic. It flows down into the mouths of rivers and goes into the sea causing low concentrations of dissolved oxygen. It's poison!"

Scott sat up and said, "Dad, we are definitely living in the last days! Doesn't it say in Revelation that all the fish will die?"

"Yes, it does. It's in the sixteenth chapter." Thomas grabbed his Bible that he kept handy in his backpack. "I'll look it up."

Thomas opened his Bible to Revelation and flipped to chapter 16. "Yeah, here it is, Revelation 16:3–4. 'Then the second angel poured out his bowl on the sea, and it became blood as of a dead man. And every living creature in the seas died. Then the third angel poured out his bowl on the rivers and springs of water, and they became as blood.'"

"Wow! That is powerful stuff, and it's all beginning now. I'm a little confused. Doesn't that occur at the second bowl judgment, which is after the seven trumpets?"

"Yes, Scotty, you're right. What we are experiencing now is the beginning of birth pangs that will lead to the seven-year tribulation. That means the rapture is at our doorsteps."

After their intense talk, the two men cleaned up the campsite from supper. They threw the remains in a garbage pail that was left for campers and travelers. Then they put out the last of the campfire's embers and were ready for a peaceful night sleep.

A couple of hours had gone by when Thomas and his son were abruptly awakened by a crash!

Scott jumped to his feet and gasped, "What the heck?"

Thomas was now up, and both men were peering out of the tent flaps. They both froze as they saw the terrifying sight of a big black bear eating out of a turned over garbage can. The bear must have heard them. With his hackles standing up on the back of his neck, the bear turned toward the two campers and let out a loud, deep growl.

4

Bowling Green, Ohio, July 1

Lorraine was spending another boring, depressing Saturday morning alone in her apartment curled up on her couch. Her mind wondered to Thomas and their kids. She missed doing things with her family. They were now all scattered in different directions.

Maybe I will give Linda a call later, Lorraine thought. *I should get dressed, comb my hair, but why? What for?*

When the doorbell rang a couple times, Lorraine was startled. She jumped up, spilling coffee all over. *Who could that be?*

Lorraine looked through the peephole, and to her surprise, there stood Christina Nelson, her best friend since middle school. They hadn't seen each other in over four years. Christina was her first real friend. Although coming from an affluent family, Lorraine had been an introverted child. It was Christina who helped her come out of her shell.

Christina's friendship came with a whole group of friends. One in particular was Tommy Perkins. Thomas and Lorraine married soon after they graduated from college. Christina married Dan Nelson, and they became missionaries. Christina's family stayed at the Perkins home when they were on leave from the mission field. Their church helped sponsor the Nelsons, so they were also missionary guests at their church.

Lorraine quickly unlocked the door, and the two friends threw their arms around each other. Christina cried out, "Oh, Lorraine, it is so good to see you! It's been too long."

"I've missed you so much, Christina! Come, sit down and excuse the mess. I jumped when I heard the doorbell and spilled my coffee all over. You remember what a klutz I am, right? Please, excuse me while I clean this mess up."

"I'm sorry I startled you. I should have called first. Thought I'd surprise you instead."

"Oh gosh, no! You know how I love surprises. I'm so happy you are here!"

Lorraine finished cleaning up and then asked, "May I get you a cup of coffee and a piece of cake?"

"Oh, yes! Thank you, I can use some. It was a long trip. Well worth it though. I have missed you so much, and I really needed to talk to you.

"Oh yes, please, tell me everything! We haven't been together for so long. There's a lot of stuff that I need to let you know also."

Christina let out a long sigh and then commented, "Lorraine, I am hurting so much, and I am having such a hard time coping. I'm sorry to lay this all on you right now because I know you are going through a rough time yourself, but I needed my best friend."

"You don't have to apologize, I need you just as bad. Now, please, tell me what's been happening. Are you home on leave from Africa?"

"No, not exactly. I'm home, but this time for good."

"Have you guys retired, or are you still doing missionary work? I have so many questions. Like, how is Dan and the kids? Are they here in Bowling Green with you?"

Christina's eyes filled with tears as she shook her head no. "Stop, stop, Lorraine," she cried out. "I'm not home because we retired! My family's not with me! And Dan! Dan's not here anymore at all! Dan has passed away!"

"What! Oh no, Christina, it can't be! I am so sorry!" Lorraine put her arms around her friend and embraced her until she had control of her emotions once again. Then she asked, "What happened to him?"

"As you know, Dan and I were running a primitive hospital in a remote part of Africa. There was so much sickness and death there. We lost two or three people a day. If it wasn't AIDS, it was the bird flu, Zika virus, or something else as bad. This past year, we had to start an orphanage for all the children who had lost their parents. It was horrible! It was so difficult trying to spread the Gospel to those poor souls while most of them were just struggling to hang on to life."

Christina had to stop for a moment to get control. She then continued, "Dan was working so hard to try to save those poor, dear people. His body was run down. I tried to get him to slow down, but he wouldn't. He contracted the bird flu and died three months ago."

"I don't have the words to tell you how sorry I am. Whatever I can do for you, please, let me know. Do you need help with the kids or anything?"

"No, not really. The girls are at my mother's in New York. Daniel is away at college. He came back to the states last year and started going to a Bible seminary. He wanted to go into the mission field like we did. Forgive me, Lord, but I don't want him to go. I don't want anything to happen to my son like it did to Dan!"

"I know how you must feel, Christina, but you must have faith that God will protect him."

"He didn't protect Dan!"

"I know, but it's all in God's hands. We are not to question Him but to have faith in Him. Jesus said in the Bible that all things work together for good for those who love God. God has a purpose for everything that He does. Maybe He was rewarding Dan's years of hard work and dedication. Just think, Dan is sitting with the Lord at this very second."

"I know, but I miss him so much!" Her voice raised. "What about me! How could God do that to me?"

In a soothing tone, Lorraine said, "I know, honey." Then she cuddled her in her arms once again. In an attempt to get Christina's mind off her deceased husband, Lorraine asked, "Christina, tell me about your girls. They must be all grown up by now."

"Yes, at least they think so. Dan is twenty. Rachael is eighteen, and Michelle is sixteen. The kids are devastated by their father's death, but at the same time, they are happy to be back in the States."

"Where are you staying?"

"The girls and I are staying with my mother."

"Do your parents still live outside of New York City?"

"Yes, Mom does. Dad is gone too. He passed away last year."

"I'm so sorry, I didn't know that. After we moved from the New York suburbs, we were so caught up in church business we weren't able to keep up with our old friends."

"I know. We were over in Africa when it happened. I couldn't even get home for his funeral."

"That had to be devastating for both you and your mother."

"Oh, yes! She was really lonely until I was finally back home. However, I am afraid I was more of a burden to her than a help. I've been a real mess since Dan's death. I had a nervous breakdown. I wanted to stay and help those poor people, but I just could not handle it! I fell to pieces. I deserted those orphans and all those sick people! I let them down, as well as I let God down."

"Christina, no one can blame you. After all, you just lost your husband. You are in mourning! I'm sure they found a replacement for you."

"But I'm a Christian! I should have had strength through Jesus."

"And He will give you strength, but first, you need to finish your grieving."

"Lorraine, don't you understand? I'm mad at God for taking my Dan from me!"

"I know, you really don't mean that. I know how much you love the Lord. You were the one who led me to Jesus back when we were kids. You are only lashing out because you are in pain."

"I can't help it! What can I do? I'm so angry!"

"I suggest that you talk it out with God. Declare to him why you are angry with Him. Maybe, you should write it down and verbalize it aloud. Next, you actually need to turn to God. Tell Him that you know that He is an all-omniscient God, that He knows everything and is in control of everything. Let Him know that you are aware that He can do whatever He pleases. Then finally realize that your prideful rebellion against Him is sin. Confess it to the Lord, and ask His forgiveness. Remember that you are not God's judge. He is never wrong."

"Of course, you are right, Lorraine. I'll try."

"You know, I was pretty angry with God myself after Thomas left me. I did a lot of praying and worked it out with Him. He has given me the strength that I need to get through it."

"Oh, I'm so sorry. I've been crying on your shoulder when you also have heartbreak to deal with. I heard about you and Thomas from a member of your last church. I was trying to track you down, that's how I found out. I cannot believe that the two of you could have ever broken up. I thought you guys had the best marriage ever. You were in love since you were teenagers. Remember when we were kids, and I was so jealous of what you and Tommy had? What went wrong?"

"It's a long story. I'll try to explain. You remember our first church?" Christina nodded in agreement. "Well, it was a small country church where I was close to everyone. I loved it there."

"Yes, I remember Dan and I visited you there a few times."

"I also had a wonderful teaching position at the local school that I loved. Then Thomas gets this great offer from a much larger church in Syracuse with lots of benefits. Thomas was so excited, how could I have burst his bubble? Besides, it would mean a better lifestyle for our kids. There was no way that I could say no. All I could do was pretend I was happy and go along with it."

"Oh yes, Dan and I visited there a couple of times too. It was a very impressive church. It was at least triple the size of your first one."

"Yeah, and it grew larger after we got there."

"I can understand that. Thomas is a very good pastor."

"Yes, he was! I still can't believe that he has left the ministry."

"Oh, I'm sorry to hear that."

"Yeah, me too. The world lost a good pastor."

"You still love him a lot, don't you?"

"With all my heart and soul."

"So what happened?"

"It was all my fault, Christina. I sinned! It all really started when we moved to the new church in Syracuse. I missed our old congregation and wasn't happy with all those new strangers. Then on top of that, Thomas asked me not to take another teaching position. He said that there was too much to do in the new church. He had me leading the ladies missionary meetings and teaching a Sunday school class. I even was involved with setting up the seniors group and, after that, a singles group! Of course, Thomas kept busy all the time with church business too. His fingers were in everything also. Unfortunately, that left little time for us. Now that I look back, it didn't leave us much time for the kids either. On top of that, I was jealous of Thomas and other women."

"Thomas! That doesn't sound like the Thomas I remember."

"No, it isn't! I am so ashamed of myself. I know now that he wouldn't have cheated on me! However, jealousy got the best of me. It bothered me when he counseled women, especially the single ones. That was stupid because I should have known that he would never put himself in a compromising position. There was always another member in the room when he counseled women. I even counseled with him once in a while. I don't know what I was thinking."

Christina had an inquisitive look on her face as she asked, "So your marriage broke up because you were jealous?"

"Not exactly. Unfortunately, it didn't stop there. My jealousy made me feel unattractive as a woman. There never seemed to be any time for intimacy between us anymore. Our lives were filled up with church business. At the end of the day, we were usually too tired to share our love. I was a fool, Christina. I let my insecurities turn into infidelity."

"Oh no, you didn't, did you?"

"Yes, I'm afraid so. I didn't mean for it to happen. It was after I bought some furniture from a flirtatious salesman. When the furniture was delivered, there was a note from him. It was an invitation to join him for lunch."

"I would hope you said no?"

"I regret to say that I didn't. After a long struggle within my soul, I drove to the restaurant. When I got there, I almost turned the car around and went home. I felt the restaurant was pulling me in, or perhaps it was that young, handsome salesman that found me attractive."

"Sounds like Satan was up to his dirty work again and leading you into temptation!"

"You're right! This guy was so attentive toward me I felt flattered. At that time of my life, I felt that I needed the reassurance that I still was desirable."

"I can't believe you didn't see through him! You didn't let it go any further, did you?"

"Unfortunately, yes, I did. It was a dark, romantic candlelit restaurant with a bar."

"Of course. Casanovas always have to have the forbidden juice to lure their unexpected prey."

"Yeah, well, he ordered a carafe of wine and then poured me a drink. I felt too embarrassed to turn it down. What would he think of me? Stupid me was feeling too sophisticated, sipping wine out of a tall stemmed glass. It was so sweet tasting. How could something that tastes so good be that bad for you? Unfortunately, I had at least three glasses of that forbidden juice."

"But you don't drink! Do you?"

"No! That was the first and last time that I ever drank alcohol."

"So! What happened next?"

"He kissed me."

"What! You have got to be kidding me! You tried to stop him, didn't you?"

"No, not exactly. I tried to pull away from him, but I still was enjoying the dangerous game we were playing."

"Tell me that's all that happened, right?"

"Not quite. I made a really big mistake. I was not thinking straight and mentioned that my husband was going to be out of town for the weekend. He got me to promise to have dinner with him that following Saturday night."

"But of course, you changed your mind the next day when you sobered up, right?"

"I wish! I know that I should have had the sense to say no, but I didn't. I had an argument within my soul about if I should go or not. Well, that rotten devil on my shoulder seemed to be winning the argument."

"Oh no!"

"Well, thanks to God, that dinner date never happened. Do you remember that accident I wrote you about?

"Sure, the one that put you in a coma? You almost died, right?"

"Yes. My heart had stopped for a while, and I was clinically dead."

"How horrible!"

"Well, maybe not so much. I swear, Christina, it was God's plan for me to have that accident. He showed me what sin would do to my life!"

"That was a drunk driver that hit you, right?"

"Yes. He was just a teenager. His mother and younger sister were also in the car. All three died. We heard later that their car reeked with alcohol, and there were traces of marijuana."

"Oh how horrible!"

"Yes, it was. I have prayed so many times that they were at least saved. However, the evidence did not point that way. I fear that they faced the Lord at the great white throne judgment and were sent to hell. That whole ordeal was parallel to the dream or vision I had when I was clinically dead. In my vision, I was that woman with those two kids."

"Wow, that's kind of supernatural."

"Yeah, it was as if God intervened. I believe He gave me a vision of how my life could have ended up if I hadn't make the decisions back when I was a young teen to accept Jesus Christ as my Savior. Maybe if I hadn't been saved in my teens, I might never have been."

"Not to change the subject, but speaking of visions, I had a really strange dream. That is one of the reasons why I had to see you. The dream included you, Thomas, and many people I didn't know. It was really weird. It was as if we were all hiding away in some mountain valley. The Antichrist had just been revealed. We were all scared that he would find us and chop off our heads. It was so real!"

"Christina, you were having a nightmare. You know that you are a Christian and that you will be raptured before the Antichrist ever signs the seven-year peace treaty, which ushers in the tribulation.'"

"Yes, of cours e, I know all that, but in my dream, the rapture hadn't happened yet. We were living in the tribulation period."

"You mean like the theory, mid-tribulation?"

"Yes, something like that."

"You've been reading too many fiction novels! Believe me, it is just a nightmare. God is not going to let us live through His wrath. Thomas has been a Baptist pastor for years, and he stands by the pre-tribulation view."

"Yes, I know. Dan and I had always believed that too. Matter of fact, most churches preach pre-tribulation. I just do not understand why it seemed so real or why I would be dreaming something like that. It really felt like God was trying to tell me something. I guess it has something to do with my breakdown, I don't know."

5

Eagle River, East of Phoenix, Michigan, July 2

Thomas and Scott both froze at the sight of a bear! Their eyes were glued on the hairy big black creature as they peered out of the tent flaps.

"Now what do we do? Did you bring a gun?" Thomas whispered.

"I don't own a gun," Scott whispered back.

"Well, how about pepper spray?"

"No, Dad, no pepper spray either."

"What the heck are we going to do?"

"I don't know! I heard if you make a lot of noise, you can scare them off."

The bear took another step toward them and let out a ferocious deep growl.

Overwhelmed with fear and anxiety, the men looked at each other. They both opened their mouths at the same time and let out a loud yell. The bear dropped down on all fours, turned his big head, and lumbered off. They both fell to their knees in relief. Thomas prayed out loud, "Thank you, Lord!"

"I don't know about you, but I'm shaking too much right now to go back to sleep."

"Me too. I don't think I could sleep either."

"I think it would be a good idea to make a fire. Maybe that will keep the bear from coming back, just in case he decides to take another look at us."

"Good idea, Scott."

"I'll fix us a cup of hot chocolate. Maybe that will calm our nerves." Soon, they were sitting in front of a blazing campfire, sipping on a mug of hot chocolate. Thomas said as he stared into the flames, "It's weird, but just before that bear woke us up, I was having a strange dream."

"Oh yeah, Dad, what about?"

"Well, it's kind of confusing, but it had something to do with those ghost towns we have been visiting. It was like you and I were in charge of a bunch of people, and we were all living in some old building. At one point, I saw all of us in an old, abandoned mineshaft. It seemed as if we were trying to hide from something or somebody."

"Wow, Dad, that is weird. I guess exploring the old towns and mines have given you a wild imagination, huh?"

"Yeah, I guess it has. The crazy part was, I believed the person we were afraid of was the Antichrist."

"What! Where did something like that come from?"

"Darned if I know! It's crazy! I have never worried about the Antichrist before because I know I am saved. I've believed all my life that Jesus will rapture his Church before any Christian will even know who the Antichrist will be. I have always believed that the rapture happens and then the seven-year tribulation. Then the Antichrist will come to power. He will reveal himself three and a half years later."

"Yeah, Dad, but what if, what if you are wrong about the timing? What if the rapture doesn't happen until the tribulation is already underway or even at the end of it? You know, like the theories of mid-tribulation, pre-wrath, or post tribulation."

"No way, son. I've believed that way all my life. Heck, every Christian I've known believes that the rapture will be before the Tribulation! If you are suggesting that one of those views could happen, forget it. That's impossible. The Bible is clear about that. In first Thessalonians 5:9, KJV, it says, 'For God did not appoint us to wrath, but to obtain salvation through our Lord Jesus Christ.'"

"Well, the Pre-Wrath believers interpret that verse to mean God's wrath. Their theory is that God's wrath will come about when he pours out His seven vials of wrath. The Antichrist lashes out his wrath at the midpoint of the seven years. Therefore, they believe that most of the last half of the tribulation period is not the wrath of God. It is the wrath of Satan. So maybe that means that while Christians won't escape the Tribulation, Jesus will save them from His wrath. After the midpoint, the Antichrist will reveal his evil self and will persecute both Christians and Jews. That is Satan's time of wrath."

"Do you really believe that one of those theories could be true?"

"Well, my mind is opened to the possibility."

"So what is the difference between pre-wrath and the post-tribulation theory?"

"One of the main differences is the timing of the seven trumpets. The late author Robert Van Kampen taught the pre-wrath theory. He made this view popular when he wrote his bestseller, *The Sign*. He wrote that the rapture will occur sometime after the midpoint of the Tribulation but before any of the trumpet judgments.

"I had a professor who believed strongly in the post-tribulation view. He offered extra credit for listening to a renowned televised pastor's series on the subject. They were very informative and interesting. At that time, he believed that five of the trumpets had already been sounded. He said that the sixth would sound ushering in World War III. So now, according to him, the sixth trumpet has now been sounded. He claims that the seventh trumpet will be the trumpet of the rapture. The last trump! It tells us in Revelation 11:15 that at the sound of the seventh trumpet, the world's kingdoms will become the kingdoms of our Lord."

"Now, son, that makes no sense at all. That's impossible! Nowhere in the Bible does it say that! None of the trumpets have sounded as yet. It does say that the first trump in Revelation 8:7 brings the world's greatest fire. The second trumpet in Revelation 6:8 and 9 brings the greatest oceanic disturbance. In Revelation 8:10–11, the third trump is the world's greatest pollution of water. In verses 10 and 11, you find the fourth trumpet, the greatest darkness. In chapter 9:1–6, the fifth trumpet brings the greatest pestilential invasion. Next, the sixth trumpet, there's the greatest army, and the last trumpet is the greatest storm. All this will occur after the rapture!"

"Of course, I'm very familiar with those verses. The seven trumpets of Revelation. However, in those DVDs, the pastor has some compelling proof that those first six trumpets have already come to pass. I'll have to loan you my set."

"Yes, I'd like to see them. Sounds like the man has a convincing argument, seeing he has your interest."

"Good! After you view them, Dad, we can discuss them in more depth."

"Sounds good, Scott. But for now, let's get back to my reasons for the timing of the rapture. What do you think about Revelation 3:10, KJV? 'Because you have kept my command to persevere, I also will keep you from the hour of trial, which will come upon the whole world, to test those who dwell on the earth.'"

"Maybe God is referring to the hour of trial as the time of God's wrath, not Satan's. The Bible also says 'Then shall they deliver you up to be afflicted, and shall kill you: and ye shall be hated of all nations for my name's sake. But he that shall endure unto the end, the same shall be saved. Matthew 24:9 & 13.'"

"Scott, I just can't believe that God will let us go through all of that."

"Dad, what about the parable of the ten virgins?"

"Well, in that parable, the virgins made provisions for what they would need to meet their bridegroom. Some were prepared, while others were not. In this parable, Jesus was telling us to watch and make sure we are ready for His coming because we do not know the day or the hour of his return."

"Yes, that's why it makes me nervous that everyone is so content about the easy way out." In a mocking voice, Scotty said, "Jesus will rapture us away from a world filled with trials." He continued on, "But what if! What if he wants us to be prepared to go through the Antichrist's persecutions? Perhaps his parable of the ten virgins is a warning to His church. The Bible tells us that we won't know the day or hour, but it says that we should know the season! Perhaps, we have been misled by today's churches, missing the signs that God had intended us to know. What if we need to make a life or death choice for Jesus? People need to be prepared! They would need to be prepared to survive the end-times. More important if this is true, they need to be prepared not to take the mark of the beast under any circumstances!"

"Well, yeah, son, that's true about those days. If any man worships the beast or takes his mark, he will perish. A Bible passage comes to mind: 'If anyone worships the beast and his image, and receives his mark on his forehead or on his hand, he himself shall also drink of the wine of the wrath of God, which is poured out full strength into the cup of His indignation. He shall be tormented with fire and brimstone in the presence of the holy angels and in the presence of the Lamb. And the smoke of their torment ascends forever and ever; and they have no rest day or night, who worship the beast and his image, and whoever receives the mark of his name.' That is found in Revelation 14:9–11, KJV. According to the Bible, anyone who receives the mark will drink the wrath of God and be tormented forever. It doesn't say 'temporarily' tormented. It says tormented forever. Therefore, if you receive the mark of the beast, there are no second chances.

"Scott, these pre-wrath and post-tribulation positions are what the Bible talks about that will happen in the last days. There will be false prophets spreading lies. Today, some churches do not even believe in hell! Others do not believe that our Lord Jesus died on the cross and arose again the third day! They say that Mary, the mother of Jesus, was not a virgin. They also say that Christ was married. You cannot believe all this stuff people come up with. There are all sorts of lies coming out of churches and universities nowadays. Like the Bible tells us, in the last days, there will be false teachers."

"Yes, Dad, I know that, but this is not a new idea! Matter of fact, the pre-tribulation doctrine originated in the nineteenth century. It is a product of the twentieth century! John Darby, founder of the Plymouth Brethren movement, was given credit for the original pre-tribulation doctrine in 1830. According to my professor, the post-tribulation doctrine goes back to when the apostles were preaching to the early churches. Who better to know the truth than those who got it firsthand from Jesus himself?"

"You surprise me! I didn't know that you were so heavy into Bible prophecy. I'm ashamed to say that I never preached in depth about that subject. The last church board that I served under frowned upon the mention of it."

"I had a couple classes on biblical rapture theories in my last year of college. My last professor was the stout believer in the post-tribulation theory."

"You almost sound like he convinced you."

"Well, it was quite compelling. The class opened my mind to the thought that it could be possible."

"Scott, I don't think you are done with the ministry yet. You sound like a preacher."

"I guess this has been bottled up in me since college. You mentioned it, and it all came back. I was quite engrossed in the subject when I was studying it."

"Well, son, I'm really tired. I believe I can sleep now. How about you?" Scott agreed.

6

Ghost towns of the Keweenaw, July 3

In spite of their late-night intruder, Thomas and Scott were up early the next morning looking forward to their next adventure. The first stop was the Eagle River Lighthouse, but before they reached the door of the lighthouse, an old gentleman walked out to meet them. The friendly elderly man said to them, "This lighthouse isn't open to the public anymore."

"Oh, okay. Are you the groundskeeper," Scott asked?

"Yep! My wife and I live here. We have been granted permission to live here until we die."

"That is really nice. Can you tell us when this lighthouse was established?"

"Yes, sir, I can. It was in 1854."

"That is really cool. I've noticed that many of the historical sites aren't opened to the public anymore. One of my buddies was up here a couple of years ago. He told me that there were lots of historical places that give tours, but we haven't seen many."

"That's right, young fellow. The tourist business has been going downhill for the last several years. With the war, bad economy, and world famine, people are having trouble just existing. What's the last you paid for gas, young fellow? The cost of living up here is getting unbearable. Our heating bills are killing us! Many of the families are closing up their homes and moving south. The summer residents stopped coming up."

"I hear you," Thomas said. "I bet a guy could pick up some of this land quite reasonable now."

The old man laughed and said, "I suppose you are right, if a guy was foolish enough to have a mind to."

"Well, thanks a lot for your time and information," Scott said as he shook hands with the elderly gentleman. Thomas gave a nod good-bye, and they left for the next historical spot.

Scott drove only a few more miles when he came upon the village of Central Mine. The village's mine was opened in 1854 and was a top copper producer. The original old town remains were located on the west side of highway 41. As they drove through the town, they saw several newer buildings. There were a couple of buildings that looked occupied; others looked abandoned. They saw the remains of the mine's buildings and rock piles that were left as they drove through. There was an old church with a plaque that read that it was built in 1868. The church looked like it had been restored.

The next stop on the tour was Delaware. It was hard to spot the once little settlement amongst the forest. There still stood one very old house, but only some cement foundations were left. There still was a plaque on the village's old mine that read it was built in 1874.

After leaving Delaware, they drove four more miles down the road. As they approached, Thomas pointed to a post, which read, Mandan. Scott jerked the steering wheel quickly to the right so he wouldn't miss the small dirt road. A few miles further, they approached the ruins of what once was Mandan. At one time, it had a population of three hundred, but then the mine had hardships. Now only a couple old abandon houses were left standing.

The men were awestruck as they scouted around for evidence of old building sites. There were old buildings that were left from a once thriving mining town. Scott pulled up to one of the old houses. They both got out of the jeep to explore. It was in bad repairs, so they were careful walking about.

"Dad, check out the foundation where part of the house has come down. It probably was one of those double houses that were built in those days."

Thomas and Scott got back in the jeep and drove slowly around the woods road looking for more evidence of an area that once was a village.

"Not too much left to see in this area. It's mostly all grown up with trees. Let's head out," Thomas suggested.

"Yes, I agree. I think we have seen all there is to see here. What do you say we head back on 41 toward Delaware? When we drove past it, I saw a sign for Mt. Gratiot. I noticed on the map that it's a fairly large mountain. It's 1489 feet in height. Also there's a large lake near it called Gratiot Lake. Maybe we can find a good spot near there to camp tonight."

"Sounds great to me, as long as we can get some old-fashioned fishing in."

Just past Delaware, Thomas saw the sign to Mt. Gratiot. It led them south down a dirt road toward the mountain. The road was bumpy and hilly, so the ride took much longer than what they anticipated. Thomas clutched the dash of the jeep and said, "Maybe we should turn back. There's barely a road here!"

"Come on, Dad. Remember, we're out for the adventure, right? Why do you think I own a four-wheel drive? Besides, this is a road. I saw it on the map. Granted it's not much of a road, but it is on the map."

They were in the foothills and about midway across the west side of the mountain range when Scott noticed a little pull off next by a creek. He pulled up and stopped. "Is this not the most perfect spot to set up camp or what?"

"Heck, yeah. It really is a peaceful place."

"Dad, would you please check on the map and see what the name of this creek is?"

"Sure thing, son. Let's see. Okay, yes, here it is. It's called Sucker Creek."

"I've heard that there's northern pike, walleye, and smallmouth bass in the creeks and rivers around here."

"Wow! Just the kind of place we are looking for. Oh boy, we're going to eat fish tonight!"

As they jumped out of the jeep, the men's breath was taken away by the beauty of the terrain. It was the ideal place to fish and camp for the night. Down the creek about fifty feet away, they spotted a doe and her two fawns drinking at the edge of the creek. Minutes later, a large fish jumped high above the surface of the water and made a big splash as it dove back into the creek. It was a beautiful site with Mt. Horace Greely to the west and Mt. Gratiot snuggled next to it. Admiring the scene, Thomas commented, "This is truly God's country! Have you ever seen a more beautiful place?"

Overwhelmed with its beauty, Scott agreed, "No, never! It's paradise."

"Yeah, I could stay here for the rest of my days and be perfectly happy."

"Me, too, Dad, but I would need someone a little closer to me than you. Not that we aren't close, Dad, but you know what I mean—a special lady."

"Like this Sheryl you told me about on our first night of camping?"

"Yeah, I guess so. Right now, I feel she is the one. She's really a nice girl, Dad. I would have introduced her to you back at my trailer, but she was sleeping when you got there. She had worked the late shift the night before."

"So are you in love with Sheryl?"

"I never thought about it before, but yeah, maybe I am in love. I guess, if I was to be stranded on this river, I would like to be here with Sheryl. How about you, Dad? Would you like to be stranded here with a special woman? Maybe, Mom?"

Thomas ignored the question and said, "Come on, Romeo, let's get our camp set up and get our fishing gear. We can't catch fish just talking."

After a relaxing evening of catch and release, the guys managed to save out enough walleye for a fish dinner that melted in their mouths. This time, they buried all the remains. They didn't want another uninvited guest that night. After dinner, they shared their day's experiences. Sitting by the campfire, Thomas commented, "Going through that village of Mandan was a really a lot of fun. I had a great time!"

"I agree it was quite a venture, but you know the best part of today was the fishing. I never fished a better river in all my life! I can't believe the size of those fish!"

They put their campfire out early that night. It had been an exciting day, and they were exhausted.

The next morning, the men were awakened by the wilderness sounds of birds, frogs, and an occasional loud splash made by a large fish in the river. The men eagerly rolled out of their sleeping bags, ready for another day of fishing. They weren't disappointed; fishing was great that morning, and they soon caught their limit of walleye.

After their tasty lunch of walleye, the fishermen were eager to cast out their lines to try their luck at catching some smallmouth bass. As they were fishing, Thomas drew back to cast out his line when he noticed a quick flicker of light out of the corner of his eye. Thomas spoke out loud, "What the heck was that?"

Scott was down the creek a ways but heard his father and called back, "What did you see, Dad?"

"I don't know."

Scott walked over closer to his dad and looked up toward Mt. Gratiot where his dad was staring. "What are you looking at, Dad?"

"I'm not sure, son. First, I thought it was the sun, but the sun is higher over there." Pointing to the mountain range, Thomas said, "Over there, by that second peak. Do you see anything that could be reflecting light?"

Scott squinted his eyes as he focused toward where his dad had told him. "Yes! I do see something! What do you suppose it could be?"

"I don't know," Thomas said. "Maybe there's a piece of metal up there or something that the sun is reflecting off of."

"That's possible, but more than likely, it's something like glass, or what if it's a distress signal? What if someone is lost up there or hurt? Maybe they're trying to send a distress message by using a mirror. Most people know that mirrors make the best light reflectors. We learned how to use them in boy scouts in case we got lost."

"Well, yeah, it's also taught in a physics 101 class."

"That too" Scott laughed. "Maybe we should investigate. I'd hate it if someone needed help, and we left them stranded."

"You're right, son. We can't just leave someone if they really need our help."

"Well, Dad, are you up to the adventure of your life?"

"Couldn't we just call the authorities? There's no roads leading up there, not even a two-track that I can see from here."

"Where's your sense of exploration? Besides, it could be nothing. I can't see getting the police out here if it's a false alarm. I don't want that embarrassment, do you? It's not that far up there, Dad. We can probably drive closer, and then maybe hike to it in less than an hour or two."

7

Bowling Green, Ohio, July 2ⁿᵈ and 3ʳᵈ

Christina spent Saturday night at Lorraine's. They talked until midnight. There were numerous old memories to talk about. They talked about their teenage years, Christina's life as a missionary, and Lorraine's life as a pastor's wife and finally talked out they called it a night.

It was Sunday morning, and the women were up early. Lorraine had invited Christina to her church for the morning worship service.

In another part of the city, Lorraine's daughter was getting off a bus. Linda was dragging a large garbage bag filled with her clothes. From the bus station, she grabbed a city transit bus and took it to her mother's apartment. Her nerves were frayed as she rang the doorbell several times. She shouted aloud, "Mother! Mother, where are you?" *Darn, where can she be? Oh, yeah, it's Sunday. She's at church. Darn, what am I going to do? I don't have any money. Dang, there's nothing to do but wait here until she gets home.* Linda reasoned that she didn't have a choice. She knew that church should get out around noon. So she figured that she'd have to wait there for an hour or so as tears welled up in her eyes.

On their way to the car, Lorraine said, "The sermon was long today but good!"

"Yes! It was such a treat to go to a church that still preaches the Gospel. Most churches nowadays are simply a community event or an entertainment center."

"Yes, I'm lucky I found it. It's small, but I always can feel the Lord's presence when our pastor preaches, and we sing the old-time gospel songs."

"Thank you, Lorraine, for inviting me. I truly enjoyed it."

"It was my pleasure! It was nice going to church with my best friend again. It reminded me of when we went to church together as teenagers."

"Yeah, but with a few more aches and pains." Christina laughed. "It was very nice. I enjoyed it."

"What time do you have to be at the airport?"

"Three o'clock."

"Good! We will have time for lunch. I'll take you to one of my favorite restaurants."

The ladies really enjoyed their meal together as they recalled their many years of friendship. Time slipped away from them. Lorraine glanced at her watch.

"Oh, no! Look at the time! Christina, we better go. I don't want you to miss your flight. I really wish you didn't have to go back to New York so soon."

"Me too, but Mom is getting old. I've already left her to watch over my two teenagers long enough. I have put too much responsibility on her shoulders lately. She was so good with the girls when I wasn't coping very well."

"Why don't you and the girls relocate here in Ohio? You don't have any ties there, do you?"

"I'd love to! I hate living in New York. The economy has gotten so bad that the crime has really gone up." She shivered and then went on, "There's always threats of nuclear bombs. I hate living there and raising my kids there. It would be great living near you again, but there is Mother. I am afraid it would be hard for her if we left again. She really doesn't have anyone close to her anymore."

"Bring her with you!"

"I've tried to persuade mom to leave, but she won't. I could never get her to leave her home. You would not believe all the keepsakes that woman has got. She has a house full of fifty years of memories, and she would not part with a one of them! Also, she visits my dad's grave at least once a month. She says she has to go there to talk to him."

"Oh, that poor dear!"

"Yeah, it's sad. She misses him like I miss Dan."

Lorraine drove Christina to the airport with only minutes to spare. They hugged, cried a little, and then said their good-byes. On the drive home, Lorraine felt sad. The thought of her empty apartment made her feel that much more, lonely.

When Lorraine approached the door to her apartment, there was Linda sleeping in front of it. She had her bag of clothes propped under her head for a pillow and was curled up against the door.

"Linda! What are you doing here? I didn't know you were coming."

Lorraine's voice startled Linda awake. She jumped up and rubbed her already swollen red eyes.

"Nice to see you too, Mother," she said sarcastically.

"Sweetie! I am happy to see you too, but I was not expecting you." Lorraine quickly unlocked and opened the door for her distraught daughter. "If you would have let me know you were coming, I would have stayed home or left a key where you could find it."

"Where have you been, Mother? I've been sitting at this door for almost five hours! I didn't have any money to go anywhere. I didn't even have enough to go get something to eat or drink, and I really have got to go to the bathroom!"

"I'm sorry, my poor baby. Didn't you know that I'd be at church?"

"Yeah, I figured that out, but I thought that you would have gotten home a little after twelve."

"Normally, I do, but Christina Nelson came for a visit, and she went to church with me this morning. I took her out for lunch and then to the airport. Honey, I'm sorry, but I didn't know you were coming!"

"I didn't know either until late last night. I didn't get a chance to call. Harold and I were screaming and yelling so much at each other I just had to get out of there. I couldn't take anymore of Harold's abuse, so I left. I had just enough for transportation, so I grabbed a bus, and here I am."

"Has Harold been physically abusing you?"

"No, not that kind of abuse! He has pushed me around some, but he hasn't hit me yet. I can't stand all the fighting and yelling. He wants to go out clubbing all the time and then wonders why we cannot pay the bills. I am so sick of him, Mother."

"Well, honey, I'll fix you a sandwich while you freshen up."

Soon, Linda and her mom were sitting at the small bar, which separated the living room from the kitchen. While Linda was in the bathroom, her mother had sat out some bread and lunchmeat.

"Linda, I only have a one-bedroom apartment," she said as she spread the bread with mayo for her daughter.

"I know, Mother! I don't mind sleeping on the couch for a while. I'll go out job hunting tomorrow, and then we'll be able to afford a two bedroom."

"Linda, I am not sure about all of this," her mom said as she handed her the sandwich. "You have been married for less than five months. Maybe you and Harold can still work it out."

"Mother! If I recall, you and Dad didn't want me to marry Harold in the first place."

"Well, yes, you are right about that, but you did make a commitment. You made a promise to Harold in the presence of God."

"That's just it, Mom. I'm not even sure if there really is a God anymore! If there is, I'm sure He wouldn't approve of the life that I have been living with Harold."

"Linda! I cannot believe you would question that! You know darn well there is a God, young lady! You were raised in church all your life. Your dad was your pastor, for heaven's sake!"

"Well, yeah, Mom, I also remember Dad saying several times in his sermons that it doesn't matter if you were raised in church or if your parents were Christians. The decision is up to the individual."

"Yes, that's correct, but you told me that you were saved, and you were baptized!"

"Mom, I was just a kid, that's all I knew back then. Did you ever think you might have brainwashed me a bit?"

"Linda, I can't believe the way you are talking! You were twelve years old when you were baptized. That certainly was an age for accountability."

"Maybe, but a person can change their mind, can't they?"

"Yes, but you went a couple of semesters to Bible college before you dropped out."

"My point! Why do you think I dropped out of college?" Linda asked sarcastically. "I was tired of trying to live the 'holy life.'"

"You started running with the wrong kinds of friends and started going to clubs, that's why!"

"Well, you know, Mom, I'm an adult now, and it is my life to do what I want!"

"That's quite an abrasive attitude for a girl who has no place to go but to her mother's."

"I'm sorry, Mom. I'm just trying to be honest."

"I know, honey. I'm sure that it didn't help when your father and I separated. I realize how upset and confused you must have been."

Linda stuffed the remaining bite of her sandwich in her mouth, nodded her head, and said, "Yeah, I guess so."

"Let's go sit in the living room, and you can tell me how you feel about it, okay?"

"Yeah, I guess."

Linda sat at one end of the sofa with her feet tucked under her. Lorraine sat at the other end. Lorraine cleared her throat and started the conversation. "Linda, I feel like you need the whole truth about what happened between your father and me." Lorraine went on to tell her daughter all about how she felt about changing churches. She even told her about the luncheon date with the furniture salesman and about the date that never happened.

Linda was shocked and hurt by her mother's confession. With tears filling her already swollen eyes, Linda cried out, "How could you, Mother? How could you do something like that to Daddy? My mother! The prim-and-proper pastor's wife, cheating on her husband! How could you do that to my dad?"

Lorraine tried to put her arms around her daughter to comfort her, but Linda pulled away. "Linda, please. It is not as if I committed adultery! I was wrong, but it didn't go that far."

"No! You said yourself it didn't happen because God stopped you with the accident. That if he hadn't stopped you, you're not sure what would have happened, right?"

"Yes, you are right," Lorraine shamefully whispered.

"You know darn well that the Bible says that if it is in your heart, you have already committed the sin!"

"Linda, we all are sinners. We have all sinned and came short of the glory of God. None of us are perfect! That is why Jesus died for us on the cross. I have confessed my sin to God and have asked for His forgiveness. God has already forgiven my sins through the precious blood of His Son.

Linda, I was out of fellowship with the Lord because I did not realize my sin at first. When I did I confessed my sins and repented. I'm still ashamed for what I did, but I know in my heart that God has forgiven me!"

"How can you live with yourself?"

"Only with the help of God's grace."

"No wonder Daddy left you. Now I understand why he could not go on pastoring a church. You must have crushed him."

"Yes, I suppose I did. He was such a godly man. He really tried hard to forgive me. He wanted to. I know he prayed about it."

"Maybe it's not too late. Maybe he still will forgive you, Mom."

"I'm afraid, Linda, it might be too late. Your dad has been seeing another woman."

"No! Daddy wouldn't do that."

"Linda, he's been lonely. We have been apart for six months."

"But neither one of you have filed for a divorce yet, right?"

"No, but I believe that your father was trying to prepare me for that at his last visit, just before he and Scotty left for Upper Michigan. He told me that he needed to make a decision either to forgive me or to start a life with his new friend."

"Daddy has never said anything about another woman! I cannot believe that he would keep something like that from me. Does Scotty know?"

"He's telling him on their camping trip."

"No matter what you have done, I don't want you guys to get a divorce!"

Lorraine reached over to hug her daughter again. This time, Linda was opened to her mother's embrace, but then the phone interrupted their special moment.

"Hello, Harold," Lorraine answered into the receiver as she looked over at her daughter.

Linda shook her head from side to side. "No! I don't want to talk to him!"

"Harold, Linda isn't ready to talk to you yet."

"Mrs. Perkins, please, will you ask Linda to talk to me? Tell her I love her, and I'm sorry," Harold pleaded.

Lorraine put her hand over the receiver.

"Linda, Harold really wants to talk to you. He says he's sorry."

"No! I do not want to talk to him. Hang up!"

"Okay," Lorraine said as she took her hand off the receiver.

"I'm sorry, Linda doesn't want to talk right now. If she wants to talk later, she'll call you. Good-bye, Harold."

"That jerk!" Linda screamed out as Lorraine hung up the phone. "How dare he call me here after what he said to me! I don't ever want to see him again!" Linda yelled as she burst into tears.

After a good cry, Lorraine asked, "How about a cup of hot chocolate? That always made you feel better when you were a little girl."

"Sure, Mom. That sounds good," Linda said between sobs.

Lorraine got a mug of hot chocolate for both of them. Soon, Linda mellowed out as she sipped on the steaming cup of chocolate.

"Makes me feel like a little girl again, having hot chocolate with my mom. That was the happy times of my childhood."

"What do you mean by that, 'the happy times'?"

"You know, before we moved away from our first church."

"I thought you were happy at the new church. Our new home was beautiful and much larger. It was in a much better neighborhood than the last place. You were so popular with all the teens at church. The teen group was five times bigger than at our old church."

"That was the time you changed, Mother."

"What do you mean?"

"We were so much closer when we were at the little church. You always had time for me then, but when we moved, you and Daddy were both too busy with church business to care about what Scotty and I did."

"No, Linda! That is not true! We always cared very much about what was going on with you kids!"

"Oh yeah, there was always a bunch of rules I had to follow. When I broke one of them, that's when I would get your attention, not when I was being good. I can't remember how many times I was told to be a good example to the other children because after all, I was the pastor's daughter. I hated that! I just wanted to be a regular kid. I'm not perfect!"

"I'm sorry I put so much on you, Linda. I really wasn't aware you felt that way."

"Of course not. You had too many other people to care about in the church. I felt like I didn't even want to go to church anymore."

"If you felt that way, why did you choose to go to a Bible college?"

"Because Scotty did. I wanted to follow in my big brother's footsteps. The two of us were always close. We had to be. You and dad never had time for us. Besides, I thought it was expected of me."

"I am so sorry, sweetie," Lorraine said as she began to wipe tears from her own eyes. "I never wanted to make you feel that way. The new church was so large it took so much of my time. Then later, I was so consumed in my own unhappiness. I was a very selfish mother! Please, will you forgive me, baby? I'm so sorry!"

"Yeah, of course. I understand it a little bit better now that I know what you were going through. It's not like you neglected us or anything."

"You had so many friends I thought you wanted your space. That's no excuse, but that's how I justified it, I guess."

After getting the past off their shoulders, mother and daughter embraced once again, and all was well between them. The day went fast, and before long, it was late. Lorraine looked at her watch.

"Where has the time gone? It's almost ten o'clock. It's time for the news. Then I need to get ready for bed. I'll have a classroom of rowdy teenagers to deal with tomorrow."

Lorraine turned on the television. The scene was in complete chaos with people running for their lives while dust and smoke was overpowering them. The reporter was talking fast as he tried to describe the disaster that had happened in New York's subway system. There had been five suicide bombers in various locations throughout the city's system. It had been at the subway's busiest time of day, and hundreds of lives were taken. There were film clips of ambulances loading the dead and injured.

"My parents! Christina's family!" Lorraine gasped.

"Mom, calm down. Grandma and Grandpa would never take the subway. I'm not real sure about Christina's family, but maybe you should give them a call."

"I've got to get my parents out of New York! I knew this was coming. What's next, a nuclear bomb? New York is the most vulnerable city, but there is no place in the world safe anymore!"

8

Mt. Gratiot and on the Sucker Creek, July 4

Thomas and Scott jumped into the jeep and drove to the two-track that led up the Gratiot Mountain. They drove for about a quarter of a mile until they found another two-track that led even further up. They drove until they were nearly to the top of the mountain. Thomas shouted out, "Stop here! I think the light came from over there."

When the jeep came to a sudden stop, they jumped out. Thomas pointed the way as Scott pushed through trees and under-brush. They followed a deer path that led in the direction of where Thomas had seen the flicker of light. When they were almost to the top of the mountain, Scott noticed a large piece of broken mirror on the ground. He picked it up and showed it to his dad. Together, they determined that this must be what they had seen from down below.

Thomas shook his head in disgust. Then with a bewildering look on his face asked, "With all the excitement and anticipation, it was a mere piece of glass? You have got to be kidding me. What a waste of time."

"Hey, Dad, look on the bright side. At least it was an adventure. It was fun while it lasted. We are so close to the top. We might as well go up and at least enjoy the view."

"I wouldn't miss it for anything," he said as he struggled up the last few feet. It was well worth the struggle to reach the top. The view was fantastic. They both gazed out over the valley below for several minutes. A perplexing gaze came over Scott's face as he got down on one knee. It was apparent to his dad something wasn't right to his son.

"Do you see something, Scott? What's got you so mesmerized?"

Scott pointed to their left down into the valley as he said, "I might be crazy, but I think I see a rooftop. Check it out! See where that straight line of trees are? I believe there's some kind of a building down there!" Thomas was unable to see what Scott was observing at first. He squinted his eyes and focused on where Scott was pointing. He barely caught sight of something among the trees. The men looked at each other and shouted out, "Let's go down and check it out!"

The terrain was steep as they made their way down into the valley below. As they got closer, they realized that what they had seen from the mountaintop was indeed a building. They reached the floor of the valley and walked another mile. Through the forest of trees, they started making out a small, old rustic cabin. As they made their way closer to the cabin, to their amazement, they could make out more buildings. Out of breath and bewildered, Thomas gasped, "Oh my gosh! There are several old buildings! Over there, across the street are two more cabins."

"Yeah, Dad, and a little ways past them, there seems to be a really big building." Scott's heart was racing with excitement. "I can't believe this, Dad! These structures appear so old, but they are still standing. They all seem to still have their roofs intact. We must have stumbled on an old abandoned ghost town," Scott excitedly said as they got even closer. "It sure looks like one of those old Western settings with one dirt road and a few buildings on each side of it. At least this looks like an old road. It's hard to make out with all the growth, but I believe it once was a road dividing this little settlement. This is a real find! It doesn't look like anyone's been here in quite some time."

"That's for sure with all this growth all over. The trees have almost consumed the buildings."

"I know, we would never have known it was here if you hadn't noticed the reflection from that piece of mirror."

"Yeah, I know, Scott! What are the odds of being one of the first to see or even find a ghost town like this? I know that I would not have been able to see it if you hadn't pointed it out to me. What were the odds of us seeing it? We were just in the right place at the right time. I'll bet this is one that the historical society doesn't know about."

"Yeah, I barely noticed it at first. I had to look twice, then I wasn't sure."

"Well, there was no way I would have spotted it without your help."

The two men looked around in wonder. Then Scott said, "Wouldn't Mom get a kick out of this place? I bet she would love it!"

"Your mother probably would, but how about your granddad? Wouldn't he love to explore a lost old town like this?"

"You know what, Dad. If the economy doesn't turn around, I bet this place will still remain a secret."

"It must have been hidden for years. If anyone knew about it, they would have turned it into a tourist trap. None of the other ghost towns have been in such good condition. You can tell that it hasn't been touched in years, though. It's a gold mine!"

Before Thomas and Scott could get to the first building, the hair on the back of their necks stood up as they heard an unusual, eerie, loud scream fairly close by. "What type of animal makes a sound like that," Thomas whispered?"

"Darn if I know, Dad. I don't think it was a coyote. Maybe some kind of cat, like a cougar. I just don't know!" Then Scott put on a ghostly gesture and, in an eerie voice, said, "Maybe, it was a ghost. After all, we are in a ghost town. The ghost is warning us to get out of Dodge!"

Thomas laughed and then said, "Okay, silly, let's go check out this ghost town."

"All right, but watch your back for wild animals or maybe even the ghost." Scott laughed. "Maybe that's why no one has discovered it was here. It is being supernaturally protected against intruders."

The men finally approached the first building, which was a small rustic cabin. The door was barely hanging in place, but it was still there. They had an eerie feeling when they carefully opened it and slowly entered. There was a thick layer of dust lying throughout the cabin. The wooden floor was missing a few boards, but it still was fairly sturdy. To the left of the room was a stone fireplace. It still had a big copper kettle, green with age hanging above its hearth. In front of the fireplace were two wooden rocking chairs and a small child's chair. On the right side of the room was a wooden table with four chairs around it. There was a kerosene lamp sitting in the middle of the table. Just behind the table was an old sink with a pitcher pump. Under the sink was a shelf where all the old pots and pans were still stacked. To its left on the back wall was an old wood cooking stove. On the right side of the sink was an opened cabinet, still filled with dusty dishes covered with cobwebs.

Scott led the way up the narrow stairs of the cabin. There they found a bedroom that was divided by a raggedy blanket hanging on a rope. There was a bed and a wardrobe filled with tattered old clothes on each side. The one window had a sheer faded curtain hanging by its threads, almost completely disintegrated. A small square table sat next to one of the beds with a lantern on it.

Scott noticed something under the bed and pulled it out.

"What the heck is this big pot doing under the bed? I wonder why it's up here," Scott asked.

"You mean that thunder jug? That is a commode. It belongs under the bed," his dad said while laughing.

"You got to be kidding me. People actually used those things?"

"Think about it, son, would you want to go out to the outhouse in the middle of the night? How about in the middle of winter? I hear the winters up here are brutal. The snowstorms and snow accumulations are enormously dreadful. I bet the people that used to live here didn't go out unless it was necessary."

After one last glimpse of the bedroom, Thomas and Scott started making their way down the narrow steps. When Thomas reached the third step from the bottom, his foot fell through. He didn't get hurt, but they both were more careful as they continued their investigation.

There were five old, raggedy cabins in all, and they all were built about the same as the first. Each building they went into was filled with years of dust and cobwebs. The old dwellings came fully filled with furniture and a household full of belongings. Amongst the small cabins was one much larger house, which had a hint of faded paint on it. As the two men walked in, they were amazed over the beauty of the home. It contained elaborate antique furnishings. The living room's vintage furniture sat on an old, faded rug, which covered part of the creaky wood floor beneath. With a look of awe, Scott said to his dad, "I'm guessing this must have been the mayor's house."

"Yeah, something like that, Scott. Maybe the mine's owner, if this towns got one. Who knows?"

After examining every room in the huge house, Scott and Thomas decide to check out the buildings across the street. The first two were the small cabins much like the others. Then they walked out in front of the large building. It was a two-story building and had an old dilapidated, wooden front porch all the way across it. From left to right, the first part of the building had some faded red letters, which could be barely made out. Scott looked up at the sign and said, "I believe it says, 'Ma's boardinghouse.'"

There was an eerie feeling in the air. It was as if Scott and Thomas were in a different dimension or time machine, thrusting them back to the eighteen hundreds. Thomas pushed opened the double front doors, which were dangling by a rusty hinge. As they walked through the creaky old boardinghouse, it was evident that it also served as the town's restaurant. The place was full of cobwebs. There were several tables throughout the large dining area. They were covered with faded, thread-bearing, red checkered tablecloths. Each one held a clogged, dusty, old salt-and-pepper shakers awaiting to be poured. In the corner of the room proudly stood a large pot belly wood-burning stove. On the same side of the room was an opened door, which led to an old-fashioned country kitchen. It even had an old wood cooking stove and an icebox. The kitchen was complete with all the dusty dishes, pots and pans of yesteryears gone by. The men took stock of all the things that were in this well-equipped nineteenth-century kitchen.

Back in the dining area at the opposite side of the room, the guys discovered a stairwell that led upstairs. When they reached the top, they realized that there was a hallway, which housed eight separate rooms. Each room was equipped with a bed and nightstand. The nightstand was graced with a lovely decorated pitcher and bowl. There was also a chair and wardrobe in each room. The bedding and curtains were all hanging by their threads from years of exposure.

The boardinghouse left a lot of images in their heads as they walked out onto the porch. They walked down the porch and walked into the next part of the building. It was just as awe-inspiring as the boardinghouse. On the left side of the store, there were long rows of shelves, which contained broken mason cans, candles, lanterns, and weather-beaten unrecognizable piles of stuff. There was a counter in front of the shelves with a big vintage cash register from the 1800s.

On the right side of the building, there was a bar with eight wooden bar stools. Behind the bar was a counter, which was the length of the bar. At one end, there sat another old cash register. Above the counter was a grand old walnut-framed mirror. On each side of it were shelves displaying dusty, cobwebbed, half-filled liquor bottles. Also behind the bar was a big round wooden barrel that stunk like stale beer. At the back of the store was a broken down staircase that led upstairs. It was risky to climb, but Thomas and Scott weren't about to miss anything that this mystical, timeworn town had to offer. At the top of the stairs, they were surprised to see an apartment. It was laid out in a simplistic manner much like the smaller homes. The broken-down furniture was still in its place as well as all the weatherworn personal items.

Back downstairs, Thomas and Scott carefully sat down on the wobbling barstools as they tried to take it all in. Glancing around the room, Scott said, "Obviously, this was the old general store, which served as a bar as well."

"Yeah. Can you imagine, a whole ghost town? Who'd have figured? It's like, so overwhelming! I feel like I'm in another world. How can a place like this still exist after it apparently has been abandoned for so many years? I love it! It is so cool! Dad, check out the railing in front of this building. It's all broken down now, but I can picture it in its heyday with horses tied up to it. I can see the old miners and their wives with long dresses walking about the town. I wish I was back in those days, living here. Life sure was a lot simpler back then. You know, Dad, I would be happy to stay right here and never go home. I could see myself living in a town like this."

"Well, do me a favor when you move up here, put in a road so I don't have to hike up these big hills again, okay?"

"That's a deal." Scott laughed. "I bet there's a way to get into this valley with my jeep. I'll bet somewhere going off that two-track there is an old road that would lead down here."

"Could be, but right now we have more exploring to do. Let's go across the street again and go through the other little buildings that we spotted."

When they reached the first small building, Scott asked, "What do you suppose this building was used for?"

Thomas walked in and looked around. He noticed that there was sawdust all over the floor. He also spotted an object hanging on the wall. "I'll be darned. This is an old pair of ice tongs," he said as he grabbed them down. "This had to be an old ice house."

"But why all the sawdust? Where did they get ice from back then?"

"After the rivers froze over, they would go down and cut out chunks of ice from them. Then they would bring the ice back and put sawdust over the ice for insulation. The sawdust would slow down the melting process."

"No kidding, where did you get that info? They don't teach that in Bible seminary."

Thomas proudly smiled. "I have read a Western or two."

Laughing, Scott answered back, "Okay, I guess that would work."

By examining all the tools and equipment, Thomas and Scott were able to tell that the next building had been a blacksmith shop. It had a forge and bellows in it for heating the metal, and there were several crude horseshoes lying around.

At the very end of the road and just beyond the row of buildings, there majestically stood an old weather beaten church. In spite of its poor repairs, it looked awesome to the men. It was a plain-looking building, but it had a steeple sitting proudly on its roof. Even though it was badly faded, you could tell it had been painted at one time.

Thomas reverently walked into the church with Scott right behind him. Other than all the dust and cobwebs, it looked like the little church was ready for a Sunday worship service. There were five rows of homemade pews on each side of the aisle with an altar in the middle. To the left of the altar was an old organ still holding a hymn-book. Thomas bowed down in front of the altar and said a silent prayer. Scott got on his knees beside his dad. He put his hand on his dad's shoulder and then bowed his head in silent prayer.

After leaving the church, Thomas and Scott slowly strolled back down the town's dirt road. Their minds were filled with curiosity about the town they discovered.

"I wonder how they supported themselves?" Scott questioned.

"There had to be a mine nearby. That is why all these small towns popped up back then. I bet that there is a mine not too far from here. There must have been!"

"You're probably right! It's getting late, or we could check it out. We don't want to be up here when it gets dark. I can find our way back to the jeep now, but in the dark, I can't promise."

9

Back at campsite, the evening of July 4

When Thomas and Scott arrived back at their campsite, all they could talk about was the ghost town that they had somehow miraculously discovered. They wondered how it could be so well preserved after all these years. It was evident by all the left-behind personal belongings, which the last people to live there were from the turn of the century. It was also evident that no one touched this place because of all the priceless antiques sitting around unprotected. All the other villages from the 1800s that they had seen were in ruins or had been restored. It didn't look like this town had been touched since the settlers moved out. Who knows what year and why? Had they been mining, and the mine gave out? Why would they leave everything behind? There were many questions and no answers.

It was dark by the time the men started a campfire and cooked up that morning's catch. Thomas and Scott relaxed as they sat around the dancing flames of the campfire. They had been silent for several minutes when out of the blue, Scott asked, "Dad, you never answered my question last night. If you had to be marooned out here, would you want mom to be here with you?"

"Scotty, you know your mother and I have been separated for over six months, right?"

"Of course, but if you were alone, forever."

"Son, I've been going to tell you. I guess now is as good a time as any. I'm seeing someone."

"Oh, I was afraid of that. I was hoping you and Mom could have worked it out. Does Mom know?"

"Yes. I told her about Diane just before we left on our trip."

"It sounds serious, is it?"

"Yes, it is. That is one reason I wanted to get away. I wanted to clear my mind once and for all."

"Have you made a final decision yet?"

"I'm getting close. I am leaning toward Diane. You know how you realized how much Sheryl meant to you since you've been away from her?"

"Yeah."

"Well, that's how I'm feeling about Diane. She has been on my mind a lot. I really miss her. I know you will like her! She is so much fun and full of spunk. I wonder sometimes if I can keep up with her. Can you believe it, she's teaching me to dance?"

"Dancing? I remember you used to preach that dancing leads to temptation."

His dad looked a little embarrassed as he said, "Well, yes, I did, but Diane really loves to go out dancing. I'm kind of enjoying it too. We go out to a really nice restaurant for dinner. Where we go, they have a three-piece band and a small dance floor. I was such a klutz the first time she dragged me up on the floor. Now we always dance after dinner. Last week, she dragged me to a dance club. To tell the truth, I did feel out of place there. A bit ashamed."

"What does your pastor say about dancing? You still attend church, right?"

"Of course. Diane talked me into attending her church. It is a mega church. It's okay, but the pastor never preaches on sins or has altar calls. I don't go along with all their doctrines, but Diane likes it there. We sometimes go to their singles group in the church. They meet a couple of times a month, which includes some dances."

"There in the church?"

"Yes, most churches as we once knew them are changing at a rapid rate."

"I guess that's another reason that I quit going."

"By the way, how old is this Diane?"

"Well, a...," quietly Thomas answered, "twenty-six."

"You got to be kidding me, Dad! She is young enough to be your daughter! I bet Mother doesn't know that."

"Scott, she is a very mature woman, and we are business coworkers. We spend a lot of time together on the job it just seemed natural that we would start to fall in love."

"Well, it's your life. If she makes you happy, I won't stand in your way. I know this is going to hurt Mom. She has been hoping that you would forgive her and take her back. I'm guessing that's not going to happen now."

"Don't think so, son."

"Okay then, I've had enough talk for one night. We need to get up early tomorrow and pack up. We have at least three more traveling days to get back home."

The next morning, Thomas and Scott packed up their gear and got ready for their long trip home. There would still be many exciting things to see along the way as they made their way down the east side of the Keweenaw Peninsula.

Before they left the area, they wanted to see the ruins of the notorious village of Wyoming, so they drove back up to highway 41. It was located across from Delaware. They read about it in a brochure. Wyoming was known back in the mining days as Hell Town.

In its heyday, the town had four saloons. Miners in surrounding towns used to come there to drink and hang out. It also had its own mine and stamping mill.

Then the men traveled down along the west side of the Bohemia Mountains to Lac La Belle Lake. They decided to pull over at the beautiful Haven Falls.

"This would be a good spot to stop and eat the sandwiches we made earlier," Thomas suggested.

"Good idea! This park even has some picnic tables."

While enjoying the waterfall and in-between bites, the two men talked about the war and the financial mess the country was in. Scott commented, "It's hard to believe that the whole world is suffering with economical strife. In the past, America always did well financially during a world war. It's not that way now."

"No," his dad answered. "We were so far in the red with China. When the war escalated, we had to go in debt even more to them to build up our armies. The United States was buried in debt with them."

Scott chuckled a little and said, "So maybe that's why President Sandaun had China annihilated two years ago."

"Quite possibly. The rest of the world said that the United States executed atrocious war crimes against humanity. The only way we could save face was to impeach Sandaun."

"He was a horrible president anyway. However, Russia was anxious to find an excuse to get into a war with us."

"Destroying Hawaii with a nuclear bomb did the trick, all right."

"Yes, but of course, we evened the score when we launched a nuclear bomb on Russia's navel facility in Tartu, Syria."

For several minutes, Thomas and Scott sat silently, staring into the waterfall. Their minds were on the thousands of lives that were destroyed and ravished by this disastrous war. After a bit, Scott commented, "On a lighter but also a troubling subject, looks like it won't be long before the world will be going to a one-currency system," Scott said.

"Yes, there definitely is going to be a one global central banking system."

"I'm afraid you are right, Dad. The government that gets control of the money, gets complete control of the world. There goes our American freedom."

"Oh, yes! The notorious one-world government! There have been many top-secret meetings on its development within the past hundred years. All the powerful nations are in on it. It is only a matter of time. I still believe that we will be raptured before all that. Then the Antichrist will sign a peace treaty with Israel, and the tribulation will begin. Bible prophecy has warned that there will be a one-world government in which the Antichrist will rule. I'm sure he's already waiting in the wings, ready to take the final stage."

"Do you have a guess, Dad, who the Antichrist will be?"

"Well, that's a good question. It could be the king of Spain or the president of the European Council, Ali Hamarat of Turkey. Who knows, maybe our own President Omidi."

"President Omidi! You're kidding, right? For the past two years, in spite of the economy, he has been a great leader. He's highly respected and loved by all our allies. I'd say, he has been the biggest advocate for peace."

"There, son. You just said it, peace! The Antichrist comes on the scene as an extremely powerful military leader. He comes under the pretense of peace! There is no other leader in the world that is liked or respected more than him. I have heard on the news and read in the newspapers that high officials from the European Union, as well as the United Nations, say that they are grooming him to be president of the new one-world government. Last year in Germany, Omidi made a speech in front of thousands of people. He said that his goals were to bring order and peace to a global world. The crowd cheered just as their ancestors had cheered for Hitler."

"Wow! I guess it could be possible, but I sure do not want to believe it."

"It's scary, but his actions sure have been pointing toward him being a good candidate for the Antichrist."

The men finished their picnic lunch and were off down the road. They continued along the coast of Lake Superior down to the historical town of Gay where they stopped to get gas. Thomas picked up a pamphlet on the town's history and read it as Scott drove on. "It says in the brochure that this town was named after Joseph E. Gay, one of the founders of the Mohawk and Wolverine Mining Companies. The Mohawk Mining Company built a stamping mill here in 1898."

They drove a little further, and then Thomas pointed to a smokestack. "See that, Scott? That's Gay's smokestack, which was used as a landmark for boats."

After leaving Gay, they drove through the Copper County State Forest. They got on highway two and headed east toward the bridge and home.

10

Detroit, Michigan, July 7

It was late when Thomas arrived home from the Keweenaw Peninsula. It had been a good trip. He had made a life-changing decision, and he also connected again with his son. He felt closer to Scott than he had in many years.

All he wanted to do now was to take a hot shower, relax, and watch a little television, but first, he had to call Diane. She was happy when she heard his voice on the line. "Thomas, sweetheart, I have missed you so much! Are you still on the road, or are you home?"

"I just got home about an hour ago."

"Why didn't you come right over?"

"Remember, my son and I have been roughing it in the outdoors for a week. Trust me, you wouldn't have been able to stand me. Besides, I'm really worn out."

"You aren't too worn out to come see me tonight, are you? I know you don't have to be back to work until day after tomorrow."

"I'm afraid so, but I'll come over tomorrow night after you get off work. In fact, I would like to take you out for dinner, somewhere nice."

"That sounds great, but how about doing something earlier too? I can call in sick in the morning so we can spend the entire day together."

"No, you can't do that. It would be a lie. Besides, you are filling in for me while I'm gone. What would the company do if both of their top sales consultants were gone?"

"I'm sure my uncle would manage. I'll try hard not to keep you out too late tomorrow night. I'll wear that red dress you like so much. It's not too fancy for where you are taking me, is it? You said it was going to be special, right?"

"Yeah, sure. The red dress will be perfect. Well, I am really tired. I'm going to watch a little television and then hit the hay."

"Good luck getting a good television show. All that's been on is breaking news. They show the same things over and over again!"

"Oh yeah, like what?"

"Something to do with the European Union and the president of Turkey."

"You're talking about Ali Hamarat, right?"

"Oh yeah, that guy. He's been saying if we want to end all the bloodshed of war, it was time for the world to unite."

"Since when did that bloodthirsty Turk ever want world peace?"

"I don't know. All I know is that he has been making speeches all week about peace and tranquility. Mainly, he was talking about the conflict between Israel and Palestine."

"Man, I can't believe it! If anything, I thought he was working with the rest of the Middle East to wipe Israel off the map."

"Maybe the war is getting too hot for the Middle East as well."

"It should! With the help of our allies, we have bombed the heck out of them."

Diane's voice changed from sounding weary to a seductive tone as she asked, "So, darling, are you sure that you don't want some company tonight? I could run over there."

"Yeah, no. I'm really tired. I'm just going to catch a little news, give Lorraine a call, and then go to bed."

The last thing Diane wanted to hear was that he was going to call his ex-wife. Her mind raced for something else to tell him. She wasn't ready to let go of him yet, so she said, "Oh, Thomas, I just turned the television back on, and there's more breaking news! Why don't you turn on your set and watch it with me. I've something else to tell you after we watch it."

"Yeah, sure," Thomas said. He quickly picked up the remote and pressed the On button. As Diane had said, the screen was full of breaking news. The cameras were focused on the outside of The Temple building in Brussels (headquarters of the European Union). Then the camera switched to inside. Television cameras were scanning around the room showing that the whole crowd was cheering as President Ali Hamarat of Turkey took the podium.

Hamarat waited until the cheers stopped and then began his speech. In part of his speech, he said, "In the past month, I have been in peace negotiations with Prime Minister Benjamin Weitzman of Israel; Yasser Kabha, acting leader of Palestine; and President Omidi of the United States. We all have been working very hard on finding a final solution for peace between Israel and Palestine. We feel confident that in the very near future, we will have a successful negotiated peace agreement between them. When this event takes place, we will share it with the world! The signing of the peace treaty will be televised. Rest assured, people of the world, everyone will be able to witness this great historical event!"

When the speech was over, the crowd stood to their feet, and a roar of applause spread throughout the whole room. Many were chanting Ali Hamarat's name over and over again.

Thomas's finger hit the Off button. He picked up his phone and asked, "You still there, Diane?"

"Yes, sweetheart, I'm here. Some speech. Thought you might enjoy it. No more war and a united world economy! It's just what we need. This guy is on the right track."

Thomas was about to tell her what he thought but was too tried and needed to call Lorraine. So instead, he asked, "Diane, you had some other news to tell me?"

"Oh, yeah. Wednesday, five suicide bombers blew up the New York subway system in various places. Hundreds of people were injured and some killed."

Thomas's voice cracked with fear as he managed to get the words out of his mouth, "That's terrible! I've got friends and relatives that live in New York!"

"Oh yeah, that's right! That's where you are from. I'm sorry, honey. I didn't think about that. Do your parents live there? "

"Not anymore. They died in an auto accident three years ago."

"I'm so sorry."

"I do have to call my wife and make sure her family and our friends are all okay!"

"Your wife! You mean your ex-wife, right?"

"Yes, of course. I'm really tired, Diane."

Without thinking, she blurted out, "Why do you have to call her? She'll let you know if anything happened to them, wouldn't she?"

"She doesn't know I'm home yet. There's no waiting, Diane. I've got to know right now! I'll call you tomorrow," he said as he hit the End button on his phone.

Lorraine was watching the breaking news when her phone rang. She didn't understand why, but she felt somewhat relieved when she saw his name show up. Even though she and Thomas were separated, she still needed the comfort of the man she loved. This was scary, terrifying news that needed to be shared with someone close. She picked up the phone and eagerly answered, "Hello, Thomas! I'm so glad to hear your voice. Are you home?"

"Hi, yeah, Lorraine just got in about an hour ago."

"I'm so glad you called. I needed to hear your voice after the last news special I just watched. Have you seen it?"

"Yes, I have."

"Oh, Thomas, I can't believe my ears. Ali Hamarat is negotiating a peace treaty with our president for peace between Israel and Palestine. I know he's been on television all the time lately talking about peace, but this throws me for a loop."

"He's a bunch of hot air!"

"Well, yeah, but do you think it's possible that he could be the future one-world leader, the Antichrist?"

"Well, I suppose it's possible. He does have an influential position in the European Union. As president of Turkey, he has developed a strong army."

"Yeah, with Russia's help. The Bible does say that the Antichrist will be a powerful military leader."

"Could be," Thomas said. "He's talking about a peace treaty with Israel."

"Yes, but remember, Israel has signed lots of peace treaties throughout the years. Now if we hear they are talking about a seven-year peace treaty, that's when we should look to the skies."

"You're right, Lorraine. I'm quite sure the rapture isn't far off."

"I'm sure you are right, and I'm looking forward to it!

"Yes, Lorraine, but right now, I'm more concerned with the New York subway bombings last week. Are your mom and dad okay?"

"Of course. Did you ever hear of my mother or father ever taking the subway? They are shook up that it happened, but they weren't anywhere near the bombings."

"Thank God for that."

Lorraine couldn't hold back the tears as she cried out, "It's not good news, though, Thomas. There were lots of people injured and killed. Mom called the next day and told me that one of the families from their church wasn't so lucky. Their pastor called and asked for prayers for Sam Olson. His wife and two sons were killed in the bombings."

"Oh no. I remember your dad talking about that family. He seemed to be really impressed with them. I remember him saying that they were a good Christian family."

Thomas could barely understand Lorraine as her sobbing got worse. "What's the matter, Lorraine?"

"It's so horrible, Thomas! It's Patricia Williams!"

"Christina's mother?"

Between the sobs, she said, "Yes. Patricia was killed in the subway!"

"Oh, no! That is awful! Poor Christina and her family."

"Yes, but if that wasn't bad enough, she was in the subway with Christina's two girls."

"Oh dear God, Rachael and Michelle are all right, aren't they?"

"They were hurt, but thank God they weren't injured seriously. They were taken to the hospital with scratches, bumps, and a couple broken bones."

"I am so sorry to hear about Patricia. She was such a lovely Christian lady. What were Christina's girls doing in New York? I thought their family was still in Africa?"

"Oh, Thomas, it's awful. That's more bad news I just found out. Christina's husband, Dan. He's dead! Christina came to see me last weekend. She was worried about me!"

Thomas was in shock to hear about his close friend's husband. His voice quivered a bit as he said, "Dan was in his early fifties like us. Why? What happened to him?"

"It happened while they were in Africa. You know that Dan and Christina ran a field hospital there, right?"

"Yes."

"Well, there was an awful breakout of diseases in that area. They had to work day and night. Dan became run down. When he was exposed to the bird flu from one of his patients, he caught it and died. Christina was devastated! She had a nervous breakdown and came home."

"Where are they living?"

"They moved in with Patricia, but now she is gone. Her son Daniel is living on campus at his college."

Tears filled Thomas' eyes as he said, "My heart goes out to that family! I'll pray for them."

"Thanks, Thomas. Christina needs all the prayers she can get. She feels guilty because she let the people down in the village they were serving. She left them before they could get a new medical team in."

"I'm sure God will send other doctors to that mission field."

"Yes, I'm sure they will. I just feel so sorry for Christina. She has had so much tragedy in her life lately."

"Yes, the poor dear has. Such a lot for her to bear. First her husband and now her mother. Are you going to the funeral?"

"Of course. I am leaving for New York this Friday. The funeral is next Monday. That way, I can support her through the visitations as well as the funeral. I'll be staying at my parent's home."

Lorraine wiped her eyes, straightened herself up, and said, "Enough of talking about this stuff tonight. Tell me about your trip! Did you and Scotty have a good time?"

"Oh man, did we ever. We had a ball! We even had a close encounter with a big black bear!"

"Oh no! What happened?"

Thomas went on to tell Lorraine the whole story of their narrow escape with the furious bear. He laughed as he told her, "We both yelled at the same time. I don't think we consciously meant to, but we did, and that's what scared the bear away."

Lorraine was laughing at the other end of the phone. Between her laughter, she said, "I'm just glad that you were able to scare him off."

Next, Thomas told her all about the old copper mining towns that they had visited. He got excited when he told her about the old, abandoned ghost town that he and Scott had accidently discovered. When he was telling her all the details about the turn-of-the century homesteads, Lorraine listened intently to every word.

"Oh my gosh, that's in creditable!" she said. "I'd love to see something like that!"

"Yeah, it was great stumbling upon that old town. Scott and I were thrilled! I felt such an attraction toward it. Maybe it was because of a dream I had about leading a bunch of people to an old town much like that one."

"Really? Was I in your dream?"

"Well, yeah. Now that I think about it, yes, you were."

"That's a good sign."

Thomas quickly changed the subject, "Have you heard anything from Linda this past week?"

"A, yeah. Matter-of-fact, Linda is here. She is sleeping, or I would let you talk to her. Thomas she has left Harold."

"They're separated already? I was unsure of that marriage in the first place, but they have been married what, not even five months."

"I know."

"So is it just a lover's spat or what?"

"I'm not sure. She said that she is through with him."

"I'll have to talk with both of them and see if there's any chance of saving the marriage."

"Speaking of that, have you made any decision about our marriage?"

"Lorraine, over the phone might not be the best place to discuss something that significant."

"Thomas, we already had this conversation! You told me that you had met another woman who you had feelings for. I know that you are having a hard time dealing with my past indiscretions. You went on that trip to clear your mind and make a decision. Well, have you decided? I need to know, Thomas. I cannot go on another minute without closure. Please, just tell me!"

"Okay, Lorraine. You deserve an answer. Trust me, I don't want to hurt you. Part of me still loves you, for heaven's sake, but yes! I have made the decision that I am going through with the divorce. I'm going to see a lawyer tomorrow about getting it started."

Lorraine had thought this might happen, but hearing the words coming out of her husband's mouth was more than she could handle.

"Why so soon?" she cried out. "Can't you just see this other woman for a while and then make sure this is what you want? A divorce is so final."

"No, I'm sorry, but I can't. I would not feel right being in a relationship with another woman while I was still married to you. If I still feel the same way about Diane after the divorce, I'm going to ask her to marry me."

There was a long pause on the other end of the line while Lorraine tried to regain her composure. Finally, she said, "Thomas, I've got to go. I cannot deal with this right now. I wish you happiness." She shut the phone down as tears rolled down her cheeks.

11

Thomas apartment, July 7th

Thomas hung up the phone after talking to Lorraine. He sat there quietly in the dark. It seemed that all the confidence he had about his decision was now out the window. His mind was in turmoil as he thought, *Have I been listening to God? I just told my wife that I was going to divorce her. Am I doing the right thing? Was I too harsh to tell her that I wanted to marry another woman? Now is a bad time for her with so much grief in her life. Should I have offered to go to the funeral with her?*

The last thing Thomas wanted to do was to hurt Lorraine. He asked himself how he could be so insensitive to the woman he had loved for over thirty years. He got down on his knees and began to pray out loud, "Why, dear God, why can't I forgive her? Why can't I be more like you? I was a pastor! I have counseled others to forgive their spouses. Why can't I practice what I preach? It says in Your Holy Bible in Mark 10:11, KJV, 'He saith unto them whosoever shall put away his wife, and marry another committeth adultery.' Although it also says in Matthew 5:28, 'I say unto you, that whosoever looketh on a woman to lust after her hath committed adultery with her already in his heart.'

"I was so sure that Lorraine was guilty of adultery because I believed that she had lust for another man, but now, I'm not that sure. However, I do know that I have had lust in my heart for Diane. God forgive me! Maybe marrying Diane is the wrong thing to do. Maybe I have been trying to get even with her for what she did to me. Am I guiltier than she is? She only kissed another man. Does that give me the right to divorce her and marry another woman?

"I know that I enjoy her company a lot. She is so young and vivacious. Maybe that is my problem. Who am I kidding, God? She is young enough to be my daughter! Lorraine said that the Romeo that took her out was young. Was it all about Lorraine being on an ego trip? She told me that she was lonely and didn't feel like a woman anymore. I was too busy to give her the attention she deserved. This guy gave her what I failed to. He wined and dined her. He made her feel desired, young, and beautiful again.

Am I going through the same thing? Is it my ego? My pride was hurt when Lorraine was attracted to another man. I thought I wasn't desirable to my wife anymore, that I had lost my appeal to her. I wanted to feel alluring again. Diane makes me feel that way! I cannot believe that a woman that young and beautiful could be interested in me. It makes me feel like a desirable man again. Is that wrong, Lord? If I have been wrong, forgive me for my pride and the desire that I have for Diane. If I am wrong for wanting a life with her, please let me know. Lord, please, let your Holy Spirit guide me! Please give me a sign as to what you want me to do."

Wiping the tears from his eyes, Thomas lifted himself off his knees and slipped into bed. It was as a burden had been lifted off from him, and he slept better that night than he had in months.

The next day, Thomas drove by the law office, but for some reason, he couldn't stop. He was not ready to face a lawyer about ending his marriage, not yet anyway. He said to himself, *Maybe tomorrow. Two and a half years ago, I would never have imagined I would be considering divorcing Lorraine. I would have sworn that nothing could ever separate me from my sweet, loving wife. What am I thinking sweet, loving wife? Why should I even be thinking that about her? Do I still have feelings for her? The woman who betrayed me?*

Thomas's mind raced on, *My life is a mess right now. Everything is changing drastically! Even the darn world is changing! The world's conflicts have escalated into World War III. It blows my mind that Russia joined the European Union. Talks of a treaty with Israel is on the news every day. Just like my personal life, the world is in chaos. What is going on? Is the rapture about to happen?*

Thomas drove around for hours trying to search for the meaning of it all. It was getting late, and he knew Diane would be getting out of work soon. He decided he better get home and get ready for their dinner date.

That evening at dinner, Thomas thought that Diane was especially gorgeous in her provocative red dress. The restaurant was dimly lit. The table was covered with a red tablecloth and a flickering candle shown just enough to give off an essence of romance. The dinner had been superb, and the mood for romance was just right, especially after a bottle of champagne.

Thomas had never touched an alcoholic beverage until he had met Diane. She had encouraged him to have a glass of wine with his meal to help him relax. The wine did make him feel less guilty when he was having a romantic moment with Diane. The wine helped cover up the guilt, but even though he had been separated for over six months, deep inside, he still felt married.

With a seductive smile on her face, Diane asked, "So why the special dinner tonight? Was there something special you wanted to say or ask?"

"Well, I've been gone over a week, and I missed you. I thought a lot about you on my trip. I did tell Lorraine last night that I was going to see a lawyer today. I also told her that I was serious about you."

"Oh, my darling, that is wonderful news! How long did the lawyer say the divorce would take?"

"I didn't actually stop today. I was going to, but it wasn't a good day for it."

"What do you mean?"

"I don't know, Diane. I just couldn't do it today. It is not easy to dissolve a twenty-six-year marriage.

"I suppose you're right. I wouldn't know. My marriage was short and sweet. I was hoping that we might take our relationship to a new level, perhaps move in together."

"Diane, I can't. You know that I was a pastor, right?"

"Well, yeah. You mentioned something about it. So what?"

"While I was a pastor, I preached to my congregation that it was wrong to live together without being married. It would be hypocritical for me to do. It would be a sin, Diane. I cannot do something that I know is sinful. I have backslid enough lately. I only pray that God will forgive me."

"What would be wrong with it? It's not sin when we love each other and are committed to one another."

"It is just wrong to live with someone when you aren't married to them, and I won't do it. It's fornication, adultery!"

In a disgusted way, she said, "All right, I'm sorry I asked."

"Come on, honey, let's not get into a fight on my first night back."

"You're right, okay. If you can wait for us to be together, then I guess I can too."

"Yeah, I need a little time. After all, I was married for a lot of years. It will take a while to get over it."

"Yes, I understand. I won't push you."

For the next few minutes, Thomas's mind began to wander again. Diane noticed and said, "Earth to Thomas. What planet are you on?"

"Oh, I'm sorry. I was thinking about a close friend that got killed in the bombing last week."

"I was going to ask you about that. Who was it that got killed?"

"She was the mother of one of my best friends. Patricia was a wonderful Christian woman. She and her deceased husband were close friends to my parents. Her daughter Christina and I have been friends since grade school. I really should go to that funeral on Monday."

"I'll get the day off and go with you."

"I really don't think that would be very appropriate right now. I am still married to Lorraine, and she will be going. Christina and Lorraine have been best friends since ninth grade. It's too soon to bring another woman to something like that. It wouldn't be right to do that to Lorraine. Besides, her parents will be there. I don't know about Scott, but I'm sure my daughter will be there."

"Thomas, do you really feel that it is necessary that you even go? After all, you just got back to work after being off for a week, and now you want to take off Monday. I'm not so sure that my uncle will be happy with you taking off for a funeral. It's not like it's a close relative."

"I'm sure when I explain it to him, he'll understand."

"Well, I don't know. Perhaps he will."

"Well, Diane, I better get you home. We've got to go to work tomorrow."

They drove the five miles back to Diane's apartment barely saying a word to each other. When they arrived at Diane's apartment, Thomas walked her to the door and gave her a quick kiss.

"Oh come on, handsome, that won't do," seductively, she teased. Then she kissed him back passionately.

All Thomas could say was, "Wow." She had kissed him with passion before, but somehow, this felt different, more alluring.

"Why don't you come in for a night cap?"

"Thanks, but I really got to get home," he said nervously, fighting the temptation. It's going to be a busy day tomorrow. "Got to get my nose back to the grindstone, you know."

Patricia William's Funeral, July 8th -12th

That next evening, Thomas was eating a sandwich that he had picked up from the deli when the phone rang. When he picked up the receiver, he was surprised to hear his daughter, Linda, on the line. Cheerfully, she said, "Hi, Daddy."

"Hello, honey, how are you doing?"

"Okay."

"I heard that you are staying at your mother's for the time being, is that right?"

"Yes, Dad. I'm sure you heard that Harold and I split up, didn't you?"

"Yeah, sweetheart, I'm sorry to hear that. We need to talk about it."

"What's to talk about? I don't ever want to see that jerk again!"

"Linda, you know what the Bible says about divorce."

"Sure, Dad, do what I say, not what I do. Mother told me that you want to get a divorce. She also told me that you were going out with some bimbo that you wanted to marry."

"Ouch! I guess I had that one coming. However, Diane is no bimbo. You can't judge someone before you even meet them, Linda."

"Well, I don't plan on meeting her, so I guess I'll just have to judge sight unseen."

"You sound a little bitter there."

"Well, yeah! I guess, I am. You really hurt Mother, you know!"

"Yes, and I'm very sorry about that."

"Me too! She woke me up a couple nights ago, crying. Well, actually, your call woke me up, then I heard her crying. How could you, Dad! Mom made one little mistake, and you cannot get past it. What kind of a 'man of God' are you?"

"Not a very good one lately, that's obvious."

"Are you going to the funeral Monday?"

"Matter of fact, yes, I am planning on it. My boss is giving me Friday and Monday off. I'll go to New York for the weekend and then go to the funeral Monday. That way, I can spend some time with Christina and her family."

"Well, that's cool. Mom needs you there. Christina's mother's death has been hard on her. She has been on the phone with Christina every night since she heard about her passing. Plus that, Grandma and Grandpa have been calling constantly. Since the bombing, all they can talk about is getting out of New York. I don't know why everybody has to lean on Mom so much."

"Your mom has always been there for people when they needed her. She has a real gift for being able to comfort people."

"Dad, I'm a little worried about her. I'm not sure if she is strong enough to make this trip alone, what with the divorce and all."

"She has you."

"I have a bug or something. If I am up to it, I plan on going to the funeral. It is just that I have been feeling sick lately. I'm afraid with this bug, I would not be able to be very supportive. She needs someone stronger. I don't suppose you could swing down here and pick us up? We could all go together."

"Linda, I'm not so sure your mother would go along with that."

"I'll talk her into it, please, Daddy?"

"I'll think about it. I'll give you a call tomorrow night."

"Okay! I'm really tired, so I'm going to go. Good night, Daddy. I love you."

"I love you too, baby. Night."

The next day, Thomas struggled with the decision. Should he go to the funeral with Lorraine or not? When he talked to Diane about his dilemma, she convinced him not to go. However, later in the day, he thought about how much Lorraine would really need his support. He remembered how sensitive she was about those she loved. He also remembered her saying that with him by her side, she could get through anything. On the other hand, he felt that it would be betraying Diane if he went. Not to mention how terribly angry she would be with him. After struggling for answers, he finally came up with the decision. He had no choice. He needed to be with Lorraine through this crisis. Not only did Lorraine need him, he needed her as well.

Thomas's phone rang. He looked at the number. It was Lorraine's. He answered, "Lorraine, hi."

"Hello, Thomas. Linda told me that you wanted to go to the funeral with us."

Thomas paused and thought, *Linda, why you little rascal!* "A... yeah, would you mind if I tagged along with you and Linda? You know how much Christina's mother meant to me."

"Yes, of course! I would have mentioned it, but I didn't want to interfere with your life. I'm sure it would mean a lot to Christina if you were there and me too."

"Great! That settles it then. How about if I pick you girls up Friday morning? We can catch a flight to New York."

"Sounds good! I'll make the reservations. I've been dreading the thought of driving that far."

"You and me both! That was a long trip to the top of the Keweenaw Peninsula. I'm not in the mood for another long road trip right now."

"Well, that sounds great! Don't worry about lodging. I'll give mom a call and let her know to get another guest room ready for you."

"Your parents won't mind if I stay there?"

"Of course not. They still love you." Lorraine bit her lip as she thought, *And so do I.* "Our separation or now a pending divorce won't change that."

"Thank you, Lorraine. That means a lot to me."

Friday morning, Thomas arrived at Lorraine's apartment. She was packed ready to go, but Linda came out of the bathroom in her pajamas. She slowly walked over to her dad and gave him a hug and said, "Hi, Daddy."

"Hi, sweetie. Come on, get ready! We need to catch the plane by eleven!"

"Daddy, I'm not going. I'm not feeling good at all. I can't keep anything down."

"Maybe we should take you to the hospital?"

"No, Dad. It's just the stomach flu. I'll be fine."

Lorraine smiled and said, "She has our cell phone numbers if she gets worse. I'm sure she will feel better with a little more rest."

Later that afternoon, James and Marge Patterson were at the airport to pick them up. Lorraine gave her mother a big hug. James gave Thomas a big bear hug as well as he said, "Great to see you, son. How have you been?"

"Great, Dad. How about you? You're looking good."

"Well, I can still play a good round of golf."

"I guess I should know better than to challenge you, right?"

"Yeah!" his father-in-law laughed. "I have beaten you a few times, haven't I?"

Marge held her arms out to Thomas and said, "I need a hug too! We have missed you, son."

"I've missed you guys too."

"Now, Dad, let's get these kids home. They must be starved and tired," Marge said with a big smile on her face.

As James drove them up to the Patterson Estate, Lorraine noticed a big For Sale sign on the lawn. "Wow, I guess you guys were serious about selling. I see you already have the estate listed," Lorraine commented.

Marge loudly spoke up, "You darn well better believe it! I have had enough of bombings. I want far away from here."

Disgustingly James uttered, "Yeah, after all those years of people wanting to buy this estate, and now nothing. Real estate in New York sure isn't moving very fast. I guess we're going to take a beating on it."

The Pattersons had their maid get Lorraine and Thomas settled into their separate rooms. Soon after, they were served an elegant dinner. Of course, it helped that Marge had a gourmet chef to prepare the dinner and a housekeeper to serve it.

After dinner, Lorraine looked over at Thomas and asked, "How about a walk around the grounds?"

"Of course, I'd love to."

It was a beautiful summer evening as the two of them strolled through the grounds. They stopped to admire the flowers as Lorraine looked up at Thomas and asked, "Do you remember all the trails we took on this estate the summer you tutored me?"

"Of course! That was a great summer. I sure was smitten with you. I thought you were the most beautiful girl in the whole wide world. I couldn't get those beautiful sapphire eyes or your long, flowing black hair out of my mind."

"And then I got old!"

"Lorraine, you still are the most beautiful woman in the world. In fact, maturity has made you even more beautiful than you were as a teenager."

"Oh, Thomas, how sweet!"

"I mean it."

"But you don't love me anymore."

"Lorraine, part of me will always love you. You are a sweet, sensitive, loving person. It is not you, it's me! I can't get past what happed two years ago."

"I know, Thomas. I understand, and it's all my fault."

Thomas put his arms around Lorraine and said, "No, Lorraine, it takes two. I was at fault too. I was good at counseling others, but I could not tell when my own marriage was in trouble. I neglected you. If I would have given you more love and affection, I'm sure this wouldn't have happened to us."

Thomas stopped walking, turned to Lorraine, and took her into his arms. For a romantic moment, their eyes melted together in passion. Lorraine was hoping that he would end this moment with a kiss. When he didn't, she was tempted to initiate one herself. Instead, she said, "Maybe we should try again. We know our mistakes now. Do you think maybe it could work this time?"

Thomas let loose of her as if he had come to his senses. "It's too complicated, Lorraine. You know I am involved with another woman. I care a lot about Diane too."

Tears began to well in Lorraine's eyes.

"Please, Thomas, can we drop this conversation. I can't handle hearing about another woman right now."

"I'm sorry. I didn't mean to be so insensitive. Maybe we should go in now."

"Yes, I believe you are right!"

The next day, Lorraine and Thomas attended Patricia William's visitations at the funeral parlor. They were there both days to console

Christina and her children. Dan, Christina's eldest child, took on the leadership role for the family at the service. The whole family was grief stricken at their loss. Christina's two teenage daughters were still recuperating from the bombing. Michelle had a cast on her arm, and Rachael was walking with crutches.

As Thomas watched Lorraine comfort Christina's family, he thought to himself, *This is the Lorraine that I remember.* He had held many funerals during his ministry, and Lorraine was always at his side as they comforted the mourners. Thomas had been proud of the way she always had the right words to say to the grieving families.

During the funeral, Thomas sat next to Lorraine. Her parents also joined them in their pew. When the funeral was about to begin, he reached down and clasped Lorraine's hand in his. They each felt a bond as if they were still that happily married couple. Sitting close to her, he was able to absorb the scent of her perfume that he had enjoyed so much in the past. Her raven hair was down—the way he liked it best. It flowed over the shoulders of her blue suit jacket, which matched the radiant blue of her eyes. Thomas smiled at her as he thought, *There could never be another woman more beautiful than Lorraine. Her beauty goes behind physical. It is inward as well. What's the matter with me, one would think that I was still in love with her? And I am. I could never stop loving this woman, but I can't forgive her either.*

After the funeral, Thomas and Lorraine went back to her parents' home. The four of them sat around the Patterson's huge stone fireplace, visiting.

"So, Thomas," Marge asked, "I hear you and Scott had quite the trip."

"Yes, we sure did! It had to be one of the best vacations that I have taken. I never realized before how many old mining towns there were in Upper Michigan. The Keweenaw Peninsula during the 1800s was thriving with copper mines! From those mines, towns sprung up.

Most are in ruins and are considered ghost towns now, but you still can see enough to relive history. But the most spectacular part of our trip was when Scott and I ran across an uncharted ghost town!"

"You guys actually discovered an uncharted town?" James asked. "How did you stumble upon it?"

Thomas reached in his pocket and pulled out a broken piece of mirror. "You see this piece of mirror? I keep it handy to remind me of the miracle of finding that old town. We wouldn't have found it in a million years if it hadn't been for this little piece of mirror. We were fishing on the foothills of Mt. Gratiot. The sun was reflecting light off from it just right, and we were able to see it. When we first saw the light, we thought it might be someone lost or hurt. We thought maybe they were sending out signals to be rescued. We didn't want to leave anyone, so we went up the mountain to take a look. We were able to drive part of the way. The rest of the way was on foot. Scotty was the first to spot a roof among the trees down in the valley. I was trailing up the hill behind him. He was at the top of the hill looking down into the valley. I wouldn't have seen the roof of that building if it weren't for Scott. The trees had engulfed the whole town. They were darn near completely covered up by them."

"Scott's always been a hawk eye." Lorraine laughed.

"Yeah," James said. "Boy scouts taught him a lot. They taught him to be aware of his surroundings."

"It made him a great camper too! He sure cooked us some wonderful meals while we were camping."

James was at the edge of his seat as he asked, "Well, Thomas, what did you find down in the valley, ruins?"

"No, nothing like it! We were amazed at the condition we found most of the buildings. All the roofs were still intact. Most of the houses could use some work, but basically, you could move right in with some patching here and there. There was one really large, elaborate house, which was filled with lovely antique furniture. Scott said that it had to have belonged to the mayor of the town. The most amazing thing was though in every residence it looked like the home owners just up and left everything they owned! The homes were full of furnishings and personal items."

Thomas went on with his storytelling about all the buildings. He told them about the general store, which was also a saloon, and the boardinghouse, which served as a restaurant. He told them about the blacksmith shop, the icehouse, the cabins, and the little church.

"That's fantastic! Do you suppose that you could get a vehicle closer?" James asked.

"There has got to be another way in. Scott and I just didn't have time to find it."

James's face was flushed with excitement as he said, "That's my kind of adventure! I'd love to have seen that."

13

Detroit, Michigan, July 16

A couple of days after Patricia Williamses' funeral, Diane invited Thomas over to her apartment for dinner. After dinner, they were relaxing, watching a movie, when a breaking news report flashed across the screen. The newscaster came on the air. His face was grim and sober as he slowly began to speak. "For the past month, I have been reporting to you about devastating earthquakes all over the globe. Today, it is my sorrowful duty to inform you that it has come to our shores. Yes, my friends, I'm heartbroken to let you know that California has suffered the long anticipated "big one.' And it was indeed the big one! It was far vast than what we feared. According to the Richter scale this morning at 10:47 Pacific Time Zone, California suffered a magnitude earthquake of 9.8. The gigantic quake of apocalypse proportion ruptured near San Francisco at the San Aderas fault. The quake and aftershocks triggered the Elsinore and San Jacinto faults including a vast interconnected fault system."

The distressed reporter stopped for a moment to get his breath and then continued, "The quake, aftershocks, and the offshore earthquakes triggered a tsunami! With all this disaster, a third of California has now dropped off into the ocean!"

The anchorman stopped for a moment to get control of his emotions. He wiped a few tears from his eyes and continued, "The residents only had a fifteen-minute warning. There's no way we can estimate the fatalities at this point, but we know it is upward of hundreds of thousands of people. Not only is a third of the state lost in the sea, but in surrounding areas, buildings, highways, and bridges have all come crashing down. Wait! I'm getting some feed from the helicopters flying over."

Thomas was sitting on the edge of his seat in disbelief. He kept repeating over and over, "No, God. No." His heart hurt for all those poor folks washed away so instantly. Diane watched silently as the reporter relayed what they were seeing on the television.

"It's hard to see with all the smoke and ash. It looks like an atomic bomb has been dropped on San Francisco and the Inland Empire. Wait, I'm getting more news in. I'm learning at this moment that the damage is going out hundreds of miles. It is even affecting bordering states. Seems the quake and the tsunami waves have caused water pipes to explode, electrical and gas lines to be cut off, and cables to be ripped to shreds. This has led to fires spreading throughout the state as well as its neighboring states."

Thomas was sitting quietly thinking about all the lives that were lost from the quake when Diane broke his concentration. She commented, "I still don't know why you had to go to that funeral with Lorraine. I understand why you didn't want me to go with you, but why go with her?"

"What? We've just watched this horrendous event, and you're worried about who I went to a funeral with? Diane, we have been through this a thousand times already. I have explained it to you. Lorraine was distraught and needed someone to help her get through the funeral."

"Yes, but not her ex-husband! She had her daughter to go with, didn't she?"

"I told you that Linda was sick and couldn't go."

"Yeah, right. Did you ever stop to think about how convenient it was for your daughter to get sick just before her mother was to go on a trip with her dad?"

"Come on, Diane, I saw her. She really was sick!"

"Are you sure it wasn't a ploy to get her mother and dad back together again?"

"Yes, I am sure! Besides, if it was, it didn't work."

"I can't believe that you actually stayed with Lorraine at her parents' home! I am sure your ex's parents want the two of you back together again, or they wouldn't have let you stay there. I can't believe that you would stay overnight with Lorraine!"

"Diane, it was all innocent! They have a large estate with several bedrooms in it. I had my own room!"

"How close was Lorraine's room to yours?"

"It doesn't matter. Nothing happened between us."

"Didn't Lorraine try to get you to come back to her?"

"She mentioned something about trying again. I brought you up, and she dropped the subject."

"All right, but I still don't like the idea that you will go running to her aid whenever she snaps her fingers."

"It's not like that. I needed to go! Patricia had been a big part of both our lives."

"My point exactly! Lorraine is your past! I am your future. That is if you will stop clinging to your ex-wife! When you have a crisis in your life, I want to be the one by your side. I want to be that woman, not Lorraine!"

Thomas smiled as he heard his phone ring. Maybe then Diane would shut up for a minute.

"Don't answer it. Whoever is on the other line can leave a message. We aren't finished talking yet."

He gave Diane a dirty look and then checked the name on his phone. "I've got to take this. It's my father-in law. He never calls. Something must be wrong."

"Oh, of course, by all means, it's Lorraine's father. It has to be important to you."

"Yeah, Dad."

Diane gave him a nasty look. He ignored her and then had the audacity to address his ex-father-in-law as dad!

On the other end of the line, James asked with enthusiasm, "What are you doing this weekend?"

"I really haven't made any plans as yet. Why what's up?" He looked over at Diane and gave her a "sorry" gesture.

"You know that ghost town that you told me about? The one that you and Scott accidentally stumbled upon?"

"Yeah, sure, what about it""

"My buddy Joe Wydeck has a private plane. When I told him about the old town, he wanted to see it too. I thought we could pick you up and maybe fly over to South Haven and pick up Scotty."

"Wow! Dad that sounds like fun, but I don't know. I've been on the go so much lately."

"Aw come on, son, where's your spirit of quest! It's only a couple of days. Come on, I couldn't find it without you."

"Okay! Okay, I'll go! I don't know about Scott, but I'll give him a call and let you know."

"All right, son. Great! See you in a couple days!"

"Yeah, sure, dad. Talk to you later."

Glaring at him, Diane blurred out, "So what in the world was that all about?"

"Remember I told you about this old mining town that Scott and I discovered?"

"Yes, I guess. Some old abandon buildings you guys found?"

"Yeah, well, James was as intrigued as Scott and I were. He wants to see it for himself. He has a buddy who will fly us there. He will even go over to South Haven and pick Scott up, if he's able to get away. From there, he will fly us to the Keweenaw Peninsula."

"Man! Isn't that rather foolish to fly an airplane all the way from New York just to go see a bunch of old buildings in the UP."

"Not if you are really interested about historical things and culture."

"When I want culture, I go to the theater, an art museum, or I read a good book."

"Well, some people still like a good quest."

"Did you really forget that we made plans for this weekend? You have been gone so much lately! And now you are telling me that you are going on an escapade with your ex father-in-law when you could have spent the weekend with me? What about our plans?"

"Diane, I'm truly sorry about that, but this is a once-in-a-lifetime opportunity. We've got lots of weekends ahead of us, but this might not happen again for me."

"Don't be too sure about us. If you keep doing things with Lorraine and her family, there just may not be an 'us' anymore!"

Later that night, Thomas called his son and told him about his granddad's plans. Scott was thrilled. "Count me in, Dad! I wouldn't miss that trip for anything. I've got to change my work schedule around a little and break a date with Sheryl, but I can do it!"

"Yeah, I know what you mean. I have to get my boss to let me take Friday afternoon off. I've been asking for a lot of time off lately. I hope he will be all right with it. It kind of helps that I am dating his niece. Okay, Scott, I'll get back with you on the schedule of the flight, and see you Friday afternoon."

14

Detroit Metro Airport, July 21

Thomas was excited as James and his buddy Joe picked him up at the Detroit Metro Airport early Friday afternoon. James introduced Joe to Thomas. Joe Wydeck was a 60-year-old man with a receding hairline, a mustache, and a well-trimmed beard. He had made his fortune as a Wall Street guru before the big crash. Now he was into real estate.

It was a short plane ride from Detroit to South Haven. Soon, Joe's plane was setting down at the South Haven Airport. Scott stood waiting patiently as he watched the men exit the plane. When they walked out of the plane, Thomas saw Scott and said to him, "Meet our pilot and a good friend of your granddad. Scott, this is Joe Wydeck."

"Glad to meet you, Mr. Wydeck! Thank you, sir, for including me."

"It's my honor. I hear you were the first one to discover the old town?"

"Yes, and it was so awesome!"

Scott motioned at Joe's plane and said, "That is some plane you have there, Mr. Wydeck. I wasn't expecting a plane that large."

"Call me Joe. Yeah, it's a nice-size plane. It will hold eight passengers easy."

Scott greeted his granddad with a hug, and soon later, Joe's plane was heading to the Keweenaw Peninsula. It was a scenic ride over the Lake Michigan shoreline crossing the Garden Peninsula and the Big Bay De Noc. The four men flew over the mainland of Upper Michigan. Soon, they were flying over Hiawatha National Forest.

The four men reached the Houghton County Memorial Airport at 5:25 that afternoon. The airport was located between Hancock and Calumet. As they were getting off the plane, Thomas asked, "What now? Shall we see if there's a car rental?"

"I've already called them, and they will have a Hummer waiting for us."

"Awesome!" Scott said. We should be able to go a lot further in with one of those babies than we did in my jeep!"

"That's the plan," his grandfather said.

"We reserved a couple of rooms at the Holiday Inn here in Calumet," Joe spoke up. "We'll check in, unload our bags, and then, I'm starving! Holiday Inns as a rule have good meals. We will eat there tonight. We also can get breakfast there tomorrow morning. I'd like to leave the hotel at six so we can get an early start. Joe and I've talked about checking out a couple spots here in town after dinner tonight. We found them on the Internet. There's this old theater they started during the mining days that we would like to see. Also we would like to check out a historical site, the Red Jacket Mine."

"That would be great," Scott said. "We missed those on our trip."

"Yeah," Thomas said. "There's so much to see up here."

After the men dropped off their luggage and had a delicious meal at the hotel's restaurant, they went to check out the historical sites. They found out that the historical town of Calumet was called Red Jacket in the mining days.

They stopped into a museum where a tour guide filled them in on the town's history. He began by saying, "In the 1900s, the population was 4,668. Then there was a big labor strike in Copper County in 1913–1914. On top of that, there was what they call the 1913 Massacre. The mine strikers and their families were gathered at the Italian Hall for a Christmas party. Someone cried out fire, and that precipitated a stampede that crushed or suffocated seventy-five victims. The majority of them were children.

During the Great Depression, almost all the mines were shut down. As a result, many miners and their families left to find work. Many went down to Detroit to get a job on the auto assembly line. Small-time mining continued in the area particularly during World War II, but they were closed down in 1968 because of a labor strike. The population of Calumet in 1950 was 1,256 people. In 2009, its population was just over 800. At present, there are a little over three hundred people living here."

"What do you contribute that to?" Scott asked.

"There's no work up here anymore. With the way the economy is, no one can afford to live up here any longer. Mainly, they can't afford the heating cost with our frigid winter weather. People throughout the whole Peninsula are heading south. My family and I are moving to South Carolina before the summer is out."

The men left the historical mining site and went to see the Calumet Theater. It was opened to self-guided tours. However, the director of the theater was there and gave them some information about it. He told them, "The Calumet Theater was opened up on March 20, 1900, and it had touring Broadway productions," the director explained. "With the decline of copper mining and the invention of the motion pictures, stage productions became less of a demand by the late 1920s. From the depression through the late

1950s, it was exclusively a movie theater. However, Summer Stock returned in 1958 and ran for nearly ten years. The auditorium was restored in 1975 and the exterior in 1988–1998."

"Do you have a show tonight?" Joe asked.

"The stage production has been shut down for some time now due to the recent economy."

"That's too bad," Joe said. "We were hoping to catch a stage show."

"Yes, it is a terrible shame. This is a beautiful theater."

The next morning, after a good-night's sleep, the men were up at six. They had a big breakfast and were on the road by seven. They were all pumped and ready to go as they drove off in the Hummer.

Scott was behind the wheel, seeing he had driven there once before and knew where to go. Joe sat in the front passenger side, while Thomas and James rode in the back.

"How long do you suppose it will take us to get there, Scott?" Joe asked.

"Shouldn't take more than an hour and a half."

"Great!"

"Oh, by the way, Thomas," James said, "Marge thought that this would be a good time to go spend some time with her daughter, so she made plans to go to Bowling Green. She even invited Joe's wife, Darlene, to come along. Then she thought about Christina Williams and her girls. She thought that it would help them get their minds off Patricia's death, so she invited them too. The woman were all excited about going. Marge called Lorraine, and she was delighted. We were flying over Bowling Green anyway, so we stopped and dropped them off."

"That's great, but Lorraine only has one bedroom, and Linda is staying with her."

"I didn't say they were all going to crash in on Lorraine." James laughed. "Marge made reservations at a nearby hotel. There's a bunch of them."

"Yeah," Joe said. "We were a bit overcrowded in the plane, but we were okay on the weight. Darlene even brought our two boys, and Christina brought her two girls along.

"Well, that's nice that they can bring the kids too. I know, Lorraine and Linda will be happy to see everybody," Thomas said.

"Yeah, Marge is always complaining that she doesn't get to see Lorraine anymore. She worries about her, especially now."

Embarrassed, Thomas said, "I know this separation has been hard on her. It's been tough on both of us."

Scott turned his head toward the backseat and asked, "So, Dad, what's with Linda? Is she going to divorce the bummer?"

"It looks that way, Scott. I haven't had much of a chance to talk to her. I've got to get some time to, though."

"Well, as far as I know, Harold's a jerk. I never liked him anyway. She's probably better off without him," Scott told his dad.

15

Mt. Gratiot, July 22ⁿᵈ

As they drove up highway 41 Thomas and Scott pointed out the old mining villages that they had visited before. Thomas explained that some of the original buildings had been restored, although most were in ruins. Both Thomas and Scott told of the stories that the Yoopers had shared with them.

James in particular got a kick out of Scott telling them about the village of Wyoming. Scott laughed and said, "Yeah, it was quite the town. Not only was it named after a western state, but was also called Hell Town. It was a hangout for the miners for miles around. There were four saloons in that small town!"

Off from highway 41, they took the same dirt road down to Mt. Gratiot. A ways down the road, Scott pulled over and said, "This is a good spot to stretch our legs. Besides, I wanted to show you where dad and I camped."

Both James and Joe were in awe of the beauty surrounding them. The mountains to the west were magnificent. As before, an occasional fish could be seen jumping out of the water. Off in the distance, they spotted a deer. Scott was sure it was a buck. Squirrels and rabbits were plentiful.

"Are you ready for the best part of the trip now?" Thomas asked.

"That's what we came for," Joe answered.

With the men all loaded back in the Hummer, Scott pulled back onto the two-track. After a ways, he veered off to another two-track that led straight up the mountain.

After they drove for a bit, Thomas said to his son, "I think this is the spot where we stopped and walked the rest of the way up."

Scott stopped the vehicle. "I believe you are right, Dad. How about this time we continue on the track and see if it will lead us closer to the valley? Maybe, we can find a better way in."

"Yeah, good idea."

Then Thomas explained to the others, "This is where I thought the reflection was coming from. We got out of the jeep and went the rest of the way on foot up the mountain. It led us up a steep path. That's when I found that piece of mirror, which led us up the mountain in the first place. We were so close to the top we decided to go the rest of the way and check out the view. That's when Scott noticed the rooftops."

"Okay, if you guys are ready, let's try to blaze a new trail into the valley," Scott said as he pushed the gas pedal and stormed ahead. He sharply turned the wheel from left to right as he steadily climbed, mowing down bushes and small trees in their way. Then they began to descend down the mountain. It got rougher and rougher as they plowed, though. They came to a sudden stop.

"What do we do now?" James said.

"Well, Grandpa, I have a strong feeling that this is the way into the valley. Notice that line of trees. They kind of form a trail of younger trees surrounded by old, larger trees. It's possible that there was a road going through there at one time. Let's get out and hoof it. Maybe it will lead us farther down into the valley."

The men got out of the Hummer and began their journey on foot. There was a lot of brush to go through, but Scott blazed the trail, with Joe right behind him. Thomas and his seventy-nine-year-old father-in-law brought up the rear. They walked about a half a mile and came upon a wide creek that crossed the trail. They were delighted when they saw fish swimming in the clear water. There was an old, dilapidated wooden bridge across the creek. It was broken up and rotten in spots, but at one time, it had been wide enough to get buggies across. Perhaps it was a way into the village. There were boards broken out, but enough was left for them to carefully walk across on.

"This is it!" Scott said with excitement in his voice. "This has got to be the way into the village! If it is, it sure is an easier way of getting here. It beats climbing up that mountain and then down again into the valley, right, Dad?"

"You've got that right, Scott! It is far better than climbing that steep mountain. However, this was still a hefty hike. Why don't we take a little break?"

James was huffing and puffing as he said, "Well, I'm glad I waited for this trip then. I thought I was fit, but this is rugged enough for me."

"I'm sorry, Granddad! I've been so eager to find the town I forgot that you aren't a young man anymore."

"Oh for land's sake I'm not that old! Come on, you lightweights, let's get going!"

The men all laughed. After a short rest, they continued their quest. They only walked a short distance when Scott pointed and said, "Would you look at that? See those old fence posts? There once was a fence of some kind here."

"Over there," Joe said excitedly. "There's a house across the field!"

"That's not one of the houses we found," Thomas said.

"Dad's right! This must be a section of the settlement that we didn't see yet."

The men hustled across the large grown up field as soon as they were able. When they got closer, to their surprise, they saw an old, rundown barn and a couple out buildings behind the house. They could see that the farm was old and abandoned. When they reached the house, they all eagerly went inside.

"It's like a typical old Michigan farmhouse," Thomas said.

The four of them walked through the house. To keep the downstairs warm, a potbelly stove stood in the corner of the living room. Like the other homes that Thomas and Scott had discovered, it had crude furniture, a wood cooking stove, and a kitchen sink with a pitcher pump. The cupboards were full of old dishes and pots and pans. There were also personal belongings scattered about, just like the town's other dwellings. Each of the bedrooms had a fireplace.

Scott told his granddad and Joe, "Even though this farmhouse has the same amount of bedrooms that the large house in town has, its rooms are much smaller. Also, all of its bedrooms are upstairs. The large fancy house in town has two bedrooms upstairs and a huge one downstairs."

The guys couldn't wait to check out the other buildings. Directly behind the house was the outhouse. Back and to the right of the outhouse was the chicken coop and a corncrib. The old barn stood tall and proud. You could see daylight through the missing boards, but it was still standing after all those years. They walked through the old barn in amazement. They could picture the cows in their stalls. Joe pictured his elderly Uncle Edward sitting on a small stool, milking one of the cows. He had visited him on the farm when he was just a small boy. There still were some farm tools hanging on the walls and some old farm machinery sitting around. To their surprise, there was even a little moldy hay in the loft above.

Scott's mind was picturing the farmer and his family that had lived there. He thought, *It is so peaceful here. I bet the people were happy. I wonder why they left such a wonderful place. They had everything they could want in a place like this. I can see the cattle grazing and the farmer tilling that field over there. Life had to be much simpler back then, but when? How long ago did they live this place, and why did they leave all their belongings behind?*

As the four walked from the barn out to the front of the house, Joe yelled, "I believe there's another farm! Looks about a half a mile away. We must be standing on what once was a road. The other farm is down this road and on the other side of the street."

Tired out but excited, the men pushed themselves to reach the second farm. To their amazement, this farm was as equipped as the prior one. Like the rest of the dwellings in this mysterious valley, it was as if the residents were snatched out of their homes, leaving all their belongings behind.

After a full investigation of the second farm, the men decided to look for the other part of the settlement. This farm was butted up against the mountain, so they were quite sure that this was as far as the road went in that direction. There was no stopping the men. They had to find the old town. They struggled on, which seemed like miles, stopping periodically for a rest. Two hours later, they came upon two cabins, which were kitty corner across from each other.

At the site of these cabins, Thomas and Scott were flabbergasted. "We never saw these houses either!" Scott yelled out in excitement. "There is definitely more to this settlement than we first thought!"

Excitedly, once again, the men began investigating the cabins. Like the others, these small cabins were also full of personal belongings.

After a half hour rest, their curiosity moved them on. Down the road a little further, they found three more similar cabins on one side and two on the other. All the same as before.

"Wow," Thomas said. "These are all new to us!"

Thomas was concerned when he looked at James. His face was red and showed exhaustion. Thomas knew he wouldn't admit it, so he said, "I don't know about you guys, but I need to take a break! I could use some food."

Scott looked at his watch and said, "I am so sorry! We should have stopped for lunch hours ago. I was so thrilled finding these new buildings I forgot to stop for lunch. I'm sorry, guys."

Joe laughed and said, "That's all right. I think we've all been too excited to think about food."

Joe and Scott had carried sandwiches and drinks in their backpacks. They took a long lunch sharing with each other all the wonders they had seen and the sights yet to come.

It was five in the afternoon when the four explorers hiked into the main part of the old town. James and Joe were as overwhelmed as Thomas and Scott had been the first time they saw this uncharted ghost town.

After a full investigation of the buildings, James said, "This is just the place I've been dreaming of. It would make a wonderful retreat for the summer. I could get Marge and me one of those really big motor homes, and we would have a blast up here. No worries about wars, bombings, or muggings."

"Only one problem with that, Grandpa. There's no electricity up here, and chances are, you couldn't get it if you wanted to."

"Oh well, that probably wasn't the best idea anyway. I would just as soon live in that big house here in the town. Marge would love it. It's sort of on the Victorian style and with all that gorgeous, expensive antique furniture."

"Yeah, Dad, but Mother wouldn't like being without electricity."

"Well, she would have to learn how to get along without it. I'd get her plenty of kerosene lamps. The big house has a fireplace in almost every room. That should keep us warm on chilly nights."

Joe looked at James in a weird way and said, "Are you really serious about buying this valley?"

"By golly, if there's a way, I think I am."

"Well, this is something that Darlene and I have been wanting for a long time. Our boys would love it up here. The boys and I love to fish and hunt. If you are serious, and you wouldn't mind, if it's possible, I would like to go into a partnership with you to buy it!"

"Slow down, you guys!" Thomas interrupted. "You have been watching the news lately, haven't you?"

"Yes," James said. "What's that got to do with the price of tea in China?"

"That peace contract with Israel! It is about to be signed any day now, and you know what that means."

"Yes, I do, but," his father-in-law said, "Israel has been making peace treaties for years, and the rapture hasn't happened yet."

"Come on, Dad, you know the signs are all here. Mark my word, if it is a seven-year peace contract, we will be raptured up with Christ in the twinkling of an eye!"

"Son, I've lived for a long time, and I've been hearing that for just about as long. I think I will be safe in buying some property. If there is a rapture, it won't matter anyway, right? Heck, for all we know, I could be dead by tomorrow anyway. In the meantime, I'm going to live my life to the fullest."

16

Detroit, Michigan, October 3

It had been a couple of months since Thomas had flown to the Keweenaw Peninsula. Since that time, Diane kept nagging him to get started on his divorce. He had good intentions, but for some reason, he continued putting it off. His mind was filled with too many other things. One afternoon, while driving to work, he thought, *How can I tell Lorraine good-bye forever? I would love to share more with her about the ghost town up north. She would be so fascinated with it. I know she would love to see it.*

Thomas's mind was also plagued with Israel and the possibility of the peace treaty. *Does this mean that the rapture is about to happen and that the seven-year tribulation will soon take place?* he asked himself. Almost every night, Hormoz or Omidi's face had been on the news with all the great humane things they were doing. The news was full of anticipation about the coming peace treaty.

That Wednesday evening, Thomas and Diane went to a dinner party at their boss's mansion. A mixture of socializing and business was always the agenda for those types of events. Whenever their boss put on a business party, it was always a big production. This one was no exception. The long dining table was full of sales representatives and their potential clients.

When the dinner was over, everyone circulated around the room, socializing with a drink in their hand. Thomas leaned down and whispered in Diane's ear, "If your uncle didn't make these parties mandatory, it would be the last thing that I would be doing tonight."

"Oh, Thomas, relax and enjoy yourself."

"I can't. I'm bored! This isn't my way of conducting business."

"Well, Darling, I look at it as an opportunity. I'm going to stir up some business. After all, that's the reason my uncle has these dinner parties. Don't be such a bore. Have another glass of wine. I'm going to mingle. I'd suggest you do the same."

Later, Thomas stood against the wall and observed the crowd. He thought, *How in the world can those jokers hold so much booze? They're guzzling it down like it is soda pop. How can they make rational business decisions?* He looked over at his girlfriend. Diane was no exception. He could tell she was feeling her drinks. She was a bit too flirtatious for his taste. Annoyed at the situation, he decided to get some fresh air.

On the way, he noticed the door was opened to the den. In the darkened room, he noticed that a television had been left on. It captured his attention when he saw the big bold letters across the screen, SPECIAL BULLETIN. Curiosity got the best of him. He slipped into the den and sat down. As he turned up the volume, he heard, "President of the European Council Ali Hamarat and President Omidi of the United States have been here at the European Union headquarters for the better part of the day. The hall is filled with EU members as well as UN members. Also, Israel and Palestine, along with other Arab countries, are all represented here today.

There was a pause, and then he lowered his voice and continued, "There have been speculations and theories as to what this world-shaken event is all about. There are rumors going around that are saying that Israel and Palestine have finally reached a peace contract. Folks, it's only a rumor, but this reporter feels there might be some validity to it. After all, EU leader Ali Hamarat, President Omidi of the United States, Palestinian leader Ahmpd Sirham, and Israel's prime minister Weitzman have all been behind closed doors for the best part of the day. You can see as our cameras are scanning the room that all the various dignitaries are all here today. Something big must be going down. I'm not sure what is happening. Wait, someone is coming up to the podium now!"

In anticipation, the enormous crowd in the auditorium became loud as their curiosity was rising. A speaker stepped up to the podium. He raised his hands high in the air and called for silence in the room. He then announced, "Ladies and gentlemen, it is my pleasure to welcome up to the podium, president of the United States, President Omidi!"

There was a roar of applause as the TV cameras focused on President Omidi walking up to the podium. Omidi stood in silence as he glanced out over the anxiously awaiting audience. Slowly but forcefully, he began, "World leaders and people throughout the world." The room broke out in applause again. Omidi held out his arms to quiet the spectators. Then he continued, "Attention, please, distinguished guests and those watching this important televised world event from your homes. President Hamarat of Turkey and the European Union's newest president of the European Council and I are about to bring you a very important historical, life-changing announcement.

Within the past three years, World War III has been raging out of control. This explosive war was activated by terrorism when they attacked the United States in 9/11. Throughout these past years all along the Euphrates River from Turkey and on down to the Persian Gulf, there has been a fiery of conflagration. The United States and her allies are firmly entrenched into the Middle East.

With most of our troops being occupied in the Middle East, North Korea decided to invade South Korea. Also China thought the timing was good for an attack on Taiwan. Former President Rosenberg of the United States showed US disapproval by launching a nuclear bomb on Tokyo, regretfully destroying the mainland of China."

Omidi stopped his speech for a moment as rage filled the president's face. He yelled out, "This has to stop! As many regions, the United States is emotionally, physically, and economically bankrupt. Our army is thinly spread all over the world. Along with our law enforcers, our homeland is now protected by the United States militia. This is an unauthorized organization by the people, but it is all we have at the present. For the best part, these soldiers are doing a good job. However, there are a few bad units among them."

Omidi took a drink of water that was sitting there for him and then began again, "That is one reason I stand before you today. Something has to change, and it needs to be very soon. That's way I am giving my allegiance and loyalties to the European Union!" The room burst out in applause. "The only way to stop all this violence is with a one-world leadership and a one-world religion! This is the EU's views, and they are mine as well!" More applause filled the auditorium.

As it quieted down, Omidi announced, "Ladies and gentlemen, coming up to the podium to join me is President Ali Hamarat, your new president of the European Council."

The crowd roared once again as Hamarat stepped up. After allowing them to applaud for several minutes, Hamarat quieted the mega-filled hall down. "Thank you so much for your generous welcome. Distinguished members of the European Union, the United Nations, world dignitaries, and people watching from your homes, as you all know, I along with President Omidi, have been promising to end World War III and bring peace to the world. Our goal is to put an end to international chaos and bring a change to the world. A world of peace and tranquility! To show that commitment today, you will witness a step closer to those goals. To honor that commitment, we bring you proof of our endeavors to achieve peace in the world." The room broke out in cheers and applause once again.

Hamarat held up his arms to quiet the crowd. When they settled down, he continued, "Three years ago, World War III was officially declared when Iran bombed the United States' 700-million-dollar-embassy compound in Baghdad. Since then, Islamic terrorism have bombed several embassies throughout Europe. ISIS terrorist have been running ramped throughout all parts of the globe.

"Regretfully, as President Omidi mentioned, the former United States President Rosenberg waged a surprise nuclear war against China. It abolished their entire governmental system. Rosenberg's official explanation for the attack was China's aggression against Taiwan. However, it is clear to the world that he wanted to take down China to abolish the trillions of dollars of United States' debt. The world looked upon this gruesome act to be an appalling war crime against China. As we have seen, this ghastly misconduct didn't work as Rosenberg had thought it might. The war continues to tear the US's national economy to shreds. United States troops are stationed in many parts of the world but especially all up and down the Euphrates River. Former President Rosenberg had worked alone to take down the powerful world giant when he gave an executive order, which led to his impeachment. Thankfully, competent Vice President Omidi was there to take his place. In his acceptance speech, he remorsefully apologized for the appalling war crimes done against China by the impeached Rosenberg.

"My point is, between the perils of war and national disasters throughout the world, almost a third of the world's population has been wiped out!" Hamarat slammed his fist to the podium and yelled,

"War must be stopped before the human race completely destroys itself!"

Hamarat stepped aside as Omidi took over once more. He braced both hands on the sides of the podium, smiled broadly, and said, "And now, people of the world, the good news! The news that President Hamarat and I have come here to share with you today! It is my pleasure to announce that after decades of talks and negotiations, Israel and Palestine have reached an interim peace solution! It will be in effect for seven years. After that time, the issues will be revisited. Hopefully by that time, we'll all be able to live in peace in a one-world government where there will no longer be any conflicts to overcome." The audience wildly applauded.

The crowd kept applauding as Hamarat took the microphone again. He raised his arms to quiet the people. With a wide smile on his face, he said, "My sentiments are the same as my distinguished new colleague and friend." He laughed a little and said, "I bet you never thought you would hear me say that, right?" A roar of laughter went throughout the room.

Hamarat continued on, "As you all know, the Middle East has played a big part in this disgusting war. As the United States, Turkey is drained as well. We are tired of wars and rumors of war." Hamarat dragged out the words, "It must stop!"

After more applause, there was compete silence for a moment. Hamarat then continued, "I too want to pledge my allegiance to the united European Union! My quest is for world peace. Which brings me to the good news that President Omidi has shared with you. The long sought-after Peace between Israel and Palestine!" The room exploded with applause and cheering.

"Thank you. For several weeks, President Omidi and I have been promising you a peaceful world. The world at present is full of conflicts and international chaos, but in its place, we want to make it a world of peace and harmony. Today, we bring you proof that peace can prevail!" There was more applauding.

When all was quiet, Hamarat began again, "Prime Minister Benjamin Weitzman of Israel and Palestinian Authority president Yasser Kabha is here with us today. Please, allow me to give you a little history as to what has led up to our negotiations. First of all, there has been an issue with the Jews that live in the West Bank/Judea. In 1967, the Arab-Israel war was waged. Israel launched a massive air assault that crippled Arab's air capability. The Israeli army captured Jerusalem and, on the Syrian border, gained the strategic Golan Heights. The Israeli war was won in six days. Many Jews returned to sites where their ancestors had lived for thousands of years. They were convinced it was their Holy Land that God had promised them. On June 7, 1967, right after the six-day war, Commander Motta Gur radioed his historical announcement, 'The Tempo Mount is in our hands.' However, defense minister Moshe Dayan ordered that it be handed over to Waqif, the religious endowment entrusted with looking after Muslim property.

Oh yes, the historical, symbolic, beloved mountain has been a long fought over piece of property for decades. The Tempo Mount, also known as the Haram, is one of the most important sites in the Old City of Jerusalem. It has been a religious site for thousands of years.

Mount Mariah is the holiest site in Judaism. They call it God's Mountain. The Jews believed it is the place God chose to rest His Divine Presence. Consequently, that is why King Solomon had the first temple built in 957 BC. When that temple was destroyed, Cyrus the Great authorized another to be built in 530 BC. As you know, that one was destroyed by the Romans in 70 AD. The spot has been vacant since that time. According to their Jewish tradition, they want to erect a third and final one at that same location.

"In Islam, this mount is revered as the location of Islamic prophet Muhammad's journey and ascent to heaven. It is also the site of the al-Aqsa Mosque and the Dome of the Rock, the oldest extant Islamic structure in the world. The right to the Temple Mount's ownership has been a great source of conflict throughout the years. It has been suggested by many that the Muslims and Jews share the Mount. Back in the year 2000, Present Clinton proposed the sharing of the Tempo Mount but was turned down. Years later, the former President Barack Obama indorsed the Clinton Partnership, that, in part, says the Tempo Mount would be placed under a sharing arrangement with UN supervision. Also, on August 8, 2012, a member of the Israeli Knesset (the home of the Israeli's parliament) submitted a bill proposing the sharing of the Tempo Mount.

In addition to Israel and Palestine's conflicts, numerous plans of partition were prosed for Palestine to become a state but without the agreement of all parties. The Vatican has referred to Palestine as a state since 2012 when the United Nations voted to recognize it as a nonmember observer state. Vatican policy has long held a two-state solution is the best road to peace in the Holy Land. In 2015, then President Obama's administration considered a UN security council resolution on a Palestinian state to pass, provided some wording could be found that would encourage a negotiated peace. In 2013, Yossi Beilin, Israeli statesman said that 'Netanyahu' was willing to establish an interim Palestinian state without a final agreement."

The Turkish ruler paused for a moment and, then in a loud strong voice, announced, "So ladies and gentlemen of the world, we have reached an interim peace agreement between Israel and Palestine! Thanks to the endless hours of negotiations between parties, the European Union, the United Nations, President Omidi, and myself now have a workable peace treaty in place. The leaders of Israel and Palestine have verbally agreed with the wording of the contract we have drawn up for them. Today, you will witness the signing of the Israeli and Palestinian Peace Treaty. This treaty will be in place for a seven-year period, giving Israel and Palestine time to reach a rational, acceptable, permanent solution. Now, I would like to summarize the two main issues of the peace contract.

"First, there will be a two-state solution, which will recognize both Israel and Palestine statehood. Palestine's borders will consist of the occupied Palestinian territories known as the West Bank and the Gaza Strip. During this interim period, Israel will maintain control of Jerusalem. At the present, there are over 550,000 Jews living in Judea and Samaria. Each Jew living in the Palestinian State will be given one of two choices. They could have the United Nations or the European Union buy out their homes and businesses and be relocate to the Israel State. From the past, we understand that there are historical and religious reasons these Jews do not want to leave. They have already proved it to be impractical to try to evacuate them by force, so we must divide the land without removing the settlers. If this tribe of Jews are interested in staying, they must live as citizens under Palestinian control. They will be a Jewish minority in a Palestinian State.

"Second, this beloved and fought over holy site, the Tempo Mount or otherwise known as the Harm Al-Sharif (Noble Sanctuary), will be shared. It will remain under a no sovereignty or God's sovereignty. The Muslims will be able to continue to worship in their al-Aqsa Mosque, the Dome of the Rock, while the Jews will be allowed to erect their third tempo on the Mount. They may worship as they wish, as they did in Old Testament times, including the sacrifice of animals."

Hamarat turned from the audience to the awaiting Prime Minister Benjamin Weitzman and the acting President Yasser Kabha. He said, "If you, gentlemen, will join President Omidi and me, we will proceed to sign the seven-year peace treaty. Omidi and I will be signing in the name of the European Union and the United Nations Organizations."

All Thomas could hear was thunderous applause echoing throughout the hall. As his head was pounding, he stood in front of the television in utter shock! It was as if a blaring red neon sign was going on and off in his head, THE ANTICHRIST SIGNS SEVEN-YEAR PEACE TREATY WITH ISRAEL! Like most Christians, Thomas believed that the signing of the seven-year peace treaty would not take place until after the biblical rapture. Thomas fell to his knees as tears flowed from his eyes, and he prayed out loud,, "No! God, no! What did I do so wrong that you didn't take me up in the rapture? I was sure that I was saved! There was no doubt in my mind that I wasn't! Dear Jesus, what did I do wrong? There is only one unpardonable sin—rejecting you. I know I have backslid, Lord Jesus. I gave up my marriage because I could not forgive Lorraine. I know that I have done the same things that I have accused her of doing. I was so upset with her because she drank wine that one time. Now I drink wine every time I go out for dinner! I accused Lorraine of lusting after another man, and I have lust for Diane. Or is it because I gave up my calling to the ministry? That must be it! When I gave up the ministry, was I rejecting You? Is that it, Lord? I am so sorry, God! Please, forgive me. Please, don't leave me behind!"

When Diane realized that Thomas had been gone for a while, she set out to find him. She walked past the den and noticed that the door was opened. There she saw Thomas on the floor and on his knees. As she walked into the room, she saw tears running down his cheeks and heard him talking.

"Thomas, get up! You're talking to yourself," she yelled at him. While trying to help him up, she scolded, "You're intoxicated!" She chuckled a little and said, "Get up, you're drunk! I never saw you drunk before. You certainly are a pathetic drunk. Come on, Thomas, get a hold of yourself!"

Thomas slowly got up and sat in a chair. He looked up at Diane and, in a daze, told her, "I missed the rapture."

"You did what?"

"Diane, I missed the rapture."

"You are really drunk."

"No, no. I am not drunk. I must be in shock or something!" he cried out, "Diane, I missed the rapture! Do you know what that means?"

"Are you talking about the Bible story about 'the one in the field and the other one was taken'?"

"Yes, Diane, the rapture that happens before the tribulation. I just saw it on TV! I just saw Israel and Palestine sign a seven-year peace treaty."

"So!"

"Don't you understand that in the Bible, it says that this happens at the start of the tribulation? Christians don't go through the tribulation. They are raptured before!"

"Oh come on, you really don't believe that stuff, do you? You're a good guy. God is not going to keep you out of heaven. Only really bad people go to hell." With a puzzled look on her face, she said, "That is if there really is a hell."

"I'm okay now," he said as he managed to get some composure back. "And oh yes, Diane, there is definitely a hell. But you are right, I had too much wine. Can you leave me by myself for a little while? I'll just sit here until I can get a grip. I'll catch up with you a little later, okay?"

"Yeah, sure, but you better lay off the booze for tonight."

"Yeah, sure."

When Diane was out of the room, Thomas dialed Lorraine's number. It rang several times but no answer. Thomas's mind was racing. *Lorraine has been raptured! If anyone would be, it would be her.*

Now how can I tell her I'm sorry qnd that I love her? My sweet Lorraine is gone. And Linda! Scott! They're probably all gone!

After several rings, Thomas hung up and tried to call his son.

"Come on, Scott, answer the phone." *What am I saying! I don't want to be left alone, but I don't want Scott to be left behind either. I don't want any of my family to go through the tribulation, even if I do!*

Thomas let the phone ring several more times and then gave up. *I can't wait to find out. I have to go to Lorraine's and see if she is really gone or not. Why, God, didn't you give me a chance to tell her good-bye? That I loved her?*

Rushing out of the den, Thomas found Diane in the crowd. She was laughing and standing a bit too close to some man. She was startled when he hurried up to her.

"You are going to have to find another way home tonight."

"Don't be that way, honey. I'm just trying to get some business going. Remember that's what this party is all about."

"No, fine. I don't care. I just have to go now!"

"Why? Where are you going?"

"Can't talk about it anymore. I've got to go to my wife's!"

"You're wife! Thomas, I swear, if you go and leave me here, you can keep going and never come back," she yelled as the door slammed in her face.

17

Lorraine's apartment, October 3rd 11:30 p.m.

Thomas drove the hour and a half to Bowling Green, Ohio. He barely thought of anything else but getting to Lorraine's apartment. He was expecting more chaos on the highway. He had expected lots of accidents along the way. He expected to see some vehicles smashed and empty, but traffic was moving normally. He wondered if the world had gotten so bad that only a few had been raptured. He tried Lorraine's phone several times but couldn't get a hold of her. He pushed the pedal of his car down until he was driving twenty miles over the speed limit. All he could think about was if Lorraine and their kids were still alive, or were they raptured?

When Thomas arrived at Lorraine's, he rushed to her apartment door. After knocking several times, he was about to give up. The door opened, but instead of it being his wife, it was Linda. She came to the door in her pajamas, yawning. She looked at her watch and complained, "Dad, it's almost midnight! What are you doing here so late? Come on in. I love seeing you, but it is late."

"I'm so sorry, baby. You must be devastated!"

"How did you find out? I just found out for sure today."

"I know, so did I. Isn't it awful?"

"Yeah, but I guess we'll all have to accept it and live with it. It's coming if we want it or not."

"You're really being brave, sweetheart. It will be hard on us with your mom gone, and I believe Scott is gone too."

"Yeah, well, Mom should be home anytime now." Linda thought for a moment and then said, "I bet it was Mom! Did Mom tell you?"

"Tell me, no. You mean your mother is still here?"

"Duh, I don't see her here, do you? Didn't you hear me, Dad? She should be home soon. She went to some urgent church meeting. Although her church meetings have never lasted this long before."

"No, I mean, didn't your mother get raptured?"

"Oh! Is that what you were talking about? I thought you...never mind."

After a brief hesitation, Linda said, "To be honest, I am getting a little sick of hearing about all that rapture stuff. Mom was all upset about it too. There obviously was not any rapture. I told Mother that the Bible is just a big fairy tale."

"Linda! Watch what you are saying. The Bible is the true word of God."

"Dad, I'm not sure I even believe in God anymore!"

Before Thomas could say anything, Lorraine opened the door and walked in. Her mouth flew open in surprise as she saw Thomas standing in her living room. Thomas ran to her and wrapped his arms around her as he said, "Lorraine, you're here!" he said with desperation in his voice.

"Yes, Thomas, and I'm just as surprised to see you, as apparently you are to see me."

"Lorraine, my dear sweet, Lorraine. I believe we are left behind. I think we missed the rapture!"

"Have you heard of anyone being raptured?"

"No, but Humarof and Omidi signed the seven-year peace treaty with Israel. You know that the Bible clearly states that we will be raptured before the signing of the seven-year covenant."

"There's got to be some kind of a mistake, Thomas! I have been at the church all night, and the pastor and all the members were trying to make some kind of sense out of it. There is no way that Pastor Nelson and his wife Sarah could miss the rapture. I'm certain of that! This must not be the covenant that the Bible is referring to."

"Oh, honey, I hope you are right! I don't know! I only know that when I first heard about the peace treaty, I was initially in shock. When I got my bearings, all I wanted to do was find out what happened to you and the kids. I was so positive that you all were raptured."

Lorraine gave out a little nervous laugh and said, "I thought that you had been raptured!"

Thomas got a weird look on his face.

"What if!"

"What if, what Thomas?"

"What if! What if our son was right! We were talking about it on our trip. He told me that while at the Bible seminary, a couple of his professors were teaching alternative rapture theories."

"Thomas, you don't really believe that, do you? You have always believed in the pre-tribulation concept."

"I only know one thing right now! Rapture or not, God has given me one last opportunity to mend our marriage. Lorraine, I love you so much. I am sure of that now. It took a crisis, but I know I can't live without you. Tell me it's not too late, my love. Lorraine, darling, will you take an old backslidden man of God back?"

With tears of Joy, Lorraine cried out, "Oh yes, my darling, of course, I'll take you back."

Linda's heart was full of joy as she watched her mother and father embrace. She joined in with a big family hug as she said, "Does this mean that you guys are back together again?"

Thomas looked at Lorraine and asked, "Well, honey, does it?"

"Of course, it does," Lorraine answered while smiling from ear to ear. "That is if you are really sure. Are you absolutely sure you want me back, Thomas?"

"With all my heart! I love you so much, honey."

"I love you too! If you only knew how unhappy I have been without you. I have missed you a so much!"

"Dad, what about that other woman?"

"Linda, I was stupid. I don't know what I was thinking. I was so lonely and missed the love that your mother and I had shared. Apparently, I was grasping for someone to take her place. I realize now that I was dating Diane on the rebound. Now that I think about it, we had nothing in common."

"Thomas, does she know that you were planning on coming back to me?"

"I didn't exactly tell her, but I'm sure she got the idea."

"My darling, you are a good man, so you need to do the right thing. You need to go to her and let her know that we are back together again. It wouldn't be right not to let her know where she stands with you."

"Yes, of course, you are right. I'll see her in a couple of days and tell her."

A loud knocking on the door startled the three of them. Lorraine rushed to the door. When she opened it, there stood her son with an attractive strawberry blond with beautiful emerald eyes. Lorraine threw her arms around him.

"Your father and I have both been trying to get a hold of you!"

"Dad? Is he here?"

"Yes, come in. Please, both of you." She looked directly at Sheryl and apologized, "I am so sorry, I didn't mean to ignore you. I was just so excited about seeing my son right now."

"Oh, no problem, Mrs. Perkins."

"Hey, this is great. The whole family is here! Mom, Dad, Linda, this is my fiancée, Sheryl."

"Your fiancée? Okay, then this is the lady you were telling me about up north, right?"

"Yes, Dad, the one I couldn't live without," Scott said with a sheepish grin. "The same one that I would like to be marooned with in an abandon ghost town." Everyone laughed.

"It is really nice finally getting to meet Scott's family. I've heard a lot of good things about each one of you." Looking directly at Lorraine and then Thomas, she said, "You have both raised a wonderful son."

Lorraine gave Sheryl a hug and said, "I'm really happy to meet you too, Sheryl. This is quite a surprise to me."

Lorraine gave Scott a playful slap on the shoulder as she said, "How come you kept Sheryl a secret from me?"

"Yeah," Linda chimed in. "Last I knew, you were dating a new girl every week."

"Hey, kid sister, I wouldn't talk if I were you. What's this I hear about you leaving Harold?"

"He's a jerk! I'm through with him," she said as tears began to fill her eyes.

"Okay, moving on," Scott said. "So where has everyone been? I've been trying for hours to get through to you guys."

"Scott, I've left you numerous messages," Thomas told his son.

"Yeah, I know. The messages all said that you had to get a hold of me right away. When I tried to call you back, either the phone was busy, or there was no answer. Then half the time, I got a recording that all lines were in use, try later. Did you get any of my messages?"

"Yes, all I could hear is that you had to get a hold of me. I also got a lot of sorry no service at this time."

"When I tried to call you, I couldn't get through either, Scott," his mother commented. "However, most of the night, I was at church with the congregation, trying to figure out what is going on."

"Well, it's obvious to me now," Scott stated. "The biblical seven-year tribulation has started!"

Scott, there has to be another answer," his dad answered back.

"Okay, please, everyone just sit down and try to relax," Lorraine said. "I'll put on a pot of coffee. I see this is going to be a long night."

"Don't you guys have to go to work tomorrow?" Linda asked.

"I don't know about anybody else, but I won't be able to work tomorrow. I'm calling in for a sub to take my place in the morning."

"I feel the same, Lorraine. I'm calling the office tomorrow to let them know I won't be in. Diane thought I was drunk earlier tonight. She'll probably tell her uncle I have a hangover. I was drunk, all right, drunk with shock and confusion."

Lorraine and Thomas were sitting close together on the couch. He had his arm around her and gave her an occasional kiss on the check. Scott noticed, cleared his throat, and said, "Dad, there's something that I have to talk to you about in private."

"Sure, son! If you ladies will excuse us, Scott and I need to get a bit of fresh air."

Standing outside the door, Scott questioned his father, "Dad, I know it is none of my business, but what do you think you are doing with Mom? Don't you think that you are being a bit too familiar with her? Do you really think that is fair to her under the circumstances? Don't you think Mom's been hurt enough?"

"Wait, no! It is over between Diane and me. When this crisis came down, all I could think about was your mom and you guys! That's when I realized that I loved your mother, and no one else could ever take her place. Scott, your mom and I are back together again!"

Scott's eyes filled with tears of joy as he threw his arms around his dad and gave him a big bear hug.

"Let's go back inside to our family," Thomas said.

"That sounds good to me!"

The Perkins family were in deep conversation about the day's strange happenings when the phone startled them. "It's after one in the morning! Who calls this time of night?" Thomas asked.

Lorraine shrugged her shoulders as she answered the phone. "Hello," she answered.

"Hello, Lorraine, this is Dad. I've been trying to get a hold of you all night! Are you and Linda all right?"

"Yes, sure, Dad. How about you and mother?"

"We're all right, just a little shook up. This has been a weird day. There was a seven-year peace treaty signed between Israel and Palestine!"

"Yes, Dad, I've heard. I guess everybody is trying to get in touch with their loved ones. Everybody must have thought they missed the rapture like we did."

"Yes, I believe so. Have you seen the eleven o'clock news?"

"No, what was on?"

"The reporter said that there is mass confusion in the world because the Christian community is spreading some radical ideas. He said that the Christians are igniting panic throughout the world. When I turned on the television, the news anchor was making fun of Christians! I have to admit that I'm really confused as to what happened, but to make fun of our Christian brothers and sisters is just not right!"

"Leave it to the media to twist this into something it's not."

"What do you think about all this? What's really going on?"

"I don't know, Dad. Maybe that signing today was the seven-year peace treaty of the Bible, and we have been interpreting the time of the rapture wrong, I don't know."

"Your mother and I, along with Joe and his wife, have been at our church tonight, but even our pastor is totally confused."

"I know, Dad, that's where I was earlier. We couldn't come up with an answer either."

"I have been trying to get a hold of Thomas and Scott, but I can't get through to them either!"

"Dad, they're right here with me!"

"Your whole family is together?"

"Yes."

"Thank God for that!"

"Wait a minute, Dad, someone is knocking on the door."

Thomas jumped up and opened the door. To his surprise, it was his son-in-law. Harold was a young, handsome, muscular man with curly sandy hair.

"Harold, what in the world are you doing here? Do you know it's after one in the morning?"

"I'm sorry, Mr. Perkins, but I had to come! Do you know that there's chaos all over the place? The news says it's something to do with Christians. They're saying something about a rapture! Linda told me a little about that when we first met. I had to see if my wife was all right!"

When Linda saw Harold, she burst into tears and ran to meet him. She put her arms around his neck and said, "Harold, you came! I missed you so much!"

"Oh, babe, I have really missed you too!"

The room was full of chatter as the family welcomed Harold into the apartment.

"Dad, can you hear me?" Lorraine shouted into the receiver.

"Yeah, what's all the commotion over there?"

"Linda's husband just got here. We didn't know he was coming. Linda was quite surprised."

"Are the kids getting back together again?"

"I don't know, Dad, but Thomas and I are!"

"What! Why, that is wonderful news! Your mother is going to be so happy. Listen, honey, we need to get together and figure this out. I'm going to call Joe in the morning and see if he will fly us to Bowling Green. Maybe all of us together can make some sense out of this! We could get a hotel suite and get together there. What do you say? Oh, darn! Do you guys have to work tomorrow?"

"No, Dad! We can't work with this hanging over our heads. We need answers too. Call me when you get the details, and we'll meet you at the hotel."

After Lorraine shut off her phone, she told everyone about what her dad had said.

Scott spoke up, "You can count me in. I'll be there." He looked at Sheryl and asked, "You can stay another day, can't you, honey?"

"Yeah, sure, Scott."

"How about you Linda?" Thomas looked over at his daughter and asked.

"Dad, if you don't mind, I think Harold and I need to stay here and try to sort out things between us. Besides, I have something very important to tell him."

Harold looked surprised and asked, "Oh yeah! What?"

"Not now, Harold, tomorrow when we are alone."

Lorraine yawned and said, "I don't know about the rest of you, but I'm really getting tired. Tomorrow will be a big day. I suggest we all get some sleep. I'm afraid that I only have one bed and the sofa. Linda has been sleeping on the sofa. I can get some extra pillows and blankets for the floor. Just like camping, right, Scott?"

"Yeah, right, Mom. If you don't mind me asking, what about dad? You guys are still married. You're getting back together again, right?"

"Yes, Scott, what's your point?" Thomas asked.

"Well, I was just saying that it's okay with me, Dad, if you and mom share a bed."

"Why waste that double bed?" Linda said as she smiled at her parents. "It makes perfect sense to me."

Thomas and Lorraine looked at each other and then burst out laughing.

"Well, Lorraine, what do you think?" Thomas asked.

"Well, you are my husband. I believe it would be the most natural thing to do."

18

Marriott Hotel, Bowling Green, Ohio, October 4

Two o'clock that afternoon, Thomas, Lorraine, Scott, and Sheryl arrived at the Marriott hotel. James and his wife, Marge, greeted them in the front lobby of the hotel. With a warm smile, James and Marge greeted their family. "I'm so glad you could make it," James said.

As kisses and hugs were exchanged, Marge asked her grandson, "Now who is this pretty lady, Scott?

"Grandma and Granddad, meet my lovely fiancée, Miss Sheryl Higgins," Scott said proudly.

Marge gently took Sheryl's hands in hers and said, "Hello, dear. We are so happy to meet you."

The group went up to the hotel suite where Joe and Marlene were waiting for their return. Joe motioned over to his wife and said, "For those of you who haven't met my beautiful wife yet, this is my wife Darlene."

After Darlene's introduction, James introduced Lorraine and Sheryl to Joe.

"Nice to finally be meeting you, ladies," Joe said as he shook their hands. "I had the pleasure of meeting your men when we flew to the Keweenaw Peninsula."

Lorraine smiled at Joe and answered back, "Well, I really enjoyed getting to know Darlene and your boys, Zach and Tim. We had a wonderful time! I know my friend Christina and her girls enjoyed it too."

"I know, I had a fantastic time!" Marge said.

"As did I," Darlene agreed.

James called for room service and ordered lunch for everyone. There had been too much going on since the controversial news report that food was the last thing on their minds. However, to their empty stomachs, food was beginning to sound really good at this point. When lunch arrived, James asked Thomas to say a blessing.

Thomas prayed, "Our dear Heavenly Father, we meet here today in complexity and confusion, but we have the assurance that you are an ominous, all-knowing God. We can rest assured in our faith that you have matters in your control and that you have a plan. We need to fully put our trust in you. Our dear God, please, give us some understanding as to what is happening. What do these current events mean? And please, guide us to do your will. We thank you for all the blessings you shower upon us, and we thank you for the meal we are about to enjoy. Amen."

After lunch, the small group got down to business, trying to make sense of what happened the night before. James spoke up first and said, "Our pastor has always preached that we would be raptured before the signing. What's going on?" He looked directly at his son-in-law and asked, "Thomas, you're a pastor. What do you make of this situation?"

"Dad, I wish I had a good answer for you. The event yesterday sure gave the appearance of the Bible's seven-year treaty with Israel. Thomas opened his Bible and said, "Let me read to you Daniel 9:27,

KJV, 'And he shall confirm the covenant with many for one week; and in the midst of the week he shall cause the sacrifice and the oblation to cease, and for the overspreading of abominations he shall make it desolate.'"

"As we are all aware, the term *one week* represents a seven-year period," Thomas continued. "The covenant that just happened is for seven years! I have believed all my life that the rapture should have happened before that signing! As we are all aware, yesterday's signing of the peace treaty really looks like the same covenant of the Bible. There is a possibility that last evening's event should have triggered the tribulation. That is why I am so baffled! I just don't see how it could be, but Scott has another possible explanation."

James turned to Scott and asked, "Grandson, you haven't been out of the seminary long, what did you learn about Bible prophecy?"

"Well, Granddad, one of my professors taught the pre-tribulation view like all of you have been taught. That of course is the most popular view of modern times. However, a couple of my professors taught different views. One taught the pre-wrath theory, which is similar to the mid-tribulation views. The differences between the two is that the pre-wrath theory goes beyond the midpoint of the tribulation. He taught that the rapture would be right after the trumpet judgments. He claims that this period of time is Satan's wrath upon the world. He teaches the vial judgments are God's wrath. In other words, after the Antichrist's persecution is poured out on Christians and Jews, God will then rapture His elect. Right after the rapture, God's wrath will be poured out onto the rest of the people left on earth.

Joe was glued to every word as he asked, "What did you learn about the post-tribulation theory?"

"Well, Professor Fischer believes that Christians will live through most of the seven years of the tribulation. He believes that six of the trumpets have already been sounded. He said that the sixth trumpet started World War III. He also believes that the seventh trumpet, the last trump would signal the rapture and would bring Christ's reign to the world. Scott took his Bible and said, "Let's read Jesus's own words in Matthew 24:31, 'And he will send his angels with a great sound of a trumpet, and they shall gather together his elect from the four winds, from one end of heaven to the other.' Also the Bible says in Revelation 11:15. 'And the seventh angel sounded; and there were great voices in heaven, saying The kingdoms of this world are become the kingdoms of our Lord, and of his Christ; and he shall reign for ever and ever.'"

Thomas looked around the room at all the anxious faces and said, "I'm still seriously doubtful about that theory."

Scott chuckled and said, "Do we have another doubting Thomas here?" The others started laughing. Scott joked, "Hey guys, don't shoot me. I'm only the messenger here. Look at Matthew 24:29-31. It says, 'Immediately after the tribulation of those days shall the sun be darkened, and the moon shall not give her light, and the stars shall fall from heaven, and the powers of the heavens shall be shaken. And then shall appear the sign of the Son of man in heaven: and then shall all the tribes of the earth mourn, and they shall see the Son of man coming in the clouds of heaven with power and great glory. And he shall send his angels with a great sound of a trumpet, and they shall gather together his elect from the four winds, from one end of heaven to the other.'"

"I've never thought about that verse that way before, son. I'm not sure if I can argue the point you are making about the rapture and God's wrath all coming at the same time period."

Scott flipped ahead in the Bible pages as he said, "I know you know this verse also. It's 1 Thessalonians 4:16 & 17. 'For the Lord himself shall descend from heaven with a shout, with the voice of the archangel, and with the trump of God: and the dead in Christ shall rise first: Then we which are alive and remain shall be caught up together with them in the clouds, to meet the Lord in the air; and so shall we ever be with the Lord.'"

"I've only preached on that verse hundreds of times. If you notice, it only says 'the trumpet of God.' It doesn't say it's the last trumpet."

"No. Maybe not in that particular passage. However, let's turn back to 1 Corinthians 15: 51 & 52. 'Behold, I shew you a mystery; We shall not all sleep, but we shall all be changed. In a moment, in the twinkling of an eye, at the last trump: for the trumpet shall sound, and the dead shall be raised incorruptible, and we shall be changed.'"

Thomas was blown away. He told his son, "I've read that passage thousands of times, but this is the first time that the words *last trumpet* has stood out to me!"

"Yes, Dad, the last trumpet is the seventh trumpet!"

"Well," Joe broke in, "I guess it's just a game of wait and see. We need to keep an eye on Ali Hamarat, President Omidi, and Israel to see what happens next."

"That's all well and good," Scott said. "But what if my professor's theory is right. We only have about three and a half years of peace. If we don't plan now, God only knows what will happen to us!"

Excitedly, James stood up and said. "That settles it, Joe. We have to tell them!" James couldn't hold it back any longer as he said, "Do we have a surprise for all of you? Don't we, Joe?"

Joe entwined his fingers, put them behind his neck, and leaned back as he said, "Oh yeah, do we ever! We haven't even told our wives about it yet."

James's words came bubbling out with excitement, "Do you remember that little ghost town that you boys discovered?"

"Yes," Thomas and Scott both chimed in.

"Well, now it is ours!"

Scott jumped to the edge of the sofa with enthusiasm. "You're kidding, right?" Scott eagerly blurred out.

"No, Scott, I'm not. Joe and I bought 1,500 acres of that mountain. We bought that whole valley including the two farms!"

Both Marge and Darlene were in shock. Marge frowned at her husband.

"James, tell me you didn't," Marge scolded. "How could you buy something that extremely expensive without running it by me first?"

"Marge, honey, it was originally a business venture. I always try to spare you with business deals. Besides, Joe and I stole it! It's been over a hundred years ago when the town's people moved out. They just left! After years passed by, the property reverted back to the county. Then by some miracle, its paperwork got lost and was forgotten for all these years. It took the clerk hours to dig up the paperwork on all its parcels. Seems they got misfiled decades ago. The files show that the last transaction on any of those parcels happened back in the 1800s."

"Yeah, it was so funny," Joe spoke up. The clerk had to call his grandfather, who had worked at the old courthouse several years ago. He thought his granddad might remember where the paperwork might be. The granddad was a retired county supervisor, who had worked for the county over fifty years. He'd been retired for over twenty years but liked coming in the office from time to time. This guy must have been in his nineties. He comes in and takes us down to the basement. After a couple hours of rummaging through old dusty files, the old man pulled out a thick file containing all the paperwork from the valley."

"We asked the elderly man if he could remember any information about the valley."

"He said that he remembered as a boy hearing stories," James added. "He told us that something bad happened there but couldn't remember for sure what it was. He thought that he remembered back then that the valley was haunted. That's why no one wanted to go near that old place. He also told us that there was some talk about an old copper mine somewhere in that valley. "

Joe laughed and said, "All I know is, that it's the best business deal that I've ever made!"

"What do you plan on doing with it?" Darlene asked her husband.

"James and I thought it would make a great summer retreat. With all the bombings and war at our door, it would be a good get-away from the city. I know Zachary and Tim will love it up there. The boys and I wouldn't have to go anywhere else to hunt and fish. It could be our recreational retreat."

"I guarantee they will love it," Scott said. "That area is beautiful. I'd move up there in a heartbeat, if I could make a living."

Scott hesitated a moment. He chuckled and said, "Maybe it would make a good safe haven from the Antichrist."

Sheryl gave Scott a dirty look and said, "Ah, what about me. Hello, you recently asked me to marry you. I don't want to go up there to live. Lower Michigan winters are cold enough! I sure wouldn't want to deal with winters in the Upper Peninsula."

Scott gave her a pleading look and said, "Oh honey, if you saw it, you would fall in love with it too! It would be a great place to raise kids."

"Scott! We haven't even talked much about our wedding yet, let alone having kids!"

Thomas looked over at Lorraine and asked, "Honey, you haven't said anything. What are you thinking?"

"Well, if this is what Dad and Joe want, I guess it would be a good place to vacation. I have heard so much about this fabulous ghost town, I'd love to see it myself."

Joe jumped to his feet with excitement and said, "Why not! I have my plane here. We could all jump on the plane and spend a few days in the Keweenaw Peninsula. That way, you women can see what we fell in love with."

"Joe, I'm a teacher," Lorraine said. "I took today off, but tomorrow, I have to go in. I really can't afford to take more time off."

"Yeah, I've got to go back to work too," Thomas said. "I need to give my boss a two-week notice."

Thomas's phone rang. He checked the name on the call.

"I'm sorry, I have to take this." Thomas got up and walked over to the window where he had some privacy. Hesitatingly, he answered, "Hello, Diane."

"Thomas, where are you? I heard you called in sick this morning. I stopped over to your apartment earlier, and you weren't there! I know you mentioned something about needing to see your ex-wife, but you were much too drunk to drive that far. Darn it, Thomas, you had me worried! I thought you might have gotten into a car accident."

"Diane, take it easy, I'm fine."

"Well, my uncle is very upset with you for missing work today. He said that you have been taking far too much time off lately. When I told him how drunk you got at his dinner party, he assumed that you were suffering with a hangover. You know how he feels about that. He doesn't care how much his employees drink on their own time, but they better not use a hangover for an excuse not to be productive or to miss work."

"Yes, Diane, I understand, but I wasn't drunk. The news about the seven-year contract with Israel shook me up."

"That's stupid to let something that petty throw you for a loop like that!"

"Diane, it is not something petty. Last night, I believed that I had missed the rapture. I thought that I had committed an unpardonable sin against God, and I would be left behind to go through the Great Tribulation."

"Oh, hogwash! Nobody was raptured, were they?"

"No, that's what has me confused. Anyway, Diane, I don't like telling you this on the phone, but I cannot keep it from you any longer. I'm going back to my wife. When this all came down, I realized that I really loved Lorraine and wanted to be with her through anything that we had to face. Diane, I'm truly sorry if I've hurt you, but it's over between us."

"Why you...how dare you! I went to bat for you with my uncle. Now you can kiss your job good-bye and me as well! Your check is in the mail, sweetheart!" Diane slammed the receiver down as hard as she could.

Thomas walked up to the others in the room with a sad look on his face. He said sadly, "I'm fired." Then a big broad smile came across his face. He laughed as he said, "I'm free to go to the UP!"

"Well, that's great," Lorraine told him. "While you were on the phone, we turned on the television to see if we could get any news. And lo and behold, the local news came on and said due to the mass confusion, our local schools will be shut down until next week. According to the news, schools all over are closing for the week." Lorraine raised her voice and shouted, "Praise the Lord, and let's go to the Keweenaw!"

19

Keweenaw Peninsula, Upper Michigan, October 5

After Joe Wydeck fueled up his plane, the eight of them left for their excursion to the Keweenaw Peninsula that Friday morning. This flight was even more beautiful than the previous flight because of the fall colors. It was a cool October day as they flew over Lower Michigan. They could see the trees as they began changing to their variety of colors. The contrast of the land and the Great Lakes was a breathtaking view. Then as they flew over Upper Michigan, the colors from the trees below became even more vivid. The color of the leaves was at its peak with a mixture of brilliant reds, yellows, and bright oranges.

As before, Joe put his plane down at the Houghton County Memorial Airport by Calumet. James had two Hummers waiting for them at the national car rental.

"How about it, Scott, are you going to be our driver again?" James asked his grandson.

"Sure, Granddad, I love getting my hands on a Hummer steering wheel."

"Good. Joe will drive the other one. He knows how to get to the inn that we booked."

"Okay," Scott said. "Aren't we going to the same hotel we stayed in the last time?"

"No. Joe and I found a real nice quaint inn at Eagle Harbor when we flew up here to purchase the land. It is really quite nice and has an excellent dining room. Best part, it's a lot closer to our ghost town."

Marge and Darlene got into the Hummer with Joe and James, while Thomas, Lorraine, and Sheryl rode with Scott. The men drove the vehicles approximately eighteen miles north on highway Forty-one/twenty-six, until they came to where twenty-six branched out from forty-one. There they took twenty-six up toward the town of Eagle River.

As they approached Eagle River, Lorraine pointed to a waterfall and said, "Isn't that beautiful!"

"Yes, it is," Thomas answered. "It is the Eagle River Falls. We saw it last time we were up here. Over there is the Eagle River Lighthouse."

The group in Joe's Hummer was enjoying the view as well. James asked, "Joe, why don't you drive up to the lighthouse so the ladies can see it?"

"Sure," Joe agreed. He pulled the Hummer into the parking lot and stopped in front of the lighthouse. The men let the ladies know that the lighthouse was no longer opened to the public. After leaving the lighthouse, the Hummers pulled away to continue the scenic drive up M-26.

"Ladies, this is the Sand Dunes Drive," Joe said. "From Eagle River to Eagle Harbor, there is seven miles of one of the most gorgeous scenic drives you will ever see. It follows the shore of Lake Superior through woods, hills, and dunes."

As they drove along the Sand Dunes Drive, Marge said, "Oh, this drive is breathtaking."

"It's absolutely beautiful!" Darlene agreed.

As they drove on, the women were also impressed with the town of Eagle Harbor and its beautiful beaches. The town had two lighthouses. After the ride through town, Joe pulled into a parking lot of an old but cozy-looking inn. Joe turned around facing Darlene and Marge in the backseat and said to them, "This is the inn that James and I told you about. We will be staying here tonight."

"Oh, it's so quaint looking, Joe. I love it," Darlene said! Marge smiled her approval.

James had a smug smile on his face as he said, "Wait till you see inside. It really is a cozy inn. We knew you girls would love it."

First, the four couples got settled into their rooms. Then as planned, they all met up again in the hotel's dining room where they enjoyed a fine dinner together.

The next morning after a good breakfast, the couples were on their way to the old ghost town. Before Joe left town, he stopped into the town's general store. Scott pulled his Hummer in next to Joe's.

Joe asked, "So, James, do you mind coming in with me? I've got to pick up a couple things."

"Of course not, Joe."

To the anxious passengers waiting in the Hummers, they seemed to take forever. Everyone waiting in the vehicles was anxious to get to the property as soon as possible. Twenty minutes later, Joe and James came back with two carts full of items.

"What's all this?" Thomas asked as he and Scott helped load the grocery bags and boxes into Joe's Hummer.

"Thought I'd pick up a little camping gear and food for later. I figure we will be out there for the better part of the day. We picked up a camp stove, some pots and pans, a charcoal burner along with charcoal and lighter, dish soap, sponge, dishtowels, gallon jugs of water, and some food. Might be a few other incidentals in there too. I thought it would be fun for us men to go out and look for a mine. Hopefully, while we are out scouting for the mine, just maybe the women would cook us up a meal."

Scott's face lighted up when he heard the word *mine*. Eagerly, his voice raised, "Man! That would be great! Your own town with a mine to boot!"

"Yeah, having your own mine, that would be great!" Thomas agreed. "By the way, Joe, The camp meal sounds good, but how do you plan on getting all this stuff to the town? That was no easy hike with backpacks on. Carrying this heavy camp gear and groceries seems impossible! Especially now that the ladies are with us."

"Well, I'm not sure, Thomas. It could be a difficult task. Maybe the women will have to make dinner out in the open by the creek," Joe answered.

Joe winked at James and said, "I guess, we'll just have to *cross that bridge* when we get there."

They drove east on twenty-six for about three miles when they spotted Silver Falls. Joe pulled the Hummer off the road and Scott pulled up behind him. They sat there for a few minutes enjoying the waterfall. As they were admiring the falls, two deer came to the edge off the pond for a drink of water. The wildlife was so abundant Lorraine suggested making a game out of who could spot the most animals on the rest of the drive.

After they left the waterfall, they drove directly toward Mt. Gratiot. The ladies were shown the place where Scott and Thomas camped at Sucker Creek. Then began the rocky ride up the mountain. It was a rough drive as everybody's head bounced about, but they were enjoying it. The higher they climbed, the rougher the road got. It was hard to tell if it was a road or not with all the growth. The Hummers plowed down small trees and underbrush as they drove through. As they approached the top, the two-track made a few sharp turns as it led back down into a valley.

When they reached the valley, they drove up to the creek. It was the same wide creek that the men had discovered the last time they were there. To Scott and Thomas's amazement, it didn't look the same; it had been drastically changed. The last time they had seen it, there was an old dilapidated bridge across it.

Scott jumped out of the Hummer and walked over to the open window of Joe's Hummer.

"What's going on here?" Scott asked in an excited voice. "The small trees and bushes are all cleared around the old bridge. Not to mention the bridge! It has had major repairs made on it!"

With big smiles on their faces, Joe and James got out of their Hummer. Thomas was dumfounded as he joined the men.

"What the heck," Thomas gasped. "What happed here? Somebody must be claiming the land and fixed up that old bridge! Now what'll we do?"

"We wanted to surprise you guys." James laughed. "We hired the work done last time we came up here."

"Praise the Lord," Thomas shouted out! "I can't believe you had time to get the bridge repaired! Is it safe to drive the Hummers over?"

"I'm not sure, Thomas," Joe answered. "Let's inspect the work, and if it looks safe. If so, I'll take it over alone the first time to check it out. The guys we hired seemed to know their business. I told them that I wanted it to be sturdy enough to hold a Hummer."

The four women got out of the Hummers as the men checked out the strength of the bridge. They were mesmerized as they watched fish swimming around in the clear creek water.

Joe kicked the pilings of the bridge a few times then declared, "This looks like a good sturdy construction. I'm confident that it will hold a Hummer, along with all of us. However, I'll test it first."

Everyone watched as Joe slowly drove the big vehicle over the newly constructed bridge. The small group cheered as they joined him on the other side.

As they stood in front of the bridge admiring it, James said, "Joe and I decided that this was all we would ask the workers to do. We made them swear not to go any further on the property. We wanted to keep it as private as possible. I could tell they were trustworthy men."

Thomas shook both his father-in-law's hand and Joe's as he said, "This is amazing! It sure is a wonderful surprise."

"I agree," Scott said. "Good job, Grandpa and Joe. I'm confident that we can get the Hummers into the main part of the town from here. We'll have to run down some small trees and brushes, but we can do it."

It wasn't the smoothest ride, but they managed to get to the first farm with no problems. The guys were excited about showing the ladies the buildings. The women were in awe as they walked into the farmhouse. They spent most of their time in the house, inspecting every piece of furniture and personal belongings that had been left behind so many years ago. Next, they went into the barn and outbuildings. Marge was the most excited out of the four women. Memories of her childhood flowed as she said, "This is so nostalgic for me! I was raised on a farm near a small town called Coopersville located in Western Michigan. This old farm reminds me so much of the place where I was raised."

"It is quite quaint like a Norman Rockwell painting," Darlene replied.

Scott stood behind Sheryl and wrapped his arms around her as he stood and looked out at the fields and admired the farm. He asked her, "Don't you just love the peace and tranquility of this place?"

"Okay, Scott, it's nice, but to live here, no way! Don't you think it would get a little boring?"

"How could it get boring when you're with the one you love? Where's you romance? I can see us living here. Maybe three or four little kids running around."

"Scotty! Please, we haven't decided on anything yet, remember? And then according to you, we only have six to seven years at the most. That is if the mean old Antichrist don't get us first."

When their daydreaming ended, they all got back in the Hummers. The excitement grew as Scott and Joe continued dodging trees and driving over bushes while they drove to the other old farm. It was the same in the second farmhouse as the first. The women's imaginations ran wild. The woman could see a different family in each house. Lorraine visualized the women dressed in long dresses from the turn of the century. Their husbands wore grubby old jeans with suspenders holding them up. She visualized the children were dressed the same as their parents, playing in a corner with homemade toys. When they left the second farm, they drove by the small country houses on the way into town. Of course, those had to be checked out by the ladies also. Then the grueling half a mile drive into the village. They were dodging large trees and riding over smaller ones until they reached the edge of town. Then the ladies saw the back of a church sitting directly in front of them. From there, the road made a semicircle around the church. The church sat proudly facing the town with buildings lining up on each side of what one time was a small dirt road.

The women could not believe their eyes. They had heard all about the ghost town, but to actually see it was quite another thing. As the men had done before them, the women had to explore each and every building. The men guided them through, giving their view of what might have taken place in each of the buildings. All three of the women were impressed with the large house filled with lovely antiques, which Thomas called the mayor's house.

They all sat around the huge fireplace in the great room talking about all they had seen. Then the possibility of the mine came up. "I don't know," Joe said. "If this town had a mine, maybe this big house was the mine owner's home. He was probably the town's wealthiest."

James laughed and replied back, "Well, perhaps you're right, Joe, but maybe he was the mayor also!"

"Just the answer I would expect from a lawyer." Joe laughed. Are you running for politics too?"

James laughed again and said, "Well, we spent more time looking around than we planned. It's getting late. If we want to find the mine today, we better get started. Come on, guys, let's go see if we can find a mine!" He looked over at the ladies and, with a playful grin on his face, asked, "Would you ladies mind staying behind and fixing us miners some grub?"

The women all laughed as Marge spoke up, "I'll be glad to stay behind! Not like my husband, I admit I am getting old. I don't think I could walk another step if my life depended on it."

Lorraine looked at her mother with a warm smile and said, "Oh you poor dear! I hope this trip wasn't too much for you."

With a big smirk on her face, Marge said, "I wouldn't have missed it for the world!"

Lorraine pulled up a chair for her mother and told her, "Well, you just sit here. There's plenty of us to do the cooking."

"Yeah," Sheryl spoke up. "At my job, when the cook doesn't show up, I take his place in the kitchen. I really enjoy cooking."

"That sounds great," Darlene said. "I name Sheryl the head cook! Lorraine and I can be your assistants, Sheryl."

The men all laughed as Scott said, "Okay then, it sounds like you women have it handled. We're not sure how long it will take, but we'll be back as soon as we can."

Lorraine walked the men out to the front porch. She warned, "Please, if you guys do find the mine, be careful. An old mine could be dangerous."

"Don't worry, darling, I'll make sure it's safe before we go in," Thomas answered as he gave his wife a quick kiss on the cheek.

"Okay, but I'll pray for your safety, just in case."

As the men set out to hopefully find a mine, they began talking about the world's circumstances. James asked Thomas, "Have you gave anymore thought to what's been happening?"

"Dad, I still don't know anymore. I'm still confused. I truly believed that we would have been raptured prior to the tribulation. All I know is that I am going to have to study some more because I do not have the answer. We'll need to pray a lot. I'm sure God will give us the right answers."

Joe rubbed the top of his head as he always did when confused. He spoke up, saying, "All I know is if that signing in Brussels was the same treaty of Revelation, we shouldn't still be here! As you, I have been taught that way all these years. It just doesn't seem like we could be wrong about something like that, does it?"

"Well, I don't know about you guys, but like I mentioned before I had a professor that believed we would live through part of the tribulation," Scott commented. "I don't know! Maybe, it's a possibility that he was on to something. Maybe he was right."

Joe got an iron-cold look on his face and said, "James and I bought this place for a nice summer vacation spot, but maybe we will need it for a retreat to get away from the Antichrist."

It grew quite as the men followed a trail that looked like it could have been a small road at one time. Maybe it was only a deer path, but it was something to follow. Scott took the lead and began following the path that led up hill.

After a couple hundred yards, Scott noticed a dark hole ahead of him. He yelled out, "Hey, you guys, I think I found something."

Scott rushed to the opening in the side of the mountain. "This is it, guys, the mine!"

Scott bent down as he started to step into the opening.

"Wait, Scott! Don't go in yet!" his dad called out.

"Why not, Dad?"

"It might not be safe! Besides, I don't think this is a mineshaft. Look at the sides and the top. Wouldn't it be a lot larger if it was a mine opening? This might be some type of cave or even a bear's den!"

"I believe you are right, Dad. It smells like rotten flesh in there."

"We don't have any lanterns or a gun. I really don't think we should take a chance by going in."

Disappointedly, Scott said, "Yeah, I hate to agree with you, but you're right."

James walked over to his grandson and patted him on the shoulder. He told him, "Don't look so sad, Scott. There will be more opportunities to find the mine. That is, if there is one. We don't know that for sure. It's getting late, and we had better be getting back, or the women will have the food all ate up. You know how this mountain air gives you an appetite."

Bowling Green, October 7

Linda and Harold were so engrossed watching the news that they didn't hear Lorraine unlock the door to the apartment. They were sitting on the sofa together when Lorraine and Thomas walked in. Lorraine sang out, "Hello, we're home."

"Mom, Dad, you're home already." Linda gasped.

"Well," Thomas said. "If you aren't happy to see us, I can whisk your mother away again. Maybe we could take a second honeymoon," he kidded.

"No, Dad. Of course, I am happy to see you guys. It's especially wonderful to see you together as husband and wife again. All I'm saying is, if you want to go on a honeymoon, go right ahead and do it."

"Oh, if only we could afford the luxury to do something like that, but I'm afraid there's school in the morning," Lorraine said with a sigh.

With a frown on his face, Harold said, "At least someone's got a job to go to."

"What do you mean, Harold?" Lorraine asked.

"Well...ah. I kind a...got fired."

"I guess we both have something in common," Thomas replied. "I lost my job as well. I was fired also! What happened to your job?"

"I was pretty bummed when Linda left me. I drank kind of heavy when she left. I missed some work. Then when I came here trying to get her back, I missed a couple days without calling in."

"Not good," Thomas said.

"I know it was dumb, but all I was thinking about was Linda."

"You're in construction, right?" Thomas asked. "Seems like there's always construction jobs in the paper."

"Not anymore! We were just watching the news, and the president finally admitted that we are now in a depression. In spite of all the thousands of men and women in the service, the unemployment has never been higher. It has been predicted that it will rise even more. There are not any jobs on the jobsites that I can do! They only hire licensed contractors now."

"Like I said, we're in the same boat. I have to hit the pavement and find a job too."

Lorraine put a big smile on her face in an effort to cheer them up. She told them, "Don't look so forlorn, guys. At least I have a job! This place is small, but we can make do until you both find work."

"What about our apartment?" Linda asked her husband.

"I got a notice that we have to move out. I missed a couple months' rent. I tried talking to the landlord, but he wouldn't listen."

"What about our stuff?"

"We can put it in storage for a couple months," her mother reluctantly added to the conversation.

"Where would we sleep?" Linda asked.

"Well, there's the sofa or the floor," her dad answered with a smirk on his face. "I remember how much you wanted to go camping when you were a kid, Linda. It's the same, only indoors."

"We could exchange the sofa for a hideaway bed," Lorraine suggested.

As the family was making plans, Thomas's cell phone rang. He picked up his phone and saw his father-in law's name.

"Yeah, Dad, I'm surprised to hear from you, we only left you a few hours ago. Is everything all right?"

"Oh sure! It's just that Joe and I got talking about something on the way home. We thought that we would run it by you."

"Great, Dad, what is it?"

"We need a lot of work done on the old town before we can spend any time up there. We were considering hiring the guys that worked for us before, but if Scott's professor was right, we need to be more discreet."

"Yes, that might not be a bad idea. Even if it is just for a summer getaway, you don't want everybody knowing about it. If we need it for a hideaway from the Antichrist, the less anyone knows, the better."

"My point precisely! That is why Joe and I would like to hire you. Maybe even Scott might be interested in doing some work up there this fall. We only have about a six-week window before it gets too cold up there. You said that your boss let you go, how about it?"

"I'm not a carpenter, Dad. Neither is Scott."

"Too bad Linda's husband is working. He's in construction, right?"

"Yeah, he is, and he isn't working anymore either. Give me a day, and I will get back with you. I'll talk it over with Lorraine and the boys."

"Great, I'll be looking forward to your call."

Lorraine had a silly grin on her face as she asked, "What was that all about?"

"Your dad wants to hire me for six weeks to do some work on the old town. He also wants me to ask Scott if he wants a job up there also."

"But, Thomas, Scott has a job."

"Yeah, I know, but he really loves it up there. Maybe he could get a leave of absence."

"Honey, he's an assistant manager. I don't think they could get along without him for that long."

"I don't know, but he did say that South Haven is a tourist town, and the fall and winter seasons are slow."

Overhearing the conversation, Harold broke in saying, "Hey, what about me? That is my line of work! I'm a construction worker! Besides, all this talk about this little old ghost town has me intrigued."

"Great!" Thomas told his son-in-law. "Scott and I don't know anything about carpenter work. That would be great if you wanted to come along."

Thomas looked over at his wife with a sheepish look on his face and asked, "What do you think of all this, Lorraine?"

"Well, you don't have a job right now, and I know how much that old town means to you. On the other hand, Thomas, we just got back together again. I don't want us to be separated anymore!"

"Oh, darling, I don't want that either! Why not see if you can get a leave of absence from school and come along with me?"

"Is anybody going to ask me how I feel about all this?" Linda snapped.

Everyone turned and looked at Linda. Her father answered, "Yes, sweetheart. I am so sorry I left you out of the conversation. Of course, you have a say."

Linda angrily lashed out at her husband as she yelled, "How could you think about leaving me at a time like this? We are trying to put our marriage back together, and there's the baby!"

Linda barely got the words out of her mouth when her father's voice rose, "Baby! What baby?"

"Mine, Dad! I was going to tell you, but I haven't seen that much of you lately. It's not something I could tell you on the phone. The night of the peace treaty, I thought by the way you were talking, you knew about the pregnancy. Boy, was I wrong. That's when I realized you were only worried about me because you thought that I'd be upset about 'being left behind.' The rest of the night was too chaotic. Then Harold got here, and I knew I had to tell him before I told anyone else. You all left for the UP the next day."

"But when. How far along are you?"

"I'm a little over three months. The due date is March 29. I must have gotten pregnant shortly before I left Harold. I didn't know for sure until after Christina's mother's funeral."

"Did you know about this, Lorraine?"

"Yes, Thomas. With all that morning sickness, I surmised she was, so I took her to a doctor."

"Why didn't you tell me?"

"Linda made me promise not to. She wanted to tell you herself."

"Well, Linda, I'm happy for you. A bit overwhelmed but happy for you. Thank God that you two were able to reconcile your marriage."

"The main reason I went back to Harold was because of the baby," she said as tears started to flow. "Believe it or not, it made a big difference when you and mom got back together again. That made a big impact on my decision to make our marriage work."

Both Linda's parents gave her a big hug as they all wiped the tears from their own eyes. Then Lorraine took her daughter's hands in hers and said to her, "Honey, I know exactly how you feel about Harold being away from you right now, but this is important. You know that there aren't any jobs right now to be had. Our men need this. Financially, we all need this!"

"Why don't you girls come along with us?" Thomas suggested. "It would be a primitive living, but it could be fun! You know, like an extended camping trip, but we would make you as comfortable as possible."

"That's very sweet of you, Thomas, but it just wouldn't work," Lorraine said. "There's no way we could afford me taking any time off work. Besides, Linda needs regular doctor appointments and pre-natal care. It's best for all of us if we stay home. Six weeks is not that long. The time will pass quickly."

"Well, if it's okay with Linda, you can count me in," Harold anxiously said.

Reluctantly, Linda said, "All right, you can go if you want to."

"That settles it," Harold said. "When do we leave?"

"Good," Thomas said with excitement in his voice. "Just give me a second to call Scott and see if he wants to go. He quickly hit Scott's number and anxiously waited for him to pick up. Scott was sitting with Sheryl on the couch, watching a movie when his phone rang. He looked at it and said, "Sorry, babe, I have to get this. It's my dad. "Hello, Dad."

"Hi, son. You are not going to believe this!"

"Oh, yeah. What is it, Dad?"

"Your grandfather just called and offered us guys a job working on that old town in the Keweenaw. He asked Harold as well. He'd like us to stay up there and work on it for six weeks. He thinks that we could get some of the old buildings livable by then."

"Wow, he sure is a fast mover. When he decides on something, nothing stops him. Did you and Harold accept his offer?"

"We haven't yet, but Harold is all for it."

"What about Harold's job?"

"He got fired."

"Sounds like him. Linda's not taking that loser back, is she?"

"Yeah, Scott. Harold and Linda are right here by the phone with me now. Congratulations are in order. You're going to be an uncle!"

"Oh no! Poor Linda."

Changing the subject fast, he asked, "So, Scott, do you think you might be interested in something like that. I know your grandfather will make it worthwhile."

"Sure, I would love an opportunity to go up there for six weeks and work on that place, but I've got a job, Dad. I've used up all my vacation time."

"You said yourself that things are slow there this time of year. Maybe if you ask, you could get a leave of absence for the six weeks."

"I don't know, Dad."

"It won't hurt to ask. I sure would enjoy it if you were there too!"

"No, right, it won't hurt to ask him."

"Can you get a hold of your boss tonight? We need to leave as soon as possible. Winter up there will be coming soon."

"Nothing like being pushy. I don't know, Dad. I will have to talk to Sheryl about it. I don't think she will be crazy about the idea."

"Well, do what you can. Call me back when you have some answers. Love you, bye, son."

As Scott turned off his phone, Sheryl looked at him and asked, "What was that all about? What won't I be too happy about?"

"My granddad wants to hire me to do some work on his place in the Keweenaw."

"Oh sure, like you don't have a job."

"Yeah, but it's only for six weeks."

"Six weeks! Excuse me, that's a long time! Can you really see getting six weeks off from work? Not to mention, you just asked me to marry you. Do you really think that I want you racing off playing pioneer boy?"

"You could go with me!"

"You can get that out of your head right now! I value my job. Jobs are a bit of a premium as of lately, or haven't you heard?"

"Things are really slow now, Sheryl. What if I could get a leave of absence for both of us?"

"No thanks! I do not want to go up there now. The weather is getting chilly down here. I sure don't want to go way up there. I would freeze to death! And I sure do not want to go up there for six weeks! Maybe a weekend or two in the summer, but that is it! We both don't share the same love for that place."

"Well, I guess that's obvious. Sheryl, I love you, but I cannot let my granddad down either. This would also give my dad and me time to study Bible prophecy. We need to sort this all out and find out what is really going on."

"Fine, but don't expect me to be any part of it!"

That night, Scott couldn't sleep. He tossed and turned all night. The decision to ask his boss lied heavy on his mind. Then there was Sheryl. She would be mad at him if he went. He loved her, but he felt the Holy Spirit tugging at his heart to go.

That next morning, Scott knew what he was going to do. He went into work and talked to his manger. To Scott's surprise, his manager was glad that he asked for the time off. He explained that business was slow, and they needed to cut down on expenditures. He had been trying to decide who he was going to lay off. Sheryl was on the short list of possibilities. A six-week leave of absence would be just the relief the business could use, and no one needed to be laid off.

On October 10, Joe flew James, Thomas, Scott, and Harold to the Houghton County Memorial Airport. When the men got off the plane, instead of going to the car rental as they had done before, Joe flagged down a taxi. He had the cabby drop them off at the Calumet used car dealership. As soon as they arrived, a middle-aged salesman in a suit walked up to Joe. With a smile from ear to ear, he said, "Mr. Wydeck, good timing! Good to see you again, sir. That 4x4 Ford crew cab you had us look for just came in last week. We have gone all though it for you. Put new brakes on her and a tune up. She is in top condition. Only 45,000 miles on her. Not even a scratch. As you can see, this truck was well taken care of."

"Well, if it runs as good as you say, and the price is right, you've got a deal."

"Here's the keys. Take her for a spin."

Joe handed the keys over to Scott and told him, "Here, you'll probably be the main driver." Scott was delighted as they all piled into the truck. After a good half an hour, Scott was impressed with the truck's test drive.

He told Joe, "Yeah, this is a good truck. It handles really well, and it would take care of all our needs. I'd say if you can get a good deal on it, go for it."

While the others waited out in the showroom, Joe went into the office to negotiate. An hour later, Joe came out of the office with the truck's keys in his hand.

21

Village of Gratiot and then to Old Town, October 10th

With keys in hand, Scotty climbed in behind the wheel of the newly purchased truck. The men were on their way to their ghost town (which now was affectionately called Old Town). This time, they took a new route off the beaten path. It was an unimproved road just east of Central. When they were about ten miles from the Gratiot Mountain, they came upon a small village called Gratiot. It was a small town with only a few stores and scattered houses. Noticing a sporting/hardware store, Joe suggested that they stop. The guys were happy to stop. After all, what man can resist a sports shop or hardware store? All four of the guys got out of the truck and went in.

The store owner greeted them with a big smile as they walked in. Joe started picking up the items that they would need for their stay. He picked up a sleeping bag, a lantern, and a few other camping supplies for each of them. He also bought a cooler and a bag of ice.

"I guess that is all we need," Joe said. Let's see, last time we were up here, we left a cooking stove, soap, towels, and washcloths. Unless anyone can think of anything else, I guess we're good to go."

"How about food?" James answered. "I noticed a grocery store next door."

Joe smiled and said, "Sounds like a plan. If everybody is ready, I'll go up and pay the bill."

While Joe paid, the others went out and loaded up in the truck.

The storekeeper had a warm, friendly smile on his face when Joe walked up to the counter. He thanked him as he extended his hand for Joe to shake.

"I'm Mark Thornton, owner of the store," the man behind the counter said. "I'm really glad to have your business. I don't get a lot of travelers way out here, mostly locals. Good to see new faces."

Joe felt a connection with Mark instantly and could sense that he was a trustworthy man. Joe hesitated a moment and then asked, "Say, Mark, by any chance, do you know of any private airports around here?"

"Yes, matter of fact, I do! I own a small airstrip straight down the road about two miles. I have a small plane that I use to pick up my supplies."

"I'll be flying into the Keweenaw from time to time, mostly weekends. I could use a landing pad nearby here. Is there any chance that you might consider renting me a small spot on your airport?"

"Sure! No problem. I'm sure we can work out a deal."

When Joe got back in the vehicle, he asked, "Do you guys think we will need tents?"

"No, I don't believe so," Thomas said. "We can stay in one of the buildings. Most of them still have their original beds in them."

"Why sure, we will have all the luxuries of home," Scott said with a little chuckle. "Remember those cabins and the old board-inghouse still have a lot of old furniture in them. Its crude stuff but useable."

"I'm not so sure," Harold questioned. "That's all well and good until it rains. I would be willing to bet, with buildings that old, the roofs probably leak."

"Yes, you would think so, but there was no sign of water damage," Joe said. "Did either of you guys notice any?"

"No," Scott said. "Dad and I remarked how well preserved the buildings were. There's boards missing here and there, but the roofs must be in good shape to keep the buildings from deteriorating all those years."

"Man, that's hard to believe a town that old could be in that good of condition when it hasn't been lived in for years and years," Harold said.

"The whole town is a bit of a miracle," James answered.

The men made one more stop next door at the grocery store to pick up food and water.

"You don't suppose you could pick us up a case of beer?" Harold asked Joe. "I always work better when I have a beer or two."

Joe gave Harold a weird look as he said, "Sorry, Harold, but I don't think beer is a necessity, do you?"

Harold was not happy but said nothing. Scott and Thomas looked at each other and chuckled under their breath.

Two miles out of town, Joe told Scotty to pull over and make a sharp right-hand turn. They pulled up to a flat field that had a large Quonset building next to a long narrow strip of pavement.

"What's this place?" Scott asked Joe.

"It's store owner, Mark Thornton's private airstrip. I've worked out a deal with him to use it." Joe pointed to the Quonset building and said, "It even has a large hanger for the plane. Mark said that there was plenty of room in there for both our planes."

"That's amazing!" Scott said.

"Yeah, this place couldn't be any handier," Thomas, added.

Harold just shook his head and said, "Man, you rich people sure know how to get things done."

Joe laughed and said, "Yes, sir, this strip is perfect. This airstrip is about eight miles from Old Town."

They pulled away from the airstrip heading for Old Town. As they were driving, Joe and his small crew made plans as to what they would like to accomplish the first few days.

"Well, tonight, we need to focus on where we will sleep," Joe commented. "I believe that the boardinghouse would be the best place. In fact, I believe that we all should stay there while we are up here working. It probably would be a good idea to make that our first project. There's enough lodging for everyone in there."

"That makes sense," Thomas agreed. "It has eight bedrooms upstairs, a full kitchen, and a large dining area down. What more could we ask for?"

"You're right, Dad. We can each have our own room if we want."

"Well, maybe," James answered. "But I was thinking maybe we should use one room for now because I hear the nighttime gets real cold up here this time of year. Until we get her patched up, the old girl could be very drafty."

"Good idea, Dad. Maybe the dining room would be a good place to sleep for now," Thomas suggested. "I noticed that there was a good sized potbelly stove in there. That's the only heat source in the entire building other than the cooking stove in the kitchen."

"We could haul down some of those old straw mattress that we saw from upstairs," Scott suggested.

"The first thing we'll need to do is clean out the chimney," Harold mentioned. "We need to make sure that it's not clogged up. In addition, we need to check the damper. After all these years, we don't want to be the ones to burn down the old boardinghouse. If it caught fire, the whole town would go up in flames. We wouldn't have any way of putting it out."

"Sounds like you know what you're talking about, Harold," Joe said.

"Yeah, I've cleaned out a few. You get into all sorts of jobs working construction. If it's got anything to do with homes, I've probably done it."

"Harold, I'm going to put you in charge of supplies," Joe told him. "Thomas, you can be the crew boss. Together, you guys can decide what you will need to get the boardinghouse in a livable condition. Scott, it looks like you will be the grunt for now. James and I will stick around today and help. After we get settled in, Harold can make a list of what supplies we will need from the hardware. Then we need to find the closest lumberyard. After we buy the supplies you fellows need, you can drop us off at the airport, and we'll be on our way back to New York."

"When do you plan on returning?" Scott asked.

"Next Saturday morning at noon. You can pick James and me up at that private landing strip outside of town. We'll spend the weekend and give you guys a hand."

Joe looked at Harold and asked, "I don't suppose you know anything about fixing old pitcher pumps, do you?"

"Yeah, a little. I don't think it should be too difficult. I would guess after all these years, the leathers are probably shot. Might be able to soak them, or we can pick up something from town that will work. We'll probably need plenty of water to prime the pump."

As always, the men's excitement soared as they drove up the mountain toward the old town. It was getting late in the afternoon, so they drove straight to the middle of the town and pulled up in front of the old boardinghouse and unloaded their gear. Even though it was barely mid-October, there was a noticeable chill in the air already.

"We better check out the stove first thing," Harold suggested. "As chilly as it is now, it's going to be a lot colder tonight."

"Good idea," Joe agreed.

The guys all pitched in and gathered wood while Harold worked on the potbelly stove. Within a couple of hours, Harold had a roaring, red-hot fire going.

The guys all huddled around the stove.

"Now that we have heat, I'm starving," Thomas said. "Anybody else?"

James was feeling worn out and famished. He spoke out, "I know I'm starving! What's for dinner?"

"How about some vegetable soup and a loaf of bread?" Scott said as he held up two large cans of soup.

The guys were all pleased with Scott's choice, so he opened and dumped the cans of soup into a big pot. Then he set the pot on top of the hot potbelly stove.

"There," he said. "Dinner will be served momentarily."

After the late dinner, the men went upstairs and pulled the old straw mattresses off the beds. They tried to be careful as they carried them down the stairs. A couple fell apart from rot. The men placed them near the potbelly stove, so they could be warm throughout the night. Joe had bought them good sleeping bags so when they jumped into bed that night, they were warm and cozy.

The next morning, the men drove into Gratiot and stopped at the hardware store to get the supplies that they would need. Joe asked Mark, "Where's the closest lumberyard?"

"Well, about five miles out of town, there's the Stevenson's sawmill. That's where everyone around here buys their lumber. Jake Stevenson owns it. He's a good man. You could go into the city and find a regular lumberyard, but Jake is fair. He will give you a good price."

The men took Mark's advice and went out to Jake's sawmill. They were pleased with the lumber he had on hand and were able to fill their list. From there, the crew of Old Town drove to Mark's airstrip where they dropped off Joe and James.

On the way back to Old Town, Thomas, Scott, and Harold were talking about the condition of the buildings. Scott shook his head in disbelief. "I can't believe how those roofs have held up all those years. I wonder what kind of roofing they have on them."

"If you want, we can find out as soon as we get back and unload the truck," Harold answered. "I can break in that new ladder we just bought! I'd be happy to climb up on the roof and check it out."

When they got back and unloaded, Harold grabbed the ladder. He climbed up on the roof of one of the homes and inspected it. He shouted down, "Man! You're not going to believe this! The roof is made out of what looks like copper. It's been dulled from age, but I really think its copper."

"No kidding," Scott said with excitement "No wonder the structure is still intact."

"Yeah," agreed Thomas. "Maybe all the buildings have copper roofs. That would explain a lot. Nevertheless, it still seems like a miracle that these old buildings are still standing."

"Dad, I agree it is a miracle, but it kind of makes sense that the roofs are made out of copper. Remember we saw buildings in other towns that had copper roofs. They had so much copper back then some used it for their roofs. It was a smart idea. The buildings weathered well."

As they had discussed before, they started work on the boardinghouse. The rest of the day was filled by replacing boards and patching up leaks. They worked until dark. At the end of the day, they were exhausted. The men cleaned up, had supper, and then sat around the old wood table. The only light was a kerosene lantern. They sat around it while they were talking and drinking coffee.

Thomas looked at Scott and said, "You have come up with some really good arguments about this post-tribulation theory, but you still don't have me completely convinced. You mentioned when we were camping about the pre-tribulation being a somewhat new idea. Can you tell me more about that?"

"Sure, Dad. My professor had some compelling facts about when it was started. He said that before the 1830s, there was no pre-tribulation rapture doctrine being taught. John Darby, who was the founder of the Plymouth Brethren movement, was credited by many of his followers for starting the pre-tribulation doctrine around 1830. Although my professor said that it has been authenticated that a few years earlier, Edward Irving was the first one to suggest this theory. However, around the same time, there was a teenage girl named Margaret MacDonald, who also was a member of the Plymouth Brethren Church. Seems she had a vision or a channeling of a spirit. Her vision occurred during a charismatic church service in Port Glasgow, Scotland. The pre-tribulation theory was based on what that teenage girl channeled."

"Channeling, that sounds like the New Age Movement!" Thomas said.

"Precisely!" Scott agreed. "They based their theory on a girl channeling!"

"I still don't know, Scott. I still have a hard time believing that God will let us go through any part of the tribulation."

"Dad, all I know at this point is that one of the main prophecies of the Bible has happened—the signing of the seven-year peace treaty with Israel. So if the pre-trib view is right, we would have been raptured by now."

"Yes, I know, but I still am having a hard time with it. I'm still not sure if this is the same signing as the Bible's or not!"

"Deny it all you want, Dad, but it sure sounds like the one and the same to me."

Harold couldn't keep quite any longer. He told them, "I'm sorry, you guys, but I can't understand a thing you are talking about.

I'm going outside to see if I can get some bars on my phone. I need to talk to Linda."

"Good luck with that," Scott told him. "You're not going to get any reception way out here."

"Well, maybe you're right, but I need some fresh air."

After Harold walked outside, Scott said to his dad, "I do believe talking about Bible prophecy makes Harold nervous."

"Yeah, I think you're right. I don't think he knows much about the Bible. In fact, there are many people in the world today who are in the dark about the Word of God. I wonder how many of them have been concerned about the peace treaty like us. How many really even care?"

"I wonder if any believe as I do that we are actually in the biblical prophecy of wrath!"

Old Town, October 13

It was Thursday evening, and the men had just finished another hard day of work. As Thomas wiped the last dish, he said, "There, the supper dishes are done. I believe we are getting this dishwashing down to a science. It only took us fifteen minutes tonight."

"Don't tell the women. They'll want to put an apron on us," Harold joked.

Scott laughed and said, "All kidding aside, we are a heck of a team. I can't believe how much work we have gotten done on the boardinghouse this week. I sure hope we can get a lot done tomorrow."

"That would be great! If we work hard enough, we can have the boardinghouse completed by tomorrow night," his dad answered back. "It would be really good to have it done by the time we pick up your grandpa and Joe."

Thomas rubbed his shoulder and said, "I can believe it! Every bone in my body hurts."

"So does mine! How about you, Harold?"

"I'm a little sore but not too bad. Remember, I do this for a living."

"Yes," Thomas answered. "Your experience has been a great help to us. I don't think I would have known which way to turn if it wasn't for your expertise."

"Yeah, Harold," Scott said. "You sure do know the construction business. I'm really glad you decided to come along with us."

"Hey, I needed the job. Besides, it gives me a chance to get better acquainted with my new in-laws. I have enjoyed working with you guys. And this old town is beginning to grow on me. Although, I do miss Linda. I would have liked to have more time with her, especially with the kid coming. It's just starting to sink in. I'm going to be a dad!"

Thomas patted him on the back and said, "Congratulations, son! Wow, that will make me a grandpa!"

"Yeah, and I'm going to be an uncle," said Scott.

The men were blissfully laughing and talking as they sat around the potbelly stove. They were each talking about their roles in the life of a child that soon would be a big part of their lives. Then all went quiet until Scott spoke up and said, "Gosh, I miss Sheryl! I don't know how I'm going to go five more weeks without seeing her."

Thomas soberly answered back, "I know what you are saying. I really miss your mother. We had been separated for so long. You don't know how hard it was for me to leave her. She is all I think about now. I don't know how I could have let my silly pride drive a wedge between us like I did. My love for her should have been strong enough."

Harold spoke up, "I know where you are coming from, Mr. Perkins."

"Call me Dad!"

"Yeah, okay, Dad, thanks. As I said, I understand what you are going through. Linda and I were not separated as long as you and Mrs. Perkins, I mean Mom, but my pride and selfishness caused our problems. I guess at that time, partying and drinking were more important to me than my wife. She tried to make me understand that times were tough and that we should save our money. I didn't listen to her because I wasn't going to have my wife telling me what to do. Since I've been up here, I've been thinking that I might have a drinking problem. I'm anxious to start over, be a better husband. I want to show her that I've changed. Not only for her but for our baby. I want to be a good dad!"

Thomas grabbed his Bible and then held it up as he told Harold, "All you need to know about being a good husband and father is all in this book. The Bible is a guideline for us to follow. It tells us everything we need to know to be happy and to live a good life."

Tears welled up in Harold eyes. He told his father-in-law, "Maybe, after your Bible study tonight, if you don't mind, I'll borrow your Bible."

Thomas smiled and said, "Great! I'll give you some verses to look up later."

Scott waited a few minutes for Harold to get up and leave. He normally took a walk right before their Bible lesson started. This time, he didn't move. Scott looked over at his dad and asked, "Are you ready for tonight's discussion?"

"Sure, Scott. Let's get started."

Harold looked a bit embarrassed as he asked, "Do you guys mind if I stay and listen this time?"

"Not at all," Thomas replied.

Surprised, Scott said, "Sure, that would be great, Harold."

Thomas smiled and said, "Okay, then, Scott, let's begin."

"Okay, Dad. I can't help but wonder what's been going on since we've been up here. I feel so isolated. I miss hearing the news. I wonder if there has been anymore Bible prophesy fulfilled since we have been up here?"

"Scott, I really doubt if this is the beginning of the Tribulation. Look up 1 Thessalonians 5:9. 'For God hath not appointed us to wrath, but to obtain salvation by our Lord Jesus Christ.' I know we both agree that the book of Revelation deals primarily with the tribulation. In part, it is a prophetic message of how God is going to pour out His wrath upon the whole world during the tribulation period. Why would God promise believers that they would not suffer wrath and then leave them on earth during the tribulation?"

"The key words here, Dad, are *God's wrath*!"

"Well, that's what the tribulation is about."

"It's also about Satan's wrath. Satan is the one who pours out wrath during most of the tribulation. While it is true that Christians will be delivered from God's wrath, the Scriptures also say that believers are not promised freedom from persecution and tribulation. Look up in your Bible, John 15:18–19. In Jesus's own words it says, 'If the world hates you, you know that it had hated me before it hated you.'"

Scott continued, "Now turn to Matthew 5:10–11, there Jesus says, 'Blessed are they which are persecuted for righteousness' sake: for theirs is the kingdom of Heaven. Blessed are ye, when men shall revile you and persecute you, and shall say all manner of evil against you falsely, for my sake.'"

Scott turned some pages in his Bible and said, "Turn to Paul's writings in 1 Thessalonians 3:3–4. It reads, 'That no man should be moved by these afflictions: for yourselves know that we are appointed there-unto. For verily, when we were with you, we told you before that we should suffer tribulation; even as it came to pass, and ye know.' Dad, let's read in the book of second Timothy 3:1–12." After they finished reading the verses, Scott emphasized part of it by rereading a portion of it. "'In the last days difficult times will come and that all who desire to live godly in Christ Jesus will be persecuted.' Now, Dad, let's look at Peter's writings. Look up and read first Peter 4:12–13."

Thomas read out loud, "'Beloved, think it not strange concerning the fiery trial which is to try you, as though some strange thing happened unto you: But rejoice, in as much as ye are partakers of Christ's sufferings; that when this glory shall be revealed, ye may be glad also with exceeding joy.'"

Scott closed his Bible and then said, "With what's happened and these Bible scriptures, it's perfectly apparent to me. Even though the Bible makes it clear that believers will escape God's wrath, it is also equally clear that they have not been promised to be kept out of the wrath of the world or Satan's wrath."

"Maybe it's clear to you, but it's not all that absolutely clear to me. Sure, I know that Christians have been persecuted for the sake of the Lord Jesus Christ. For that matter, Christians have been persecuted in some countries for decades. That doesn't necessary mean that we'll have to go through the wrath of the tribulation."

"Dad, the Bible only promises us that we will be raptured before God's wrath! Remember Jesus never said that we would not be persecuted for His sake. In fact, He tells us we will be. All He really promises is that He will keep us out of the wrath of God. I guess the main question is what God's wrath is, and on the opposite side of the scale, what is Satan's wrath? In Revelation 12:12, KJV, it says, 'Woe to the inhabiters of the earth and of the sea! For the devil is come down unto you, having great wrath, because he knoweth that he hath but a short time.'"

"Scott, what about Revelation 3:10, KJV?" Thomas opened his Bible and started reading, "Because you have kept My command to persevere, I also will keep you from the hour of trial which shall come upon the whole world, to test those who dwell on the earth."

"Well, Dad, I believe the key word here is *hour*. Look at the seventieth week of Daniel. We know that in this text, it means that the seventy weeks are weeks of years. Thus, seventy times seven equals 440 weeks. It would seem to me that an hour out of one of those weeks would be a fraction of those years. That tells me that this hour of time could be at the end of the tribulation. The time that God pours out His wrath!"

"I see where you are coming from, son, but what about the restrainer? Let's look up 2 Thessalonians 2:6–8, KJV. It reads, 'And now you know what is restraining, that he may be revealed in his own time. For the mystery of lawlessness is already at work: only he who now restrains will do so until He is taken out of the way. And then the lawless one will be revealed, whom the Lord will consume with the breath of His mouth and destroy with the brightness of His coming.'"

"Sure, Dad, that's the verse that says that before the Antichrist is revealed, the restrainer will be taken. He can no longer protect believers from Satan."

"Right! That verse proves that the church will be raptured before the Antichrist is revealed because the restrainer is the Holy Spirit. The Holy Spirit lives within the hearts of each Christian, so they must be raptured out before the revealing of the Antichrist."

"That's if the restrainer is the Holy Spirit! There is nowhere in Scripture that actually says that the Holy Spirit or the church is the restrainer."

"If not the Holy Spirit, then who?"

"Michael the archangel, Israel's prince! He is the one who stands guard over Israel as well as the spiritual kingdom of God. Michael's job is to keep Satan from persecuting Israel. God will remove Michael's restraint. Thus giving Satan power through the Antichrist the freedom to purge Israel. They must go through the fiery testing. Michael's restraining stops, letting the demonic forces of Satan to allow the Antichrist to reveal his true identity to the world, thus venting his full fury on God's people."

"Scott, I remember Daniel calling Michael 'the one who stands firmly against,' which means 'restrains.'"

"That's right, Dad! In addition, in Daniel 12:1, KJV, it says, 'At the time Michael shall stand up. The great prince who stands watch over the sons of your people.' So you see, Dad, the restrainer's power might have already been taken out of the world, leaving Israel and the church wide open to the Antichrist's wrath."

At this point of the discussion, Harold interrupted and said, "Hey, you guys, you're beginning to scare me."

Scott looked up at Harold and said, "You don't have to worry. If I'm right, we still have about three and a half years before Satan begins to lash out his terror on us."

"Gee, thanks! I got a child coming. How am I going to protect him from all of this?"

Scott smiled and said, "Maybe that's what we are doing here, getting our safe haven ready."

Thomas put his hand on Harold's shoulder and said, "Harold, the way to be ready for all this is to give your heart and life to the Savior, Jesus Christ. Then you will be ready to face anything that Satan might pour out on you."

Tears welled up in Harold's eyes as he said, "I want to, but I don't know anything about God or the Bible. The only time I was ever in a church was at my wedding. I wouldn't know where to begin."

Thomas had a big grin on his face, and he gave his son-in-law a hug and said, "Son, all you need to do is accept Jesus Christ in your heart, and He will do the rest." Thomas opened his Bible to John 3:16, KJV and read, "'For God so loved the world that He gave His only begotten Son, that whoever believes in Him should not perish but have everlasting life.'" Thomas turned to several other Gospel passages and read them to Harold.

"You see, son, the Gospel of God is a free gift of salvation."

"Please, help me. I want to be saved."

Thomas put his hand on Harold's shoulder and said, "Harold, pray this prayer with me: Lord, I know that I am a sinner. If I died today, without You, I know that I would not go to heaven. Lord Jesus, I believe in Your death, burial, and resurrection. I believe that if I accept You as my savior, you will wash away all my sins through your divine blood. Please, forgive my sins, come into my life, and be my Savior. Help me live for you from this day forward, in Jesus's name. Amen."

Harold repeated each word after his father-in-law. With tears flowing down his checks, he said, "I can feel God's Spirit. It's like a load has been lifted off my shoulders."

"Praise the Lord," Scott shouted! Both men gave Harold a bear hug. All three men had tears of joy in their eyes.

Thomas told him, "Linda is going to be so happy!"

Later that evening, Harold was daydreaming. Scott noticed and asked, "A penny for your thoughts, bro?"

Harold chuckled a bit and then said, "Wouldn't it be fun for all of us to live up here in this forgotten valley? One big happy family. You guys, Mom, Sheryl, Linda, me, and maybe a kid or two. Wouldn't that be great?"

"I'm not so sure about Sheryl," Scotty said sadly. "She isn't all that interested in this place. Besides, after I tell her that I have decided to rededicate my life to God, I don't know if she will even be interested in me anymore. For that matter, maybe we shouldn't even be together."

That following night's Bible study was centered on Harold, giving him an outline of what the Holy Scriptures were all about. Harold was captivated with all the Bible stories that Thomas and Scott told him about. He also was very interested when his father-in-law explained how to rightly divide the Bible. He then understood how the Old Testament dealt mostly with Israel and the New Testament was about the Gospel of Jesus and Christ's church of believers.

23

Mark's airstrip outside Gratiot, October 14

The long, hard first week of Old Town's renovation was finally coming to a close. The men felt that Joe and James would be happy with their progress. The boardinghouse was now ready to be lived in. It was crude but livable in a pioneering sense. The work crew of handymen was quite pleased with their finished product.

Saturday morning, Thomas, Scott, and Harold were on their way to the airstrip by 11:30 a.m. They arrived there at a quarter to twelve, fifteen minutes before Joe's plane was to land. The plane flew in forty-five minutes later. The men sat in the truck while they waited for Joe and James to exit the plane. When the plane's door opened, they were in for a big surprise! Thomas and Harold's mouth flew open when they saw their wives coming out of the plane. The three men jumped out of the truck and ran to the plane. Both Thomas and Harold embraced their wives as they gave them a passionate kiss. Scott looked at the door with anticipation. Was Sheryl coming out next? Was she waiting to be the last one out so she could surprise him? To Scott's great disillusionment, James was the next exiting the plane. James looked at his grandson as he stepped off the plane. He could see the hurt and disappointment on his grandson's face. He walked over to him, gave him a hug, and said, "I'm so sorry, Scott! Sheryl wasn't able to come."

Turning from her husband, Lorraine sadly looked at her son and said, "I'm sorry too! I called and talked with her, though. She is doing fine and sends her love. I called her when dad told me that they wanted to bring us up to surprise you guys. I asked her if she wanted to come, but she said no. She had to work. Besides, she said it was too cold in the UP." With a sheepish look on her face, his mom said, "At least she sent her love."

He tried to hold back the hurt in his voice as he said, "Thanks, Mom, for asking on her."

Thomas knew his son was hurting and wanted to do or say something to boost his spirits. He told him, "Come on, son, and smile! Aren't you happy to see your mother and sister?"

"Sure, Dad!" Scott gave both his mom and sister a hug, along with a kiss on their cheeks.

Joe was the last off the plane. He had a big smile on his face as he said, "Sorry we were late, but we knew you would forgive us when you saw your wives. It always takes a little longer when you put women in the equation."

Thomas gave Joe a pat on the back and said, "The wait was well worth it. What a wonderful surprise. Thanks, Joe."

"Well, it was kind of your father-in-law's idea. He knew how much a visit would mean to you guys."

"It was a great idea," Lorraine said. "Linda and I were so excited when Dad called us. We have missed you guys so much!"

Harold was beaming as he looked at his wife. He could not wait to give Linda the good news. He asked, "I'm sorry you guys, but I really need to talk with my wife alone a minute. Do you mind?"

Joe laughed and said, "Young love! Sure go ahead. We'll be waiting in the truck. You kids take all the time you need."

"Thanks, man. Come on, sweetheart, let's take a little walk."

Harold and Linda walked down the side of the runway holding hands. Halfway down the tarmac, Harold stopped and turned to his wife. He looked her directly in the eyes and said, "Darling, I have some wonderful news! I have accepted Jesus as my Savior!"

Linda raised her voice and shouted, "You did what?"

"Your dad and brother helped me to understand God's salvation plan. I accepted Jesus, and now I am saved! Together, our little family will be with Christ for all eternity!"

"How could you let them talk you into that fairy tale?" Linda yelled. "Harold, they have brainwashed you! Just like they did me ever since I was a child. I'm sick of it! I don't want anything to do with religion or church! All this talk of the rapture and the tribulation! I'm sick to death of it all! I thought our marriage would have a chance, but now I have serious doubts."

Harold was stunned and confused. The joy left his face. "Guess we better head back to the truck," he told his wife. Walking back to the truck, it was evident to the rest of them that something was wrong between Linda and Harold. They were no longer holding hands, and both looked upset.

After a quick stop at the grocery store, they went back to Old Town. Thomas and Scott were anxious to show off their handiwork as they gave a tour of the work they had accomplished on the boardinghouse. James and Joe could not believe how much progress the three men had made. Lorraine was thrilled at their workmanship and know-how. Still upset with Harold, Linda walked around with the group, barely uttering a word.

Thomas patted Harold on the back as he said, "We couldn't have done it without Harold. Linda, your husband is a very knowledgeable guy when it comes to carpentry and home repair. You should be very proud of him."

"Yeah, sure, Dad."

All went silent for a few seconds, and then Lorraine spoke up, "Okay then, Linda, let's go into the kitchen and get these groceries unpacked. We'll need to get lunch started."

As the women were unloading the groceries, Linda was glaring at the old wood cooking stove. "How in the world are we supposed to make dinner on that old relic?"

"Linda! The guys worked hard getting it in shape. They had to rebuild the chimney and replace some of its insides. Remember, your dad told us that Harold had to fabricate the parts because they couldn't get them around here. I don't know, maybe they don't even make parts for them anymore."

"Yes, Mother, I know. I realize they spent a lot of time getting this old thing to work, but why? We could have used the camp stove."

"Yes, dear, but they want to restore things to their original state. I think it is a lovely idea. Besides, you can cook more at one time with all this area. And look, it even has an oven."

"Sure, Mom, but do you know how to get this thing working?"

"No, but I bet that we could get the guys in here to get it going. What do you think?"

While Lorraine and Linda were peeling potatoes, Scott and Harold started a fire in the old wood stove.

For the first time since they arrived at Old Town, Linda had a smile on her face as she said, "At least this old artifact warms up the kitchen nice."

"Yes, isn't it cozy in here?" Lorraine said with a smile on her face.

Cooking dinner on a wood stove takes a lot longer, but at least that gave Lorraine and her daughter more time to talk. Lorraine was anxious to know what had her daughter so upset with Harold. So she asked, "Linda, you don't seem yourself today. Is there something bothering you?"

"No, I'm all right, Mother."

"I noticed that you and Harold seem a little distant with one another. Is everything okay with you guys?"

Linda turned away from her mother and said, "Mom, I really don't want to talk about it! It's between Harold and me."

"Honey, you know you can talk to me about anything. I've had a lot of experience with marriage problems."

"Yes, I know, Mother, but I wouldn't brag about it if I were you. Just look at what happened to you and Dad!"

"All right, you got me there. But you know, I helped your father with marriage counseling."

"Mother, please, knock it off! I am not one of your church members! I don't want to talk about it now! We're okay."

Lorraine felt hurt that her daughter would not confide in her but gave Linda her space. Changing the subject quickly, Lorraine asked, "So what do you think about this place?"

"It's like living in another century. I guess it would be okay if someone wanted to vacation here once or twice, but I think it would get old fast."

"Really? I'd love to come here often. It's so quiet and peaceful."

"Maybe when I get old. Now I like the excitement of the city. I would miss the nightlife. Oh, I'm sorry, Mom, I know you don't approve of nightclubs and such."

"Linda, I know you are a grown married woman, but I'll never stop being your mother. I am sorry, but you have changed so much. Before you met Harold, you were in Bible college. Your life revolved around God and church. What happened to you?"

"I grew up, Mother! I was tired of being good all the time. I was experimenting with life."

"You mean you want to live for the pleasures of this world? The Bible says that no man can serve two masters, 'For either he hates one, and loves the other; or he will hold to one, and despise the other. Matthew 6:24.' Linda, you cannot love the way of the world and love God!" Lorraine picked up her Bible and said, "Here, Linda, let me read to you 1 John 2:15 & 16. 'Love not the world, neither the thigs that are in the world. If any man love the world, the love of the Father is not in him. For all that is in the world, the lust of the flesh, and the lust of the eyes, and the pride of life, is not of the Father, but is of the world.'"

"Mom, that's just the point! I don't know if I even believe in God anymore! I'm confused. I have heard about God all my life. I was taught to live a holy life. Now I need to find out for myself! I'm a young woman, and I want to see what the world has to offer. I enjoy going out dancing and partying. That is, until I got pregnant."

"Look where that kind of lifestyle has gotten you and Harold. It broke up your marriage for a time. Harold lost his job and then your apartment."

"Oh, don't worry about Harold anymore. Mother, Dad and Scotty brainwashed him since he has been up here."

"What? Are you saying that Harold has accepted the Lord?"

"Yeah, that's what he claims."

"Praise the Lord! That is wonderful news, Linda!" Lorraine looked into her daughter's gloomy face and said, "Don't tell me that's why you have been so upset with him?"

"Well, yeah. Now that I have decided to change my life to be more like him, he decides to get religion. I liked him the way he was. He was a lot of fun."

"Fun? You told me that he drank and partied too much that's why you left him."

"Well, he did overdue it a little, but we did have good times together most of the time."

"Linda, he was leading you down the wrong path! You have a baby to think about now. It is important for you to be a good, godly mother. Furthermore, it is wonderful that Harold has been saved because a child deserves to have Christian parents. It takes God in your life to do a good job raising a child."

"Please, Mother, can we drop this now?"

Lorraine stopped talking and tried to think of more pleasant things. She let her imagination run wild as she visualized the woman that had last ran this old boardinghouse. In her mind's eye, she watched her as she stood slaving over the old cookstove. Lorraine saw her hair up in a bun, wearing a long dark dress covered with a white apron. There were little children tugging at her long skirt for attention. She saw the door open. The woman's husband walking through the door with a rifle in one hand and the next day's meal in the other.

After the meal was ready, Lorraine and Linda were out in the dining room setting the table. Their men were coming in from outdoors. As Scott walked through the door, he said, "Man, something smells awful good. I sure am hungry!"

James took a big whiff and said, "Anyone would feel hungry with that sweet aroma coming from the kitchen."

"Yeah, I sure have missed my wife's cooking," Thomas said. "She is the best cook in the world."

James laughed. "She sure didn't get that from her mother!"

After Thomas said grace, they all settled down to a good old-fashioned dinner of chicken and dumplings. There were also side dishes of vegetables. There were hot rolls that were right out of the oven. To top off their delicious meal, there were two fruit pies cooling. Lorraine had picked up the frozen pies at the store, hoping she would have the right equipment to bake them. The oven on the old wood stove did not let her down. The pies came out beautifully.

"Mom, this is great!" Scott said. "I sure do miss your cooking. The grill where I work makes good food, but they sure can't compare to your home cooking."

"Don't give me all the credit. Your sister was in there doing the cooking right along with me."

194

"Wow, are you telling me that my wife can cook like this!" Harold kidded. "Seriously, honey, you never cooked like that for me."

"Haha, very funny, Harold. You guys don't have to give me any credit. I only was mother's assistant. She was the one that really cooked it."

"Linda, I couldn't have done it without you. You were a big help."

Joe raised his coffee cup and said, "Here, here, I'd like to make a toast to the best meal I've had in a long time and to the two lovely ladies that prepared it!"

The men raised their coffee mugs toward Joe's, and each said, "I'll drink to that."

"Ladies, this is truly an excellent meal," Thomas said.

Lorraine modestly said, "Thank you, guys. I'm glad you enjoyed it."

"Hey, kid sister, how you been feeling lately? Any morning sickness?"

"No, actually not, Scott. I've been feeling pretty good lately. I guess I'm all done with that."

"So how far are you along now?" Scott asked.

"It will be four months at the end of this month. The baby is due March 29."

"Cool! I can't wait to be an uncle. You know I'm going to spoil it, don't you?"

"If you do, you're going to have to babysit."

"Now wait a minute. I heard that grandparents can spoil their grandkids and then send them home to their parents. Shouldn't that apply to uncles too?" Everyone around the table laughed, including Linda.

Thomas glanced up at Joe and then James as he asked, "Have either of you guys had any luck selling your estates?"

Joe spoke up, "James and I both have our estates listed through my agency. There have been several candidates, but few can come up with the cash, or they're afraid to invest in these troublesome times."

"Yeah," James said. "Over half of the homes in the New York area, and for that matter the rest of the country as well, are in foreclosure."

"Wow, that's really bad news," Thomas said. "Speaking of news, I'm dying to know what's been going on in the world this past week. We have not had any communication with the outside world all week. We've been in the dark. Please, fill us in."

Lorraine stood up from the table and said, "Oh boy, this will take some time. Come on, Linda, let's clear the table and then go clean up while Granddad and Joe fill them in. I've heard enough news this week."

24

Boardinghouse at Old Town, October 14ᵗʰ

As Lorraine and Linda cleared the dinner table, Joe rubbed his forehead and said, "Where do we start? The past week was very news worthy. So much has happened."

James broke in, "I'd say the biggest news was President Omidi's pushing for uniting the world for global peace. Wouldn't you agree, Joe?"

"Yeah, that has to be the biggest news. He mentioned that after centuries of fighting, Israel and the Middle East were now living in peace. This led him into bringing up the subject of a one-world government. He said that the people of the world would be able to appreciate the joys of peace by uniting. Plus it would help the economy."

Scott shook his head and said, "We had the signing of the seven-year peace treaty with Israel and now talk of a one-world government. I knew this was next!"

Still reluctant to admit that they were into the tribulation, Joe said, "There have been talks for years about the formation of a one-world order, but this is the first time a president of the United States has publicly announced it so vigorously."

"Not that a United States president hasn't mentioned it before," James said. I remember years back when President Obama made a speech in Germany promoting forming a global world government. At that time, there was very little mention about his speech on the news, but *USA Today* did an article on it."

Thomas looked sad and said, "As much as I hate to admit it, it is getting to look very much like we are living in the seven-year tribulation. Scott and I have had several discussions on the subject while up here. Is it possible that I was wrong? That most of the churches have been wrong? We have all been misinformed, deceived! I now believe I was wrong about the timing of the rapture!"

Disgustingly, Joe said, "I guess I have to agree! It's definitely looking that way!"

"Oh yeah," exclaimed James. "On top of that, there was breaking news that the Jews are beginning to rebuild the temple in Jerusalem. As we know, that was in part of their agreement. They are even making plans as to what animals they are going to use for their temple scarifies."

"Oh my gosh," Thomas said. "It's Bible prophecy unfolding right before our eyes! In the chronicles of the Bible, it tells about the first temple that the Jews used to worship in."

Scott spoke up, "Yes, it was called Solomon's Temple. King Nebuchadnezzar of Babylon destroyed it sometime around 590 BC."

"That's right, son. Then seventy years later, it was rebuilt under Zerubbabel and Joshua's reign. Next, that temple was desecrated by Antiochus Epiphanies, a Greco-Syrian ruler who brought a pig in the temple. This was the first act of desecration to the temple. In 20 or 21 BC, Herod the Great rebuilt and enlarged it. Then in 70 AD, Titus, a Roman general, formed the western nations of the old Roman empire. That was the time in history that he smashed down the temple and drove the Jews out of Israel into all corners of the world."

"Dad!" Scott anxiously said. "This is just one more piece of the puzzle that proves that the tribulation is well on its way! There hasn't been a temple in Jerusalem since Titus destroyed it. Nor has there been another Jewish nation until 1948."

Joe and James listened intently as the Bible scholars remembered details of Bible prophecy. James asked, "Doesn't the Bible say somewhere that when Israel became a nation once again that our generation was to be in the last days?"

"Absolutely!" Thomas said. "It's in Matthew chapter 24 where Matthew writes about the budding of the fig tree. In Matthew 24:32-34 'Now learn a parable of the fig tree; When his branch is yet tender, and putteth forth leaves, ye know that summer is nigh: So likewise ye, when ye shall see all these things, know that it is near, even at the doors. Verily I say unto; you, This generation shall not pass, till all these things be fulfilled.' In the Bible, the fig tree refers to Israel. In Joel 1:17, Joel pictures Israel as the fig tree.'"

"What does rebuilding the temple have to do with end-time's prophecy?" Harold asked.

Thomas went on to explain, "Well, Jesus predicts in Matthew 24:15 that there will be an abomination of desolation in the Jewish temple. In the Bible, it is predicted to happen sometime around three and a half years into the tribulation. By this time, the Jews will have already built the temple and will be having animal sacrifices. The Antichrist, who by that time will claim to be God, will ride a pig into the temple, imitating what Antiochus did back in approximately 520 BC. It will be the final abomination of desolation."

In a defeated tone, Joe said, "It's all falling into place. We are living in the Bible's seven-year tribulation! "

Thomas looked up at him sadly and said, "As much as I hate to admit it, Joe, I have to agree.

Scott smiled slightly at his dad and said, "I don't mean to say I told you so, but, Dad, I told you so. Hey, why all the gloom and doom? I think this sounds exciting to be in the very last days of this dispensation! Seven short years and we'll be living in God's kingdom. I am looking forward to it!"

"As am I," Joe agreed. "It's the seven years before God's kingdom that's got me worried."

Scott smiled and said, "Look, guys, we have a beautiful place that God has led us to. I believe that it was nothing short of a miracle from God that we found this place. He protects His own. This could be our safe haven to ride out the tribulation until the rapture does take place!"

"You're right, son," Thomas said. "We have a lot to be thankful for."

There was a minute of silence while each man digested the inevitable reality.

James was the next to speak up, "Anyway back to the news. The news reporters have been talking a lot this week about the militia. The secretary of Homeland Security has intelligence information that says that the militia from most states have joined up with several other militia groups in surrounding states. Michigan militia already has enough soldiers to make it a small army. Can you imagine the size of their army if they all decided to unite?"

"Yeah," Joe said. "I saw a spokesman from the Michigan militia on the news the other day say that they are only being good Americans. They said that they will do whatever it takes to keep our God-given patriotic freedoms."

"Yeah, Joe, I saw that too," James said. "Only problem is, the militia has two fractions, and one is very radical. No telling what they will do. I hear they are really unhappy with our law enforcement."

"Well, yeah!" Scott said. "Each of our states have become a police state! Everybody is disgusted with the way they brutally rule."

"Right, son," Thomas said. "However, it's the law of government. We have to live by the rules. That is, until they start demanding we take the mark of the beast or worship the world leader."

"Well, on the lighter side." Joe said. "The news also talked about the new communication center, the Beastavision."

"Those are awesome!" Scott said. I've been wanting one, but they're too expensive for me."

"I've got one," James said. "They are pretty cool. You have one, don't you, Joe?"

"Yes, I've had one for a couple months now. Once you have one, you never want to go back to a regular television again."

Thomas looked confused and asked, "I've heard something about them, but what all do they do?"

Joe answered, "They do all your communication jobs. It's all compacted into one unit. It's a computer, television, virtual reality, security, and phone all wrapped up into one neat package."

"So like, do you have to watch TV programs on a small computer screen?" Thomas asked.

His father-in-law laughed and said, "No, no. It is altogether on a flat screen and comes in any size you want. I have a sixty-four-inch screen. You can be watching a television program, and it goes on pause mode. Then a beautiful blonde-haired woman with a sultry voice will come on telling me that I have a phone message from a particular person. If I want to accept the call, I say okay. Then she says if I want the caller to see me, to say okay once again. I press the red button if I don't want to be seen. After the call, your programming comes back on from where you left off. Even my electrical power is programmed into it, along with my security system. It runs the whole estate."

"That's right," James said. "The news report said that most all other means of communication will become obsolete in three months. It is an all brand-new digital technology. Our telephones, computers, and televisions will only work on the new system."

"So you mean our television, the phone, and our computers won't work after three months?" Thomas asked.

"That's right!" James answered.

"What about my cell phone?" Scott asked.

"You can still use a cell phone, but the new ones come with all that stuff. They work much like the big set only much smaller," Joe answered.

"But how can all people be able to afford them?" Scott questioned.

"The government has already thought about that," James answered his grandson. The news report said that prices on the Beastavision will be coming down. In addition, there will be government programs based on income to pay for them. And get this: the government has passed a bill that each household will be required to own one, or they could be jailed."

Scott got frustrated as he asked, "How can the government force people to do that? What happened to our freedoms? This is still America, isn't it?"

"Where have you been, Grandson?" James said. "We lost our freedom of rights a couple presidents ago. This is now a socialistic nation run by a few politicians in Washington. However, what can we expect? It's a prerequisite to a one-world government."

The following weeks passed quickly. Old Town's renovation crew got a lot of work done on the old ghost town. Joe and James flew up a couple more times and spent the weekend. Lorraine and Linda didn't go back for another visit, so when their men were finally home again, they were really happy to see them.

25

Bowling Green, Ohio, March 2

Several months had gone by, and it was now spring. Lorraine and Thomas were relaxing in their apartment when the phone rang. "I'll get it," Thomas said. On the other end of the phone was his father-in-law. Cheerfully, Thomas answered, "Hello, Dad. Good to hear from you. It's been a while."

"Yes, son, it has. Have you or Harold gotten any work yet?"

"No, nothing. We both get up early every morning and go looking for work, but there's nothing out there!"

"Yeah, that's too bad. It must be awful crowded in that little one-bedroom apartment."

"Yeah, it sure is, but we get by just fine. We're family. I've really gotten to like my son-in-law. He is quite a guy. As far as Lorraine's concerned, she loves having our daughter here. She is so excited about being a grandmother. We bought a new sofa that has a hide-a-bed in it for them. It works for now."

"That's great," James said. "I called because I've got some good news. Joe and I both have sold our estates! The same company bought them both. It was some company out of Germany. We got close to the asking price!"

"That's great, Dad! So what are your plans now?"

"It's got to do with Old Town, son, but it's too important to talk about on the phone. Can you, Lorraine, Harold, and Linda meet us again at the same hotel we met at last time, Thursday evening at seven?"

"Sure, Dad. I'm sure it will be all right with the rest the family. What about Scott?"

"Already a done deal! Anything pertaining to the Old Town, Scott's onboard."

"Great! Then we will see you Thursday night. Good-bye until then."

* * * * *

Thursday evening, the families all meet at the Marriott in Bowling Green, Ohio. When they got settled in, James got right to the point. He said, "As I told you all on the phone the other day, both of our estates have been sold! Joe and I have given this a lot of thought. With the events going on today, it looks like we could have war on our shores at any time."

"But, Granddad," Linda reasoned, "I thought that President Omidi was talking peace. Israel and Palestine aren't fighting now."

"Linda, it doesn't matter what Omidi wants at this point. The world is too unsettling right now," James explained to his granddaughter. "North Korea, Syria, and Iran all have access to nuclear weapons with the capacity to do great damage. Russia is always threating. God help us and Israel! Long before the peace treaty, the leader of Iran said he was going to annihilate Israel. He still is unhappy about the treaty. Iran might take its aggression out on us. The United States is its number-one enemy next to Israel."

Joe looked from Thomas to Scott and then said, "James and I have given a lot of thought to what you men have said to us about being in the tribulation. We have come to a conclusion. There is no doubt in our minds we are in the Bible's seven-year tribulation! It is evident that last October, the Antichrist signed that pact with Israel. The only question is which one of those monsters is the Antichrist? Is it Ali Hamarat, the President of the European Council, or our very own president of the United States, President Omidi? They both signed the treaty with Israel."

James cleared his throat and said, "Whoever the Antichrist is, it doesn't matter. All we need to know is he will be showing his true self so soon. When we hear that we are no longer the United States of America but part of a one-world government, we will know. Whoever is leader of the world will be the Antichrist. Our time is short. Thomas, how long would you say we have?"

"Well, I suppose we could learn very soon who the Antichrist will be. Although he won't reveal his true identity, Satan incarnated until about three and a half years from the signing. The signing took place about five months ago. That gives us a little over three years. The Bible tells us that there will be peace for Israel for three and a half years. Then the Antichrist will break his contractual agreement with Israel. He then will turn his wrath toward the Jewish people, along with Christians. That's when the false prophet comes on the scene. He will lead a new one-world religion. It's only about three short years away!"

James pounded his fist on the table as he sprang out of his chair. It was as if he was making a profound statement at one of his high-profile court cases. "We must move quickly! Joe and I have decided to pool all our resources toward restoring Old Town. It had to be God that miraculously led you guys to that forgotten valley. God also gave Joe and me the means to buy those sections of land. If it were not for you, my dear grandson, we would not have realized that the tribulation had started. I thank God that he gave you knowledge of the post-tribulation theory. We have three months before we have to be out of our homes. Joe and I are moving up to Old Town to get it prepared. We are asking you three men to join us. I feel strongly that our families should move up north to our secret valley as soon as possible. I hope that we can be hidden away from the rest of the world, including the Antichrist!"

"But, Dad, after the three years, when we can't buy or sell without the mark of the beast, then how will we feed our families?" Lorraine asked.

Filled with excitement, Scott spoke up, "We can grow our own! There are the farms! I would love to live on one of those farms and raise food for our families. I could even get some chickens and a cow or two. Who knows, maybe I am cut out to be a farmer! Besides that, there are plenty of deer, fish, and wild life to live on."

Harold joined in with Scott's enthusiasm and said, "Scott, that's a great idea! I would like to farm one of those farms myself. Between the two of us, we could support all our families. Besides, a farm would be a great place to live with a family. I'm sure the baby will like it when he's a little older."

Linda frowned and said, "The way you all are talking, 'she' might not even see her third birthday."

Scott turned to Marge and asked, "Grandma, didn't I hear that you were raised on a farm before you married Granddad?"

"Yes, Scotty, I was, but that was a long time ago. I do remember all the chores, though. However, I really loved living on that old farm."

"Did you ever learn to do canning? You know like the old days when they canned anything, from vegetables to meat?"

"Well, I do remember helping my mother do some canning, but I can't recall exactly how we did it. I could look it up in a cookbook."

James broke out laughing and said, "Marge, you haven't owned a cookbook since I married you!" He looked around at everybody in the room and said, "My wife never cooks!"

Joe looked at Scott and said, "Not a bad idea you have, young man. The old farms will take a lot of work, but it sure would be a reassurance to have our own food supply. I like the idea! How about you, James?"

"Absolutely! Scott and Harold will be our residential farmers. They will be in charge of the farms. As soon as we get up there, we'll buy a tractor, plow, or whatever they need to get started."

"That's great, Granddad! We can get the fields worked up as soon as the ground thaws out. We can do our planting this spring and have a harvest by fall."

Thomas added, "That's great for now, but what happens when we run out of gas and can't buy anymore because we don't have the mark of the beast? Remember, in Revelation, it says that no man will be able to buy or sell unless he has the mark of the beast? Again, I must warn you. We only have about three years before those events will occur."

Scott was quick to answer his father's question and said, "We'll get a couple of good work horses that can pull the plows and other equipment that we'll need."

Joe smiled. "You know, I believe that will work! Our small community will survive. Now unless someone has anything more to say, I make a motion that this meeting be adjourned."

Thomas spoke up, "Just one more thing I'd like to say, if I may. God's divine intervention brought us to that forgotten valley in the first place. I am sure he wanted us to have a place where we could survive the perils of the days ahead. That forgotten valley reminds me of the vows I took and how I broke them. Like the forgotten valley, I forgot how much I loved God and the promises I made him. I turned my back on God and the church!" Thomas stopped talking a minute, and then turning toward Lorraine said, "I even forgot my love for you and broke our wedding vows. Maybe God has given me this opportunity to move to this forsaken valley so I will always stay faithful to God and my precious wife. I do not want to be separated from either of them again! Thank you, everyone. That's all I have to say."

There was an intense moment of silence, and then James spoke out, "If no one has anything to add, I suggest this meeting is over. Now I would like to spring for dinner down in the hotel's dining room. Then you can all go home and digest what we talked about today."

"Yes," Joe said. "Sleep on it tonight. We will need an answer by tomorrow. Our plans are for us men to leave for Old Town no later than this coming Monday. We want to start work as soon as we can. Our time is short. We need to have everything ready to move up there permanently as soon as possible."

26

Bowing Green, Ohio, March 2nd

The meeting at the Marriott was over, and Scott's family was walking him back to his car. Linda gave her brother a hug, and Harold shook his hand as they told him good-bye. Then they left in their car.

Thomas asked, "Son, why don't you come stay with us tonight? I know it's crowded, but South Haven is so far away. It will be so late when you get home."

"Thanks, Dad, but I need to see Sheryl. There's a lot I need to talk to her about."

Lorraine looked puzzled as she asked, "I thought that you said you and Sheryl broke up a few months ago."

"Yes, Mom, we did. We broke up last winter just after I got back from Old Town. While at Old Town, I rededicated my life to the Lord. I explained to Sheryl that the Holy Spirit had convicted me. I knew in my heart that it was wrong for two people to live together without marriage. Sheryl got all upset. She didn't understand and took it the wrong way. She thought that I didn't love her anymore. Sheryl told me that she thought that I wanted out of the relationship. I believe it was the other way around. I think it was her that wanted out! Now that I'm living closer to God, I'm afraid Sheryl doesn't look at me the same. I stopped taking her out to clubs. One night, we had a fight over it. She called me a religious fanatic!

"I really don't want it to be over between us. I love her so much, but once I make the move to Old Town, I'll probably never see her again. I still really care for her. There has to be a way that I can get through to her. I want so much for her to know the Lord and be saved."

Lorraine gave him a comforting little hug and said, "Maybe, son, it's for the best that you guys break up. You know what the Bible says about being unevenly yoked."

"I know, but I keep hoping that she will accept Jesus as her Savior. I really need to talk to her again about salvation."

Lorraine and Thomas both gave Scott a big hug as they said good-bye. When they arrived home, Thomas put his arms around Lorraine and said, "Well, honey, this will be a big step in our lives. What do you think about it?"

"I would hate being separated from you again, but I know we have no choice. You have to go. We definitely won't last long if we don't go into hiding."

"I know, honey, I don't want to be away from you either, but yes, it is imperative that we prepare for the last days. You get out of school June 7. That will give us two months to work on the place. By that time, Linda's baby will be over two months old. She'll be old enough to travel."

Both Linda and Harold were sitting close enough to hear her parent's conversation. Linda jumped up from the chair and yelled out, "Whoa! Wait just a minute! Put on the brakes! For starters, I never said that I wanted to go! Second of all, you can forget about my husband going." Linda put her hand against her stomach and said, "I want him by my side when this baby is born! It could come early. I could have the baby anytime now!"

Lorraine walked over to her daughter and patted her hand. "I'll be here for you, honey."

"No! I want my husband to be with me. Tell them, Harold! You don't want to be away from your wife at a time like this!"

Harold stammered for words and finally said, "Linda, sweetheart, there is no place that I would rather be than with you at the birth of our baby, but this is important to our wellbeing. I know that you have been questioning your faith lately, but I feel this threat is real. You have to trust me on this one! Think of all the other women in the world whose husbands are fighting in the war. Uncle Sam doesn't let soldiers get out of the war just to be with their wives when they are having babies. This is our war, honey. I have faith that getting my family to Old Town will keep them safe from the war that the Antichrist is about to start."

Sarcastically, she asked, "So, wanna-be farmer, you're going to do this if I say okay or not, aren't you?"

"Yes, Linda, I am."

"Well, I'll stay here with the baby. I'll divorce you!"

"Come on, Linda, how do you think you could support yourself and the baby? Your dad and I cannot even buy a job. What makes you think you could get one? Everybody close to you will be gone. You won't even have your mother around."

"I'll go on welfare."

"I know better than that! You're too proud to go on welfare. Besides, it was just on the news that welfare has been bankrupted."

The argument between Linda and Harold continued. Lorraine thought they should give them their privacy as they ironed out their problem. She took her husband's hand and said, "Come on, darling, it's almost twelve o'clock. We need to sleep on it. We can talk more tomorrow."

Lorraine and Thomas snuggled into bed. As they cuddled, she whispered, "I love you so much. Wherever you are, that's where I'll be happy. I feel safe when I'm in your arms. You are so strong. I believe I could endure anything through your strength."

Thomas kissed her forehead and whispered, "It is God's strength that will get us through this."

Lorraine cuddled tighter to her husband and said, "I can understand why Linda feels the way she does. I hate the idea of being separated from you again. I know it is harder for her with the baby coming. I remember how much it meant to me that you were there when I was in labor. The birth of a baby means so much more to a woman when her husband shares the experience with her."

"I absolutely agree, honey, but these are not normal times. The most important thing right now is our survival. Harold wants to protect his family, just as I do. I really hate the thought of leaving you too! Last winter, when we went up north, I was miserable without you. The nights were especially hard."

"Oh my poor dear, I have been so selfish! Here I am only thinking about myself, and you're going way up there to that desolate place."

"Desolate place? Honey, I thought you liked it up there. It will only be desolate until you are able to join me, then it will be our little paradise."

"Yes, my darling, it will be paradise as long as we are together. I know what you are doing is for the best. We have no choice. You must go."

Later in the living room, lying on the hide-a-bed, both Harold and Linda lay next to each other, barely touching. Harold was the first to break the silence. "Come on, Linda, talk to me. I don't know why you're so mad at me."

"You don't! How stupid are you? Right in front of my parents, you tell me that no matter what I want, you are moving to that old rundown ghost town! You could care less what your own wife wants. You don't even care not being here when your baby is born! You are just caught up in all the hype about the end days. That the Antichrist is out to get us."

"Linda, don't make fun of all this. When I first met you, Bible prophecy meant a lot to you. Can't you see that some of the events you tried to tell me about have actually happened? There was the signing of the peace treaty with Israel for Pete's sake!"

Scornfully, she answered, "Yeah, yeah, but I'm still not sure about any of it. I still don't know why you cannot understand my feelings at a time like this. Harold, I need you here when I go into labor! I thought you would want to help deliver our baby!"

"Linda, darn it! Don't you think as a dad that I'd want to be part of the birth of our first baby? If there was any other way, don't you think I would do it? The safety of you and the baby must be my first priority right now. I love you! You don't know how much I love you. Please, try to understand that it is important that our families pull together right now."

Linda cried out, "But, Harold, I'm so afraid of having the baby without you. I am so afraid that this whole thing is real! I am about to bring a baby into the world, and I have to worry about protecting her against the monstrous Antichrist! If this is true, we have only a short time to be with our child. Harold, I want to see my baby grow up. I want to buy her dolls and all that goes with it. Maybe when she gets a little older, put her in a dancing class. Dress her up in fancy little dresses and take her to church. I want to see my child off to her first day of school, watch her go to college, and see my daughter walk down the aisle in a beautiful wedding gown."

"What if it's a boy?"

In between her sobs, Linda giggled a little and said, "Well, in that case, I would want to buy him cars and trucks, not dolls so much. I think it would be fun to see my son in little league baseball. Maybe even be in football or basketball. I can see us going to college football games and our son being the quarterback."

"What if he is a studious nerd?"

"That would be okay too. Maybe he will become a lawyer like Grandpa. As long as he's happy, that's okay with me. Harold, I want at least two more kids. We're just getting started. I don't want it to end!"

"Honey, I understand where you are coming from now. You are so full of fear. So am I, but the three of us will live for all eternity together with Jesus. Your father showed me in the Bible that all children who are under the age of accountability will go to heaven. So there is no problem about our child. He will be with us in glory. Linda, darling, you have to open up your heart to God again! If you continue to reject Him, you will surely go to hell! I cannot stand the thought of you in hell. I want you in Jesus's kingdom with me. I want the three of us together, forever! Your dad told me that there was only one unpardonable sin and that is the rejection of Jesus Christ."

"I guess deep down, I know it's all true, but I still don't want it to be so! I want to experience a normal family life."

"I know, Linda, but this is our reality. According to your brother, we will have approximately six years before the rapture."

Linda scowled and said, "That is if the Antichrist doesn't get us first!"

"True! That is why it is so important that we seek refuge in Old Town. So many people of the world, including Christians, are completely unprepared for all of this. A great majority of them still don't realize we are in are in the seven-year tribulation. We are fortunate that your brother had some knowledge about all of this ahead of time. Together with your father, they were able to figure it all out. I believe stumbling on Old Town was no accident. No one had known about the place for years. The condition that they found the old buildings in was nothing but a miracle in itself! Then your granddad and Joe got involved. Without their money, we could have never done it. I do not believe it was a coincidence that they both sold their estates when they did. Linda, I truly believe God led your brother and father to Old Town and made it possible for us to make it livable. I believe it was all God's plan. He is in control. I feel we really have a chance to survive until the rapture because God's hand is in all of this."

27

South Haven, Michigan, October 3ʳᵈ

The sun was rising as Scott pulled up to Sheryl's apartment. His mind was racing. What was he going to say to her to convince her that these were perilous times? That she should turn to Christ and accept Him into her heart. Even though they weren't dating anymore, he still cared deeply for her. While sitting in front of her apartment, Scott dialed her number and woke her up. His heart melted when he heard her soft, warm but sleepy greeting. She answered, "Hello, Scott. Are you all right? What time is it?"

"I'm sorry to wake you. I didn't think about the time. I just needed to talk to you. I've just drove all the way back from my parents in Ohio."

"Scotty, I just got out of work at two. I've only been sleeping for less than an hour. Can it wait until later? No, never mind. I'm awake now. If it is that important, come on up."

"Thanks, beautiful. Sorry I woke you up. I'll be right there!"

"Okay then. I'll put the coffee pot on."

Sheryl greeted Scott with open arms as she said, "I've missed you, Scott Perkins! When you ran off to Ohio yesterday to meet with your family, I thought I had lost you for good. I figured that your grandfather would have all of you on a plane flying away to that ghost town."

"Not yet! That's why it was so important that I talk to you tonight."

"What do you mean not yet? Scotty, don't tell me that your grandfather has talked you into going up to work on his place again?"

Scott cleared his throat and said, "He doesn't want me to just go up there to work. He wants all of us to move up there."

"What?"

"That is why I am here tonight. Sheryl, I love you so much. I really don't want to leave without you. Please, reconsider and go with us. I'm hoping that if you learn more about God, you'll ask Him into your heart."

"No! I love you too, but I already told you that I could not see myself living in that cold, boring place. Scotty, why don't you stay here? If you really love me, we could get married!"

"As wonderful as that sounds, I still have no choice but to move up to Old Town. Sheryl, God has led us there! I have to do God's will. Remember, I told you about the signing of the peace treaty with Israel?"

Disgustingly she nodded, yes.

"Well, that ushered in the tribulation. In addition, The Jews have begun to rebuild the temple in Israel. That also is a sign that we have entered into the tribulation. In approximately three years from now, a man will emerge and take rule over the whole world. The Bible calls him the Antichrist. He now is a powerful politician waiting in the wings to take the position of leader of a new-world government."

"Scotty, it's no secret there's going to be a one-world ruler. It is on the news all the time. I think it is a good idea. The economy is bad all over. If the world unites, the problem could be resolved. I also like the argument of a one-world religion. So many wars have been started because of religion. President Omidi is even in favor of it. It could give us world peace!"

"Sheryl, that's what I'm talking about. That was all prophesied in the Bible thousands of years ago. What the Bible prophesied then is coming true today! Maybe this new one-world government sounds good to those who don't understand God's prophecy, but to us that do, we know it's a lie. Israel has been promised seven years of peace, but according to the Bible, their peace will be broken in about three years from now. Then war will be waged against the Jewish nation. The world leader (Antichrist) will desecrate their temple and declare that he is the one and only God, the Messiah. Satan will actually enter his body at that time. The religions leader (the false prophet) will order everybody in the world to give allegiance and worship to this counterfeit Jesus. If the Jews, Christians, or anybody does not comply with that order, they will be put to death. Each person will be ordered to have a mark on their forehead or right hand to declare their allegiance to him. No one will be able to buy or sell or do any business transactions without that mark. If anyone does not worship him or take his mark, they will be put to death. Revelation tells us that this mark will consist of either the name of the beast (Antichrist) or his number 666. It also says that if anyone takes that mark or worships the Antichrist (who is the devil reincarnated) will never enter heaven. Instead, they will go straight to hell. There will be no hope for those poor souls."

Sheryl shivered as a chill ran through her body. "How can you believe all that silly hogwash? I thought you were an intelligent guy."

"Sheryl, I can prove it by showing it to you in the Bible. Do you still have the Bible I gave you?"

"Yes, somewhere. Scotty, what makes you think that a book written by men is true? You have heard about fiction writers haven't you?"

"Of course, but this is different. Why do you think that the Bible is hundreds of years old and still the bestseller ever? Yes, men did write the Bible, but every word was inspired by God."

"Oh, Scott, that's preposterous! How can you prove that?"

"By the Bible itself. The Bible has hundreds of prophecies written in its pages. Most have already been fulfilled. If the Bible wasn't true, then answer me, Miss Smarty, how could that happen?"

"Like what prophecies?"

"Do you know that it was prophesized in the Bible about automobiles, planes, atomic bombs, and the vast knowledge that we have today to create all our electronic gizmos?"

Sheryl tossed a pillow at Scott and said, "Now you are pulling my leg, Scott Perkins!"

Scott chuckled as he grabbed the pillow. "No! Go see if you can locate your Bible, and I'll show you."

Reluctantly, Sheryl got up and, a few minutes later, came back with the Bible. Scott thumbed through the crisp new pages. "Ah, here it is! Here in Nahum 2:4, KJV, it reads, 'The chariots shall rage in the streets, they shall jostle one against the other in the broad ways: They shall seem like torches, they shall run like the lightings.' This is the prophecy of Nahum's vision of the last days. He had no way to know what to call what he saw in his vision. He related it to what he knew in those days. The verse is talking about the horseless carriages or the automobile. The torches are the headlights of cars, and we know how they rage in the streets. Jostle one another in the broadways. Definitely, he saw our great expressways. As I read this verse, I can see a busy expressway at night.

Then in Isaiah 31:5, KJV, it says, 'As birds flying, so will the Lord of hosts defend Jerusalem; defending also he will deliver it; and passing over He will preserve it.' That Bible passage is referring to the airplane. The Lord is talking about defending Israel in the air, flying just like birds. Now let's look in Daniel 12:4, KJV, 'But thou, O

Daniel, shut up the words, and seal the book, even to the time of the end; many shall run to and fro, and knowledge shall be increased.'"

Scott pointed to Sheryl's computer and said, "Look how much knowledge has increased in such a short time. Personal computers have only been in mass market since 1977. The knowledge of the world was much the same until around the turn of the 1900s. Since then, it has been rapidly increasing."

Scott flipped the pages until he got to Matthew and said, "Even the New Testament is full of end-time prophecies. Matthew also tells about the signs of the end-times. It tells us that there will be false Christs and false prophets. These are men that try to make people believe they are God or teach false doctrine. Like pastors who preach that there was no virgin birth of Jesus or that there is no hell."

"You mean like that cult leader Jim Jones? I read about him awhile back. He got his followers to commit suicide in the name of God. What about the satanic cults?"

"Yeah, precisely! Matter of fact, here, let me find it. Yes, here in Timothy 4:1–2, KJV. It reads, 'Now the spirit speaketh expressly, that in the latter times some shall depart from the faith, giving heed to seducing spirits, and doctrines of devils.' The Antichrist will be the last and most terrifying tyrant of them all."

Sheryl shivered as she said, "Well, yeah, if he does have the devil reincarnated in him! If what you say is true, I certainly wouldn't want to be anywhere near him."

"That's my point, Sheryl! We have to hide away from him. I really feel that God is going to protect us from him. That's why he led us to Old Town."

"Scotty, are there any other signs?"

"Too many to name tonight. Although 2 Timothy 3:1–5 comes to my mind. There are nineteen signs about the condition of people during these last days. He says that in the end-times, people will be lovers of themselves. Remember the conversation we had that nobody cares about the other guy anymore? Everybody just cares about themselves."

Scott cleared his throat and continued, "Then in Matthew, it talks about the condition of the world that there will be wars and rumors of wars. We have had three world wars in recent times. In the past decade, there have been wars all over the world with terrorism running rampant."

Scott was on a roll he couldn't stop. "Also in Luke 21:11, it talks about famines, earthquakes in diverse places and pestilences. All these things have been increasing more and more each day. Then over two thousand years ago, it was prophesied that because of their disobedience to God, He would scatter the Jews out from Israel to all corners of the world. The Word of God says that they would be persecuted and hated. In Jeremiah 31:10–11, God also guarantees that He will return the dispersed nation back to the land He promised them. Israel became a nation again in 1948."

Scott turned the Bible to Matthew 24:32–34, KJV and read, "Now learn a parable of the fig tree: When his branch is yet tender, and putteth forth leaves, ye know that summer is nigh: So likewise ye, when ye shall see all these things, know that it is near, even at the door. Verily I say unto you, this generation shall not pass, till all these things be fulfilled."

Scott continued, "The fig tree and its branches symbolizes Israel. The generation that sees these things shall not pass till all these things be fulfilled. Therefore, prophecy is right on target. We are in the last days."

"Well, Scott, I'm learning a lot about the Bible. It's kind of scary, if it is true."

"Yes, Sheryl, and you can bank on it. It is true! Do you know that the birth of Jesus was even prophesied in the Old Testament hundreds of years before it actually happened in Bethlehem?"

"Really? I never knew that before, but for that matter, I never knew much at all about the Bible. I wasn't raised in church like you were."

"I understand. I thank God all the time that he gave me good Christian parents. However, that is not what saves a person. It certainly gives one a good foundation to make the right decision, though."

"Yes, I'm sure it does. You're proof of that. If I had been raised in a Christian home, I am sure my views would be quite different. Now, Scotty, I'm really tired. Please, go home and let me think about all you have said."

"Okay, but don't wait too long. Time is getting short. I'm leaving with the guys Monday. Mom and Linda will join us after school is out in June. By that time, Linda's baby should be about two months old."

Scott embraced Sheryl and gently kissed her on the lips. He then told her good-bye. He fought back tears. Could this be his finally good-bye to his beloved Sheryl?

28

Destination Old Town, March 6

Monday morning, Joe, James, Thomas, and Harold flew into South Haven to pick up Scott. As soon as Scott was aboard and settled, he said, "I don't know about you guys, but I have had very little sleep since we decided to go back to Old Town. My mind has been spinning with ideas about all the things that we need to do."

"I know what you mean, Scott," his granddad answered. "Joe and I have been going over everything we can think of. I'm sure we've missed something. We are concerned that there's not enough of us to get all the work done in the time we have!"

"Well, Dad," Thomas broke in, "Harold and I have been doing a lot of talking about this as well. We came to the same conclusion as you. We probably will need more help, maybe an electrician. Harold brought up the fact that we'll need some kind of power to run things. I naturally thought about windmills since I used to work at a turbine company. The only thing I'm concerned about is that they would be seen by planes flying over."

"I really don't think they would be seen all that well on the valley floor," Joe answered. "The trees should help to give some camouflage for them. Hopefully, in the winter, it will be too stormy for planes to be flying over the area. Maybe the snow will act as a camouflage also. I'll fly over the area and check it out. My biggest concern is will there be enough wind down there to run a windmill. What do you think, Thomas?"

"I'm quite sure there is. It doesn't take very much of a breeze to get them moving. However, I'm not sure if that's what we should do, they are fairly costly."

"Well, guys," James said, "we have a good many concerns. Just as soon as we get there, we better sit down and make a list. Then maybe we'll be able to figure out what to do first."

Joe landed the plane at his rented small airstrip. After exiting the plane, the men loaded their personal belongings into their parked truck.

They drove the two miles back to Gratiot to get lunch. After the meal, the men sat around drinking coffee and throwing out ideas. James pulled a notepad out of his jacket and said, "Let's make a list so we can put a plan together."

"Good idea," Joe agreed.

Scott was the first to throw out ideas. "To me, one of the most important thing to do is to think about getting the fields worked up so we can get some crops planted. I'm not exactly sure what kind of crops we will need. For starters, I'd say we need hay, corn, and a large vegetable garden. Also, we will have to have some way of working up the ground so we can plant and harvest the crops."

"I agree, that's important," Joe said. "But it's too early to actually start plowing. However, we need to keep our eyes and ears open to where we can buy some of the equipment that we will need. Maybe you and Harold could get some information from a local feed mill as to when and how you should plant."

Excitedly, Scott agreed, "Yes, because we will also need to buy seed by the bulk. We definitely need to locate a local feed mill."

"What about animals like cows, horses, chickens, and pigs?" Harold asked. "They will need a barn or a pen to stay. We will eventually need to raise animals to survive, so we'll have to fix the barns up. Thank God all the buildings have copper roofs. That's why every building is in decent shape, but they'll still take a lot of work."

"You're right, Harold," Thomas told his son-in-law. "However, the most important thing right now is getting the houses in town livable. Next, we can work on the farm buildings. If we don't get the farmhouses done by the time everyone moves up, the farm families can stay in the boardinghouse until they are ready. Scott and Harold, seeing you guys are in charge of farm business, each of you should live in a farmhouse."

"I agree," Joe said. "It will make a good home for Harold and his family. Scott, you might ask someone to join you at the farm. They could be a farm hand for you and Harold."

"Good idea," Thomas said. "Are there any more pressing concerns or ideas?"

Joe spoke out again, "Well, my idea would be to get a good used tractor if we can find one. Next, we need to keep an eye out for other pieces of equipment to go with it like a plow, disk, drag, cultivator, and maybe a wagon. Oh, and of course, we'll need a corn picker and a mower to cut the hay and a baler. That should get the farms started."

"Which brings me back to the subject of electricity," Thomas mentioned. "We still need to decide about what we are going to do about the electricity problem. Should we go with the windmill idea, or something else? Or maybe we should forget about electricity altogether! How about it, guys, what do you think?"

"Personally, I like the idea of the windmill," James said. "I think it's a good idea, if it's not too easily seen from the air. It appeals to me because later on, we won't be able to get fuel without the mark of the beast. With air energy, we can at least have some power for important things like refrigeration, limited lighting, and various equipment we might need to run. Maybe we'll even be able to get news broadcasts on the radio."

"Wow, I don't know about you, guys, but I'm not an electrician," Harold said. "I can do some basic wiring, but that's about it."

"Don't worry, Harold," Joe said. "James and I have been talking, and we might know just the two guys that could help us. In fact, they attend the same church we went to in New York. If it is all right with you, guys, I will talk to them when we make a trip back home. I'll see if they will be willing to come up and give us a hand. Who knows, they just might want to stay up here! Of course, that's if it's agreeable with the rest of you." The other men were quick to agree.

Joe continued, "Great, some good ideas. I believe the first thing to do when we get to Old Town is to evaluate what materials we will need to fix up the town's houses. Harold, I'm going to put you in charge of that. You did such a fine job with that last fall."

"Okay," Thomas said. "I believe we have covered some of our main concerns. I realize that all of this is a bit overwhelming. I pray that God will open the doors that we need and bless this undertaking. With that said, let's end the meeting and go home to Old Town! Let's build our families' new future! All in favor, say amen." Each man said a hearty amen!

The guys stopped at the town's grocery store to pick up their week's supply of food. They also bought some blocks of ice for the coolers to keep their perishables from spoiling. Next, they went over to the hardware store. Mark was happy to see the men as he welcomed them back. He shook each of their hands as he said, "Good to see you men again."

"Good to be back here in God's country," Joe answered. "Mark, I don't remember if I introduced you to the rest of our guys or not. "

"Oh, I have become quite familiar with each of them from last fall. They were good customers. So are you boys coming all the way up here to fish?"

Scott gave Harold a quick glance and then looking back at Mark said, "Yeah, we're up here for the fishing."

James could sense that Scott felt uncomfortable about the cover up and said, "Joe and I bought a couple of acres for rest and recreation. Plan on slapping up a cabin and doing some fishing. Maybe we'll come up in the fall and do a little hunting also."

"Yeah," Mark said. "From what I hear, there are getting to be fewer and fewer places to fish without finding some kind of pollution or contamination in the rivers and lakes. So far, man hasn't ruined it up here."

"Yes," Scott spoke up. "It's sad to see what man has done to God's creation."

"Amen," Mark answered back. "God created such a beautiful planet, and man is destroying it."

Thomas looked over at Mark and asked, "Sounds like you're a Christian, Mark?"

"You bet I am! I have been saved for six years now. Good thing God is a forgiving God because I sure needed a lot of forgiving!"

"Praise the Lord," Thomas said. "God will even forgive a murderer when he surrenders his life to Him."

"You boys are welcome to visit our little church anytime you want."

"Thanks, Mark," Thomas said. "We just might take you up on that sometime."

"That would be nice. We are a small congregation, about ten families, but we're a friendly bunch. And oh boy, our women are some of the best cooks. I love it when we have our monthly potluck. That would be a good time for you boys to visit. We'll be having one in two weeks if you boys are still around. You would be warmly welcomed."

"Sounds good," Joe said.

"Yeah, we have a bunch of good Christian people that go there. There's Jake Stevenson. You might know Jake. He runs the sawmill I told you about."

Scott smiled and said, "Yes, we have met Jake. We bought some lumber from him last fall. Seemed like a real nice guy."

"Yeah, he's a good man. Then there's Carl Jenkins right next door. He owns the grocery store. He cuts up his own meat. Buys his beef from Clarence Masterson, who has a cattle farm and is also a member of our church. Carl buys pigs from George Olson, who by the way goes to our little church. We also have a few retired couples in the church. Then there's the Westhoff brothers, Todd and Sidney. They do general contracting. They're also members."

Joe spoke up, "We know the Westhoff brothers, right, James? Remember those were the men we hired to rebuild the bridge?"

"Yeah, you're right! Those guys did a great job for us."

"So you're the people they were talking about. Had us all wondering what you were up to. We wondered why would you want to buy a piece of land way up here."

The five men looked at each other for a tense moment, and then James answered, "After living in a New York City most of our lives, we needed to find a place as remote as we could. We wanted to be away from all civilization. Just a handful of us and some good fishing and hunting."

"One of our neighbors got curious and drove his truck up there to take a look, but he didn't go beyond the bridge. He saw the sign that read, Private: Keep Out! We like to respect the rights of others around here, so he didn't intrude."

"We appreciate that," Scott said. "We value our privacy."

"Oh, I understand where you boys are coming from. This is a great little community, and we like our privacy too. That's why we live in this small town. We enjoy the passerbys and tourists, but our personal lives belong to us. But you boys are more like our neighbors now."

Joe smiled and said, "We really appreciate that, Mark. You have been a good friend, and this is definitely a friendly town."

"Yep, it's a good God-fearing town!" Mark said as he smiled proudly.

Just then, a lightbulb went off in Harold's head. Reluctantly, he asked, "Mark, would you mind doing us a big favor?"

"Sure, anything. Name it!"

"Would you mind if we tell our wives that they could leave emergency messages with you? My wife is expecting a baby at the end of this month. I'm very worried about her. Our cell phones don't have signals up in the mountains."

"Why, of course, Harold, no problem, but how will I get a message to you?"

Harold thought for a moment and said, "We need to come to Gratiot a lot to pick up supplies. We can check with you when we are in town."

"But what if it is something that can't wait," Mark asked? "How would I get the message to you?"

Harold though a moment and then said, "You could have someone drop it off at the bridge. I'll rig up a jar or something and hang it on the bridge. I can check it at least once a day."

James spoke up, "Coming way out here would be an expense and an inconvenience, so I would make it worth your time and effort. If our families have an emergency, it is important for us to know. We sure would appreciate it, Mark."

"No problem! I've got two sons of my own. I know it's important for my wife and me to know that our boys and their families are doing okay. I'd be happy to see to it that you guys get your messages."

Mark laughed a little as he asked, "Harold, my wife didn't want me out of her sight when she was near her delivery date. How did you get away with it?"

"Well, to tell the truth, Mark, she wasn't too keen on the idea, but this trip was such an opportunity for me. She understood."

Noticing that Harold was a bit squeamish about Mark's question, Joe quickly changed the subject. "Say, Mark, do you know of any used farm equipment for sale around here?"

"Matter of fact, yes, I do. Old Chad Wilson is retired from farming and is having a huge farm auction next Saturday. When you pull out of here, just follow the auction signs. He's about five miles out of town." The men thanked Mark again and then picked up some nails and other hardware items that they knew they would need at Old Town.

After they left the store, they followed the auction signs and checked out the farm where the auction would be held the following Saturday. From the road, they could see the farm equipment lined up for inspection. The guys got out of the truck and looked over the machinery and equipment. There was everything that the men thought they would need and more. After spending a good hour of checking it all out, they got back in their truck and headed back to Old Town.

By the time the five men got to Old Town, it was already five thirty. They brought all their supplies into the boardinghouse. Harold started a fire in the cookstove while Scott started one in the potbelly stove. Joe and James put the groceries away, leaving out four cans of chili, a loaf of Italian bread and butter for the men's supper that evening. The guys were all in good spirits, even though deep down, they were apprehensive about the work that lay ahead of them. On top of that, they were missing their wives already. Harold's mind was on Linda most of the time as he second-guessed his decision of being there.

The week that followed was extremely busy as the men pushed themselves to get the old homes restored. Harold, Thomas, and Joe worked on the large house that they called the mayor's house while James and Scott worked on the house next door.

By Friday evening, the men had completed work on both houses. James decided to reward them by taking them out to a restaurant for breakfast Saturday morning. After that, they all went to the farm auction, which started at ten o'clock. Joe and James could not believe how reasonable the equipment sold for. They bought an old truck, a tractor, a hay baler, a corn picker and planter, and several small pieces of equipment. They even bought a large trailer to haul the equipment. Not everything they bought was a necessity, but they had a whole lot of fun.

The sale had taken up a good portion of the day. Even though the men felt a little guilty about the amount they spent, they were thrilled at the good deals they had made. Scott was the most excited of them all. As they unloaded the tractor, Scott said, "I really think that I should start working the ground right away."

"Slow down, partner." Joe laughed. "The snow has barely left. The earth is still frozen. It isn't even mid-March yet. Don't worry, there'll be plenty of time to get the ground ready."

29

Bowling Green, Ohio, March 17

It was Saturday morning, and the deliverymen had just finished installing the new Beastavision that Lorraine had ordered. Her old TV set had been having advertisements running about how time was running out on getting Beastavision installed in homes. The ads reminded the public that they would be committing civil crimes if they did not comply. Even though Lorraine knew that she would be using the Beastavision for only a short time, she did not want to take a chance on going to jail. She filled out and sent in a government form that lowered her monthly charge on her Beastavision. Her cost was minimal because of her wage and household expenses.

Lorraine and Linda spent the rest of the morning getting acquainted with the new system.

After a light lunch, the women settled down in the living room to watch a movie. At the most exciting part of the movie, the screen went blank for thirty seconds. Then President Omidi's face appeared on their set and said, "Hello, Lorraine Perkins and Linda Weber, welcome to our new Beastavision. Thank you for allowing me into your home. I am President Omidi of the United States of America.

From now on, whenever there is any important world or government news bulletin, I personally will come into your living room and keep you informed."

When the message was done, Lorraine was in shock! She quickly shut off the Beastavision and said to Linda, "Do you believe that?"

"No, Mother, I don't! How did he know our names? It was as if he was actually in the room. Like he was looking right into my eyes."

"I know! I thought he was looking into mine. I don't know how he could have been talking directly to us. It is a televised program. I just don't understand."

"Maybe, he got our names from when you signed up on that low-income government program. You had to list me for living here, right?"

"Yes, but still, like I said, it's a program, which goes out to everyone. I heard that these sets were required all over the world."

"Mom, this is freaky."

The ringing of Lorraine's phone interrupted their troubling thoughts. Christine Nelson's name appeared on her cell. She quickly answered, "Christina, what a wonderful surprise to hear from you."

"Hi, Lorraine. I've missed you so much! I can barely remember our last time together, with Mom's funeral and all. Thank you so much for supporting me through the ordeal. I finally sold Mom's home. I had a big estate sale. I've been doing a lot of thinking as to what I'm going to do. There's nothing left for me here in New York anymore. Besides, it is too dangerous. Remember how you tried to talk me into moving to Bowling Green so we could be close?"

Lorraine's heart stopped for a moment. She wanted nothing more than to live close to her best friend. When she tried to talk Christina into moving to Ohio last fall, she had no idea that her family would be moving to the Keweenaw Peninsula. What could she say? Lorraine knew that it was imperative that Christina should get away from New York, but now, she didn't want it to be because of her. She was sworn to secrecy. She trusted Christina with her life, but until she cleared it with the rest of the group, she couldn't say a word. Lorraine didn't know what to tell her. She loved her so much and wanted to spend time with her before she was off the grid. At least they could be together for three and a half months. Selfishly, she didn't discourage her friend. Biting her lip, she said, "Christina, that's wonderful! When are you coming?"

"I can leave in three days! Daniel dropped out of Bible college, so he will be living with us. We will need a three-bedroom apartment. Are there any openings at your apartment building?"

"You know, I think there might be. I know of a family who just moved out last week. I don't believe anyone moved in yet. I'll find out and call you back."

"That would be great! Love you, Lorraine!"

"Love you more. Can't wait to have you as my neighbor, girlfriend."

Lorraine called the landlord as soon as she got off the phone with Christina. Fortunately, there was an empty three-bedroom vacancy. She was able to secure it for Christina and her family. Three days later, Christina and her three children were moving into the apartment above Lorraine's. Lorraine and Linda helped them move in. Boxes were stacked everywhere as the movers finished delivering the last of them. The top of the boxes were marked as to which rooms they belonged.

"Linda," Christina called out. "Please do not lift any heavy boxes, and please do not overdo it. I don't feel like delivering a baby today."

Linda smiled as she patted her huge baby bump and answered, "I won't. The baby isn't due for almost two weeks. Actually, twelve days. I don't want to have it early either! However, if I did, I know I am in good hands. Mom told me that you delivered lots of babies in Africa."

"Well, I helped, but Dan was the doctor. There were a few times that I had to do it solo when he couldn't get away from a critical patient, but most of the time, we did it together."

"Don't worry, honey," Lorraine said. "The first baby it's usually a long labor, and the hospital is only twenty minutes away."

A couple of hours later, Linda picked up a box that was marked with Daniel's name. She carried it into his room where he was unloading boxes. "Here you go, Daniel, looks like this is your last box."

Daniel gently took it from her as he said, "Great, here I'll take it. Why don't you sit down on that chair for a few minutes and rest. You've been working too hard for a lady that is getting close to her delivery date."

"Yes! I think I'll do just that. I'm exhausted."

"Yeah, it will give us a chance to talk a little. Even though our parents are old friends, we didn't get to see each other that much."

"Yeah, I know! The only time we were able to visit was when your parents would get a vacation from Africa. Then your mom and dad would come and speak at our church about their mission field. We always had a potluck dinner when you guys visited. Remember how much fun we had when your family stayed at our house when you were in town?"

"Yeah. I remember how silly my sister Rachael acted around your brother Scott. Last time we were there, she was only fourteen. She had such a crush on him. He was a freshman in college already. I know he thought of her as a little girl."

"I remember that! I bet you didn't know that I had a crush on you too, did you? You're a little younger than me, but I didn't care. I thought you were cute. We were always giggling about something."

"No! I didn't know you liked me that way. I was just starting to like girls about that time. I liked you so much that all I could do was stutter when I was around you."

Linda laughed and said, "I thought you had a speech problem."

Daniel smiled at Linda and said, "Now that we are going to be neighbors, maybe we can become good friends again."

"I'd like that. I don't have any friends here. My husband is far off trying to save his damsel in distress."

"I heard something about your dad, Scott, and your husband working on an old ghost town in. I heard that your granddad and Joe Wydeck bought some property in the Keweenaw Peninsula. Your mom told my mom that your dad and brother are convinced that this peace contract with Israel is the seven-year peace treaty of the Bible. When I heard that, right away, I thought, I bet they bought the property as a refuge. The whole thing is stupid."

"No, not really. The way things have been going, I've been thinking the same thing! I'm thinking we have been wrong about the timing of the rapture. I might have done the same thing if I had the money and know-how."

"Not you too? I thought you dropped out of Bible school for the same reason I did."

"Why was that, Linda?"

"You know, both of us being brought up in the church. Having to be an example all the time. I got sick of being a goody two-shoes. Things actually changed for me when a couple girls on campus talked me into going to a club with them. I had so much fun it became a regular event."

"Did you drink at the clubs?"

"At first, I only drank sodas, but I've got to admit, with peer pressure, I eventually started ordering mixed drinks. Then I met my handsome husband, Harold. It was love at first sight. I was so tired of religion! I turned to a whole new way of way of life. I wanted to experiment with my newfound freedom. Harold was a good teacher." Linda's mood changed from jovial to serious as she said, "Now I'm struggling with my beliefs, especially now that Harold has been brainwashed into becoming a Christian."

Daniel smiled and said, "Praise the Lord! Your husband became a Christian?"

"So he says."

"Linda, I understand where you are coming from. There was a short time in my life when I questioned my faith. It was when my dad died. I also gave into temptations, but then one day, I looked around at God's creation. I knew without a shadow of a doubt that He was the almighty God. From that day on, He has been the Lord of my life."

"Then why did you drop out of Bible college?"

"Well, I went to the same college where my mom and dad had gone. Back then, it was a very good Bible seminary. Today's Bible colleges are not the same. My first year wasn't bad, but this past year, it went downhill. The Bible colleges have gotten a lot like the modern churches of today. They teach peace and love but no sound Bible doctrine. Some are even teaching that Christ was not God, that He was merely a man. Some are even promoting Chrislam."

"Oh yeah, that's the merging of the Christian and the Islamic churches, right?"

"Yes. There's a possibility it could be the one-world religion."

"If our world had a one-world religion, at least they wouldn't have that to fight over. That doesn't sound all that bad."

"Linda, I'm sure you know enough about Bible prophecy to realize that the one-world religion will be the worship of the Antichrist. In the Bible, it says that in the end-times, the Antichrist will say he is God and make all worship him. It also says that he will fool even the elect. The Antichrist will be reincarnated by Satan himself."

Linda's face showed pain as she clenched her hand on the chair's arm. "Ouch," she cried out.

Daniel rushed to her side as he asked, "What's the matter, Linda, is it the baby?"

"I don't know."

Daniel yelled for his mother. Both Christina and Lorraine came running into Daniel's room. Linda described to Christina how hard her pain was and how long that it lasted. Christina then looked at her watch and said, "Let me know when you have another pain. I'll time them."

Christina kept a close eye on her watch as she timed her for the next hour. Her pains were now getting closer and lasting longer. Christina looked at Lorraine and said, "It's time to call her doctor."

When they arrived at the hospital, Linda was sent to the maternity ward and given a room. As soon as she was settled into a bed, Lorraine tried to call Thomas on his cell phone. She couldn't get through to him, so she called the emergency number that he had given her. Mark, the storeowner, answered the phone and wrote down her message. He promised her that the message would be delivered within the hour.

30

Old Town Keweenaw Peninsula, 7:30 p.m., March 17

As the men ate supper that evening, they also discussed how much they had accomplished these last couple of weeks. Joe proudly said, "Well, in town, we now have three cabins and the large home ready. Also we have two farmhouses almost ready to move into. I would say, men, we have done a good job!

Joe looked over at Scott and said, "In a couple of weeks, I believe the ground should be ready to plow."

Smiling from head to toe, Scott answered, "Can't wait!"

Thomas looked over at his son-in-law and noticed the sad look on his face. He asked him, "What's the matter, Harold, aren't you feeling good?"

"Yes, sir, I feel fine. I'm just worried about Linda, that's all."

"Yeah," Scott said. "The baby's due in a couple weeks, right?"

"Actually, sooner than that. It's due this month on the 29."

James looked over at the others. Then he suggested, "Let's give Harold a break on kitchen detail tonight." He then turned to Harold and said, "Why don't you take this break to go down and check the bottle, just in case there's a message."

Harold sprung to his feet and shouted, "Thanks! Are you sure you guys don't mind?"

Thomas smiled broadly as Scott threw him the keys to the truck. Joe yelled out, "Go on and get out of here!"

It seemed to take forever as Harold drove out past the cabins, then the farms, and finally to the bridge. He jumped out of the truck, hoping to find some kind of message from home. To his surprise, there was a message in the bottle. It was a message from Lorraine letting them know that Linda was in labor at the hospital. The way back to the town seemed to take longer than the trip there. Tears flowed down Harold's cheeks. He wrestled with the decision that he had made to come up here. His wife needed him. He was nearly seven hundred miles away from her when she needed him the most. He worried because it was too early for the baby. Would the baby be all right? What about Linda? He asked himself, *How could I have been so insensitive to leave her at a time like this?*

When Harold got back to the boardinghouse, he told the rest of the men about the message. They were all concerned. Joe looked at James and whispered, "You know what I'm tempted to do?"

"No, Joe, what?"

"I'm tempted to fly Harold over to Bowling Green tonight for some R&R."

Harold jumped from his chair and said, "What! Did I hear right? Do you really mean it, Joe?"

"Yes, son, you have been working really hard, and I believe your place is with your wife right now." Joe turned to James and said, "In fact, why don't you come along, and we'll fly from there over to New York and check on those men we were talking about. Sam Olson is an electrician. With the economy like it is, he has been struggling. He also had a guy named Albert Cline that was his apprentice. Both good men. Maybe we can convince them to work for us awhile. I know we can trust these men. They are good Christian men."

By nine o'clock, the three men were boarding Joe's plane. All the way over to Bowling Green, Harold was tense and nervous. James patted Harold's back and told him, "Try to relax, son, we'll be there soon."

"Yeah, Mr. Patterson, but I'm worried that the baby will be born before we get there. I should be there to help her through this. I hope she can handle the pain."

"Harold, my boy, first of all, call me Granddad. After all, I'm going to be great-grandfather to your new baby."

"Relax, Harold," Joe said. "There is nothing we can do about it. I've got the plane flying at her top speed. When Darlene had our first child, she was in labor for twenty-one hours. Those first babies take longer."

Harold squirmed in his seat and said, "According to Lorraine's message, Linda has been in labor since four o'clock. So she has been in labor for over five hours already. Maybe we will get there in time." Struggling to get it out of his mouth, Harold asked, "Granddad, how long was Mrs. Patterson in labor with Lorraine?"

With hesitation, he confessed, "I believe she had labor only six hours before she delivered. I hear that's unusual. Most first deliveries take longer."

"Yeah, just my luck, she'll probably take after her grandmother. Linda never does anything slow."

Trying to get Harold's mind off Linda's delivery, Joe changed the subject and said, "If Sam and Albert agree to come to Old Town for a couple of months, it won't be necessary for you to come back before we move the women up. I think it would be in our best interest to leave one of us behind to help get Lorraine and Linda ready for the move in June. We can fly down and pick up our wives when they're ready. How about it, Harold? Would you mind staying in Bowling Green until the move? With the new baby and all, the women could really use the help moving."

Harold could hardy hold it together as he excitedly said, "If it's all right with me? Of course, it is all right with me! To be with my wife and new baby? You bet it's all right with me!"

Joe's plane finally landed at the Wood County Airport in Bowling Green, Ohio. James handed Harold some singles and six one hundred dollar bills. "Here, son, you'll need this. You will be able to grab a taxi easy enough here. Call us when you get the news if it's a boy or a girl." Harold gave each man a hug and thanked them for their kindness.

Upon arriving at the Wood County Hospital, Harold went straight to the reception window. When the clerk asked if she could help him, Harold nervously blurted out, "I'm having a baby!"

The clerk chuckled under her breath as she glanced at his physique then said, "So how far along are you?"

Too nervous to see the humor in it, Harold faked a smile and said, "No, no, I mean my wife is here in labor. I was out of town when I got the message. I got here as soon as possible. Please, miss, what room is my wife in?"

"Name?"

"Linda Weber."

"One moment, sir, while I check with the maternity ward." To Harold, it seemed forever as the clerk waited for answers. Finally, she hung up the phone and said, "Mr. Weber, your wife was released at nine thirty last night."

Chills ran down Harold's back as he thought the worst. He asked, "The baby, is our baby all right?"

"Mr. Weber, seeing that your wife has been discharged, I'm not at liberty to give out any more information. I would presume she is at home. Maybe you should go check there."

"Yes, yes, of course," he said as he turned and rushed to the door. Outside of the hospital, Harold impatiently waited for a taxi. Finally, one stopped and picked him up. Within a half hour, he was at the apartment pounding on the door. Lorraine was half-asleep when she looked through the peek hole and was flabbergasted to see her son-in-law. She opened the door and threw her arms around him. "What a wonderful surprise to see you, Harold. I tried to get a message to you at about five thirty last night, but I wasn't sure you got it. I didn't think you would get it until morning. Linda will be so happy to see you! She's sleeping in my room. I've changed places with her because she has been so uncomfortable lately."

"The baby, Mom. Is the baby okay?"

Hearing the commotion, Linda was awakened. She walked out into the living room, holding her large baby bump. When she realized it was her husband, she awkwardly lumbered up to him. She fell into his arms as they kissed one another. Then he looked up and down at his wife as he asked her, "Sweetheart, are you okay?"

"Yes, honey. More than okay because you're here!"

"But the baby, and why are you home from the hospital?"

Linda's smile went to a scowl as she said, "It was false labor! Which at first I thought was a good thing because it was too early. Then the doctor assured me that a week early was not dangerous to the baby. So then when the labor stopped, I was upset. All that pain for nothing! The nurse told me that even false labor counts toward the actual labor. So maybe I won't be in labor so long when the real thing happens."

"That's wonderful news, honey! Now I can be here when you do go into labor!"

Linda screamed, "What! Do you mean it, Harold? Can you really stay for a while?"

"Honey, I'm going to be here until we all go to Old Town together. The guys knew how much I wanted to be with you when our baby was born. They also felt that you ladies could use some muscle for the move."

Both Harold and Linda slept better that night than they had in weeks.

31

Old Town Keweenaw Peninsula, March 30

When Joe and James landed back at the airstrip this time, they had with them Sam Olson and Albert Cline. Sam was a master electrician, and Albert had been his assistant. After approaching the men about working at Old Town, they were both excited and intrigued about the job. Joe explained to them that the work would not be limited to their trade, but they would be asked to do a variety of jobs.

Before heading to Old Town, Joe and James stopped into the hardware with Sam and Albert to pick up some more gear for them. Mark approached them as soon as they walked through the door. Smiling, he said, "James, glad to see you guys! I just got a message from your daughter, James. I was trying to find someone to take the message up to the bridge when you walked in."

Anxiously, James asked, "What did she say?"

"Congratulations, James! Your daughter says that you have a granddaughter! Linda gave birth to a seven-pound. six-ounce baby girl! Her name is Brianna Lynn. In addition, Lorraine told me that mother and baby are doing well!"

Mark laughed and then continued relaying the message, "Then Harold grabbed the phone and shouted, 'Tell the guys all hello and that I'm a dad!' "

Beaming, James said, "Praise the Lord! I am so glad that we decided to let Harold go home to be with Linda. He really needed to be there when his baby was born!"

Joe patted James on the back as he said, "That's wonderful. Congratulations on your new great-granddaughter."

Mark looked over at the new men and said, "I don't believe we've met."

Joe apologetically said, "Oh, I'm sorry. With all the great news, I forgot to introduce you. These men are a couple of our buddies from New York. Thought we would take them on a fishing expedition."

After Joe made the introductions, the men started their shopping. As Mark watched the men gather new gear, his mind wondered. He questioned to himself why they had bought farm equipment. They even purchased an old truck at the auction. He wondered, *What's up with that?* Not that he minded their hefty purchases, but it was curious that they were always buying so many hardware items. A few days back, he had had a conversation with Jake Stevenson about how many truckloads of lumber the men had bought from his sawmill. The two business men couldn't help but be curious. And now, two more men adding to the mix? He could feel something strange was going on!

Even though his curiosity was getting the best of him, Mark kept his questions to himself. Instead, he said, "Like I mentioned last time you guys were in, you are welcome to visit our church anytime you want. Worship service is at ten in the morning. This Sunday, we are having a potluck after the worship service. Would love to have you stop by. Don't worry about bringing anything. The women always cook way too much. Darn good food, though!"

"You know, that doesn't sound bad," James said. "I'll talk to the others. Well, better run now and get that important message back to camp. Thanks, Mark. We'll be seeing you soon."

At Old Town, Thomas and Scott were working on a cow stanchion in one of the barns. Thomas said to his son, "I can't wait until I get your mother and sister up here. I really miss them. I am so lucky to have your mother back in my life. God is so gracious."

"That's for sure. I'm really happy for both of you. You and Mom love each other so much. You guys truly belong together. I thought Sheryl and I would be together forever. I love her so much, Dad. It still hurts that she is out of my life. I thought being up here would help me forget her, but it hasn't helped at all. I can't get her off my mind. I have prayed so hard that the Holy Spirit would get a hold of her heart and save her. Her salvation means the most to me. However, if she would accept Jesus as her savior and she still wanted to marry me, now that would be fantastic! I'd love to live here on this farm with Sheryl as my wife."

"I'm sorry, son. There's not much more I can say, except you are obeying God by not allowing yourself to be unevenly yoked to an unbeliever. All you can do is pray about it."

"Yeah, I know, but it still hurts!"

The men looked up as they heard a truck come over the bridge and down their primitive road. Scott ran out of the barn and saw that it was Joe's truck. He yelled to get his attention. Joe saw him and stopped. Thomas heard and came walking up as the four men were getting out of the truck.

James said, "Thomas, Scott, I'd like to introduce you to our new team members, Sam Olsen and Albert Cline. Sam, Albert, this is my son and grandson, Thomas and Scott Perkins." The men shook hands as they greeted each other.

After the introductions, Thomas asked, "Any news from home?"

With a beaming smile on his face, James said, "Let's see, any news from home? Well, nothing except I'm a great-granddad, and, Thomas, you're a grandpa!"

"What!" Thomas shouted. "Did Linda and Harold have their baby?"

"Yes! Brianna Lynn Weber is a beautiful seven-pound, six-ounce girl! Mark had a message for us when we stopped into the store. Mother and baby are both doing well. He talked to Harold for a minute too. He was all excited. Wanted to let us know that he is a daddy now."

"Hey, that makes me an uncle," Scott said. "Thank God everything went well!"

"Yes, we have so much to be thankful for," Joe said. "The sandwiches we picked up in town are getting cold. Come on, let's get to the boardinghouse and have lunch."

Scott smelled the aroma of the sandwiches and said, "Great! I am starving! I am hungry enough to eat a cow, but as you see, there aren't any in the barn yet, so a sandwich would be the next best thing! Thank you, guys, for thinking about us."

The men all laughed at Scott's attempt at humor as they scrambled to get into the truck. When they got into the town, the men went straight to the boardinghouse. They all settled down at the old wooden table to eat. Before they started their lunch, Thomas bowed his head and prayed. "Thank you, God, for the sandwiches we are to about to devour, and we pray that they will give us strength to do Your will. Thank you so much for bringing these blessed new members into our family. And thank you so very much for bringing my new granddaughter, Brianna, into our family! Please, keep Linda and her new baby girl happy and healthy. Dear, God, please, bless our labor and endeavors, and lead us to make good decisions. Again, we thank, you, for our new members. Please, put a protective hedge around our new family and keep us safe. Amen."

When lunch was over, James suggested that they have a meeting to decide what had to be done next. All agreed, and the meeting began. Joe began by saying, "James and I have completely disclosed the reasons why we are here at Old Town to Sam and Albert. They realize the importance of complete secrecy in this matter. We have chosen these men for their skills as well as for our complete trust in them. Sam and Albert attend the same church that James and I did. Their actions have proved over and over again that they are both good Christian men."

"In addition to those fine qualities," James added, "we were aware that Sam recently lost his wife and two boys in the New York subway bombing. I am hoping that this expedition will help ease his pain. James looked directly at Sam and said, "I'm truly sorry for your loss. We hope that your involvement with our community will help in the healing of your disastrous tragedy."

With tears welling up in every man's eyes, the rest of them gave Sam their condolences.

Then Joe continued, "We chose Albert because he is a strong young single man with no ties. He has been living on his own for a couple years now. In addition, he has worked for Sam as his apprentice. Due to the plunging economy, both men have been having a financial struggle. Therefore, Sam and Albert were elated over our job offer. Now with introductions out of the way, does anyone have anything they would like to comment on?"

"Yes," Thomas spoke up. "I believe that I can speak for all our missing members, myself included, as I say, I feel that we would be privileged to have these two men working for us." Scott readily agreed.

"Okay," Joe said. "Now are there any other problems or suggestions that need to be addressed?"

Thomas spoke up again, "Yeah, there's been something that's been weighing heavily on my mind lately. Our ladies, and now a baby, will be up here before we know it. Thank God, we now have more than enough places for us all to live. There are four houses in town, along with eight rooms in the boardinghouse that are ready. The two farmhouses should be ready by the time the families arrive. But what worries me is how we all will be able to take baths! So far, we have been using a plastic camp shower. It is heated from the sun. After the weather turns cold and gloomy, that won't work! Besides, we would freeze up here if we had to use it in the winter. The locals say up here there are only two seasons—winter now and the winter that's on its way."

After they stopped laughing, James said, "Yes, son, you have a point. Joe and I both are planning on bringing our wives up here about the same time you are bringing your family up. As you know, both our wives have lived in the lap of luxury for most of their lives. We have always lived very comfortably. Since we have been married, Marge has always had a cook and a housekeeper! I am a little worried how she will handle the discomfort of a pioneer lifestyle. She got a kick out of camping for a couple of days. However, from a day's visit to a permanent living arrangement is a whole different ball game. To tell you the truth, I don't know how she will handle it. On top of her countless salon treatments and her daily afternoon bubble baths, I don't know how my dear wife will adapt to all of this."

Joe laughed. "Darlene complained about the outhouses when she camped here for a few days. I don't how she is going to do it on a daily basis either."

"Yeah," James answered back. "I have to admit, when you're almost eighty, it's not easy using the outside john. We haven't even gone through a winter here! What's that going to be like?"

Joe scratched his head and said, "Well, there's really nothing we can do about it. We'll all have to get used to it. There are always the commodes under the beds. However, the big problem, like Thomas has pointed out, there aren't any way for our folks to bathe. I have been mulling this over in my head too. What we need is some sort of a bathhouse."

Scott spoke up, "Like a shower house in a campground?"

"Yes, something like that."

Sam looked puzzled and said, "I've noticed that there isn't any electricity coming into this valley. Showers take water pumps and heaters!"

"Yes, I know," Joe answered back. "That was part of the reason I picked you and Albert to join us."

Sam answered back, "Yes, but you could never get the electric company way up here to hook up anything. You would need your own power, like wind turbines."

"Bingo!" Thomas spoke out. "We have been talking about the possibility of putting in one or two of them."

Albert asked, "Wouldn't something like that be easily seen from the sky?"

"Not that easy," Joe spoke up. "I flew over the valley, and to the best of my judgment, I don't think they would be all that visible. We talked about camouflaging them with paint. I also did some checking and found out that no major airlines are routed to fly over this valley."

"Do you plan on bringing electricity and plumbing to all the buildings and houses?" Sam asked.

"Gosh, no," Joe said. "That would be too big of a job. We would just like to have electricity in essential places. I was thinking maybe we should consider two windmills. One here in town and one out by the farms. In town, we could use it to run the electric for the bathhouse and the boardinghouse. We have some large freezers in the kitchen at the boardinghouse. It would be nice to be able to plug in a radio to keep up on world events. Electricity out at the farms would be useful for running some of the farm equipment."

"But, Joe," Scott said, "couldn't we have electricity in a few of the houses? Once we start milking cows, we'll need to keep the milk cold."

"Son, that probably wouldn't be a good idea. We don't want the valley all lit up at night. You never know when a stray plane might fly over. However, you have a good point about keeping the milk cold."

"Well, it would be fairly easy to extend electrical lines to the houses. Just one simple outlet in the wall and use it very minimally," Albert explained.

Joe looked at Sam and asked, "What do you think?"

"Well, it could be easily done. If we don't have to wire the whole house, it would be fairly easy just bringing electricity into the house. It would be for simple things like a small table light or refrigerator. Do you have any idea where we can purchase windmills?"

"No, but Thomas used to work for a company that sold and installed them. I'm sure he could get things set up for us. Couldn't you, Thomas?"

"Well, I can aim you in the right direction, but I don't think it would be good for me to show my face at their office. I was a sales consultant until I was fired."

Sam perked up, "Oh, a sales consultant! Do you know how to install one of those babies?"

"Not really! I could do the talk but not the walk. I never actually was on the job installing one."

"Well," Joe said, "sounds like we've got a good team going here. With your book knowledge, Thomas, along with Sam and Albert's experience with electricity, I'm sure we'll have no problem installing a windmill or two! I think we should fly over to Detroit tomorrow morning and see about ordering the windmills. Sam and Albert, you men can fly over there with me. Thomas, after our meeting today, you can fill Sam and Albert in on what you do know."

"Okay, sure, I would be glad to. One thing would be very helpful is be sure to remind them to give you a manual and blueprints."

"Yeah, great idea, Thomas," Sam said.

Joe turned to Thomas and asked him, "Oh by the way, how does this company deliver the windmills?"

"By semi. They come in sections for easy transport."

"Okay, good. "I'll stop into the hardware and ask another favor of Mark. Maybe he won't mind if I have them dropped off at his place."

Joe leaned back in his chair and said, "Okay, that settles it then. Sam, Albert, and I will fly out tomorrow to Detroit. Scott and Thomas, you guys can keep working on the farmhouses and buildings." He looked at James and asked, "Do you want to fly along with us tomorrow?"

"No, I'm sure that the three of you have it covered. I will stay behind and give my boys a hand. I can't do as much as I used to, but I'll do what I can."

"Oh come on, Grandpa, Dad and I can't keep up with you."

James laughed. "Yeah sure, son. Being an attorney all those years never quite toughened up my hands. I guess now is the time to toughen up."

"Okay," Joe said. "Let's get started. I will work with each of your teams today. Anything you need, just let me know, and I'll make note of it."

32

Gratiot Grace Church, Sunday, April 5

A couple of days earlier, Joe had suggested that it might be a good idea to take Mark Thornton up on his invitation to attend his church. It was now Sunday morning, and all the men had agreed to attend the small church in Gratiot.

Mark and his wife Brenda were door greeters that Sunday morning. When Mark saw the six men walk in, he was eager to shake each of their hands. He told Joe, "I can't tell you how happy I am that you and your friends are joining us this morning!"

After everyone was seated, a man stood up at the pulpit. He looked over to the pew where the six visitors were sitting. "I see some new faces at our church this morning. For those of you who are visiting, my name is Carl Jenkins. I've seen most of you at my grocery store here in town. I believe I cut some lunchmeat for a couple of you. On behalf of our congregation, I would like to welcome you, men, to our service this morning. I am the acting pastor for the day. Pastor Davis retired three years ago, and we have not found anyone to take his place. So the four of us deacons take turns teaching the Word of God to the congregation."

Carl Jenkins continued, "My message this morning is found in Ephesians chapter six, putting on the whole armor of God. However, before I start, please stand and turn to page 257 in your hymnbooks. Let's all sing together this old favorite, 'Amazing Grace.'" Next, Carl lead prayer, made announcements, and then the collection plate was passed. After a couple more songs, Deacon Jenkins began his sermon.

Acting Pastor Carl Jenkins opened his sermon with the reading of Ephesians 6:11–18, KJV. "'Put on the whole armor of God, that ye may be able to stand against the wiles of the devil. For we wrestle not against flesh and blood, but against principalities, against powers, against the rulers of the darkness of this world, against spiritual wickedness in high places. Wherefore take unto you the whole armor of God, that ye may be able to withstand in the evil day, and having done all, to stand. Stand therefore, having your loin a girt about with truth, and having on the breastplate of righteousness; And your feet shod with the preparation of the gospel of peace; faith, wherewith ye shall be able to quench all the fiery darts of the wicked. And take the helmet of salvation, and the sword of the Spirit, which is the word of God: Praying always with all prayer and supplication in the Spirit, and watching thereunto with all perseverance and supplication for all saints.'"

Immediately after the service, Mark walked over to the Old Town visitors and insisted that they stay for the potluck. In fact, several others approached them and invited them to stay for the dinner. Feeling welcomed, the men agreed to stay, but Joe insisted on donating some money since they didn't bring a dish to pass. He told Carl that they could use the money for food or whatever needs the church might have.

In the banquet room, there were several large tables. After filling their plates with food, the children all went to one table while the other tables soon filled up with the adults. James, Thomas, and Scott sat with one group. Joe, Sam, and Albert went over to other table.

Then Carl Jenkins gave thanks for the meal. Mark had been right; the ladies of their church were great cooks. The friendly down-to-earth mannerisms of the church members made it easy for the men of Old Town to feel right at home. The potluck meal and fellowship was enjoyed by all.

Thomas was sitting next to Carl Jenkins and commented to him, "That was a very good sermon. I really enjoyed it! Have you had any theology training?"

"No, not at all. I've got a degree in business. I have run that little grocery store here in town for twenty-five years. None of us four deacons have studied for the ministry. We just love the Lord and wanted to keep our little church going. As you can, see we have a good-size group of kids, and they need a good structured church where they can hear the Gospel. It is hard to get a pastor to move up here. When we think we have found the right one, he wants too much money. Seems like nowadays, a lot of preachers are in it for the money. No doubt, we sure could use a good pastor."

"You did a marvelous job, but I do understand what it means to have a pastor to lead the flock," Thomas said.

Carl looked at Thomas and the other three visitors at his table and asked, "Do you men attend church when you are at home?"

James spoke up first and said, "Yes, I attend a church outside of New York City. Our friends at the other table attend the same church as I do."

Thomas looked a bit sheepish and said, "Yes, I've been attending a church near Detroit. It is not the type of church that I normally would attend. I have to admit, because of personal reasons, I have strayed from my spiritual convictions. I am ashamed to say that I have strayed from God. Of all people, I should have been more faithful! I was a Baptist pastor for over twenty years. I should have had more strength! I let my problems influence my conviction. Although, since I have been up here, by the grace of God, I have rededicated my life to the Lord."

"No, you got to be kidding me! You're a pastor?" Carl asked. "That's great! Maybe you wouldn't mind being a guest speaker some time?"

"Perhaps, but," Thomas put his hand on his son's shoulder and said, "My son here has recently graduated from a Bible seminary."

Scott looked embarrassed and said, "Yes, but I haven't actually been preaching." Then he proudly turned to his dad and said, "Now my dad is a very experienced pastor. One of the best, if I may say so myself."

Scott's expression changed rapidly as he confessed. "I'm ashamed to admit that I have strayed from God also. However, like my father, I too have rededicated my life to Jesus Christ."

James spoke up, "I would stand behind either of these two men for spiritual guidance. If it weren't for my son-in-law, Thomas, I probably would never have been saved. I was stubborn for a good many years about accepting Jesus as my Savior. Thomas never gave up on me. Finally, one evening, I went to one of his services, and while he was preaching, the Holy Spirit came into my heart. I'll always be grateful to him for that."

James pointed to Scott and said, "If it weren't for my grandson, I wouldn't have understood about the confusion the world is in today. For that matter, I wouldn't have understood that we are living in the last days."

Mark Thornton joined the conversation as he said, "That's an interesting statement you made, James. The other deacons and I have been pondering that these days have to be near the end-times. Now more than ever, we feel that the rapture could be at any second. We are looking for the rapture very soon!"

Scott stared into Mark's eyes for a time, wondering if he should say what was about to come out of his mouth. Then he said in a low, clear voice, "What if I was to tell you that we believe that we have been in the seven-year tribulation for close to a year now?"

"No offense," Mark said, "but I can't believe that! You might have fallen from grace, but once you are saved, you are always saved! I have been strong in the Lord Jesus Christ for six years now, and nobody will convince me that I've been left behind! I know that I'm saved! The Bible verses that comes to my mind are Corinthians 3:15 & 16. 'If any man's work shall be burned, he shall suffer loss: but he himself shall be saved: yet so as by fire. Know ye not that ye are the temple of God, and that the Spirit of God dwelleth in you?'" Mark continued, "So don't you see, Thomas and Scott, once you are saved, you are sealed by the Holy Spirit. You guys didn't miss the rapture. It didn't happen yet. The Bible tells us in Ephesians 4:30. 'And grieve not the holy Spirit of God, whereby ye are sealed unto the day of redemption.'"

Scott smiled a broad smile and said, "You are absolutely right, Mark. We haven't missed the rapture. We believe that it will not take place until sometime after the midpoint of the tribulation. Maybe even just before the end."

Mark laughed and asked, "Wait a minute! Are you trying to tell me that you believe that we are now in the seven-year tribulation, and the rapture hasn't even occurred yet?"

"That's exactly what I'm saying! When I was in the seminary, one of my professors taught this theory. At the time, I thought he had some sound teachings on the subject, but I still had doubts. When President Omidi and the EU president Ali Hamarat drew up that seven-year peace treaty with Israel and Palestine, I knew he must have been right."

"Yes," Thomas broke in. "Scott told me about those teachings before the signing. We had quite the debate on the subject, but after the signing, I too began to wonder what if I had been wrong. Had the tribulation started without the rapture happening first? We shared our strong convictions with my father-in-law and Joe."

Carl looked from Scott to Thomas and asked, "Would you men mind sharing your views on this subject with the congregation next Sunday evening? I have to admit we have been confused about all the things that have been happening in the world these days. We did do some serious wondering about that peace treaty."

Thomas spoke up, "We'd be honored."

At the other table Joe, Albert, and Sam were in deep conversation with Jake Stevenson, Clarence Masterson, and Sidney Westhoff. They talked about the disasters of the world and how they had been magnifying in intensity.

Sidney brought up the subject of the Michigan militia. "Have you heard about the Michigan militia fighting against cells of Muslims lately? The Islamic people have this stupid idea that they can take over the world."

"Yeah," Albert answered. "It's been mostly around the Detroit area. Detroit has the largest population of Muslims in Michigan. I also heard that it is happening all over the United States. A lot of the militia are calling themselves the United States militia. They feel our government is in danger of being taken over by the Muslims. President Omidi does not do anything to stop the militia because our US Army is scattered around the world in too many places. All we have for homeland security now is the militia, so our government ignores them and pretends they do not exist. The fighting is throughout the United States. You might as well say we're in a civil war."

Clarence Masterson cleared his throat and said, "I heard the other day that the European Union and the United Nations were talking about joining together to form a one-world power."

With that, Joe added, "There was an article in the *USA Magazine* that stated that there was already in place a list of the ten divisions that would make up a one-world empire."

Amazed at Joe's statement, Clarence answered back, "In Revelation, it talks about the ten horns. In addition, Nebuchadnezzar's dream in Daniel was about the ten toes on the image. The ten toes and the ten horns represent the ten-nation confederacy that the Antichrist will come out of to form his one-world power."

"You're absolutely right!" Joe said.

Jake spoke up, "Sounds like the end of this world as we know it is coming soon!"

"Absolutely!" Joe repeated.

* * * * *

That evening back at Old Town, the men had a lot to discuss about the new friends they made at church that morning. Thomas admitted, "Scott and I let some of the men at the church know that we believe we are living in the tribulation period. At first, they didn't believe us. However, they did wonder about the treaty with Israel. They showed an interest in what we had to say. Carl Jenkins even asked us to give a talk on the subject in church next Sunday night, and we agreed."

"Do you think that was a good idea," Joe asked? "Do we really know them well enough to trust them?"

"I feel really good about these people, Joe. They really seem like good Christians. I'll only give them our views. Of course, I won't reveal Old Town. I would never share our secret of Old Town unless we all agreed."

33

Lorraine's apartment, Sunday, 3:00 p.m., April 12

When Lorraine and Linda were finished cleaning up the kitchen from dinner, they joined Harold in the living room. He was giving his new baby a bottle as he watched the Beastavision. One of their favorite programs was playing. Abruptly, President Omidi broke into the broadcast. He stood tall and proud as he began his speech. "People of the world, as you know for the last fifteen years, our world has been in a state of political crisis! The economy of the entire globe has been going on a downward slide. World War III has killed over a billion people. Natural disasters and diseases have killed another billion. There is mass confusion between nations as to what to do about global warming."

He paused for a moment and then raised his voice as he continued, "People of the world, we need a joint effort to save our planet. And that is exactly what I have been working toward. My long hard efforts have paid off! For the past several months, I have been working on merging two great superpowers together. With the help of President Ali Hamarat, we have been able to solicit the unification of the United Nations and the European Union! Emerging these two regimes together, we have created the most powerful governing body in all the world! The name of this new regime is called One-World United. This powerful government body will bring peace and prosperity to the entire world!

During a closed-door session, leaders of the One-World United have emerged. Today, people of the world, I am going to share with you who will be the new leaders of the One-World United! I am honored to announce that I have been named as president of the One World United Council! My role as president of the council will be as follows: I shall be in charge of the newly formed government. Second of all, I will lead the executive branch of the government. And thirdly, I will be commander-in-chief of armed forces. Our armed forces will consist of all countries that were members of the former United Nations and the European Union. This, of course, includes the United States of America. All these nations combined will produce the strongest armed forces in the history of the world!"

Omidi took a sip of water and then continued, "Rest assured, Americans, for the time being, I will continue to be president of the United States. I will be leading both the united One-World government and the United States government from my new office here in Brussels. For that matter, the United States is under the One-World government umbrella. I will commute back and forth to Washington D. C. as deemed necessary.

He stopped for a moment and then continued, "I am privileged to announce that the members of the One-World United has named Ali Hamarat president of the One-World United Commission. His role will be to assist me in the government legislature. He will implement policy and be administer of the budget. He will also ensure compliance of the law. Together, President Hamarat and I will lead this world into blissful utopia." Applause rang out through the hall as Hamarat took the stand.

Hamarat held up his arms to quiet his standing ovation. When there was silence, he began. "Hear this, people of the world! All nations that are members of the One-World United will be in compliance to the new ruling or will face the consequences. As President Omidi stated before, over two billion people have been exterminated from the world in war, natural disasters, and various diseases. The world has been in turmoil for years! The One-World United is going to take control and turn this world around!" The crowd roared with applause and cheers.

After the applause quieted down, Hamarat continued, "Earlier, President Omidi proclaimed that the One-World United Government is the most powerful organization in the world. Also, the One-World United has the largest, most powerful army of all the nations! Therefore, as our first act of restoring our world, the One-World United has compiled a strategic plan. The plan consists of dividing the world into a ten-nation confederacy. Each nation shall have its own king. The nations will be divided in this fashion: First of all, Canada and Mexico will join the United States of America. President Omidi will step down at that point and select a new king to rule that empire. Second, South America will form an empire. Third, Australia and New Zealand will emerge as an empire. Fourth, all of west Europe will emerge. The fifth empire will be all of east Europe. The sixth, Japan. The seventh, Central Asia. The eighth, South Asia. The ninth, North Africa and the Middle East. Lastly, the tenth nation will be all of the rest of Africa. These plans will be effective in one month from today!

"For nations that are members of the One-World United Government, all militia groups will cease and desists all illegal activity! Any acts against the authority of the One-World United Government will be considered illegal activity and be punishable by incarceration or death! All weapons from this day forward are illegal in the hands of civilians. All arms are to be dropped off at your local police department. There will be a One-World United armed forces stationed in all of the member nations.

Rest assured, with these united world changes, you will be living in a virtual utopia, as long as you are in compliance with the rules of the One-World United. President Omidi and I would like to say good night and sleep well in a united world."

Lorraine shut off the Beastavision. Stunned, they all just sat still for a couple seconds. Lorraine was the first to speak. She said, "Well, I suppose we shouldn't be surprised. We knew what was coming. The Bible clearly talks about the ten-nation confederacy. The Bible says that the Antichrist will be the leader."

Harold asked his mother-in-law, "So is this the Antichrist's one-world rule?"

"Well, Harold, I'd say it is a fairly good start to one, but it's not quite there yet. Some of those nations are not members of the one united world. Sure, Omidi and Hamarat are flexing their muscles, but they still have some powerful enemies. Look at north Africa and Middle East nations. I would say we'll be in war for a while yet."

Harold brought up another point. "According to what dad has said, I'm surprised they didn't say that they were enforcing a one-world religion as well."

"Oh, I'm quite sure that's already started," Lorraine answered. "He might already have a one-world religion started. I'm sure it will seem somewhat familiar. You know, some kind of a broad, genetic religion that would fit most people. Hopefully, true Christians will see through it."

Linda nonchalantly added to the conversation, "Actually, that sounds like the Chrislam church. The newer churches made up of Christian and Muslim faiths. The church actually started in 1970 in Nigeria. Some Americans became aware of it here about 2001. Now they are all over the United States. Although now it has become more Islamic than Christian. In their church services, they teach out of the

Holy Bible and the Koran. They teach that Jesus was not God but only a profit like Moses and Abraham."

Her mother answered back, "I suppose it's possible. Maybe the Antichrist will use the Chrislam church to convert the whole world over to the Islamic religion. However, the Muslim's haven't infiltrated any of the Catholic churches yet. They have been getting stronger as the other Christian denominations are dwindling. All I know is that there will be a one-world religion promoted by the false prophet. He'll tell everyone that the Antichrist is the true God and force everyone to bow down and worship him."

"The 'bow down' stuff is supposed to happen after three and half years into the tribulation, right, Mom?"

"Yes, Linda, that's right."

Fear filled Linda's face as she looked at her mother and then her husband. "That's not very far away! It's only a little more than two and half years from now! That is if the tribulation really started last summer when Israel signed that treaty. What about our baby! What are we going to do?"

Harold laid Brianna down in her bed. He went over to his wife and put his arms around her as he said, "Honey, don't panic, it'll be all right! That's the reason why we have been working so hard to get Old Town ready."

"What makes you think we will be safe there? If the Antichrist wants to get us, no one can stop him!"

Harold held his wife close and said, "God will keep us safe. Linda, sweetie, you have to have faith. We need to turn over all our worries and fears to God. Your family believes that this is where God wants us to go. Your dad and Scott believe that God led them to that valley. They believe that God will protect us against the Antichrist's wrath."

The phone rang, and Lorraine answered. She squealed out, "It's Thomas! Darling, what a wonderful surprise! How far did you have to go to get bars on your phone?"

"I'm visiting at Mark Thornton's home. Remember last week, I called and told you that we went to their church last Sunday and they asked me to speak this Sunday night?"

"Yes, dear, I remember."

"Well, all of us guys went to their church this morning. Mark and his wife invited us over to their house afterward. Mark turned on his Beastavision, and lo and behold, guess who was on?"

"The president Omidi and Hamarat!"

"Yes, you saw it too?"

"Yes, Thomas, we did. It was shocking, but we knew it was coming, so we have to accept it."

"Are you guys going to be ready to move as soon as school's out?"

"Not a minute later! Oh, Thomas, I have been wanting to ask you something that is very important to me."

"What is it, honey?"

"I want to invite Christina and her family to join us. They don't have anyone else but us. I don't know of anyone godlier than her. Having a doctor assistant would come in handy, especially with the baby. She knows as much as a doctor. You know how close she worked with Dan in their clinic in Africa. We could use her medical expertise."

"Honey, you don't have to sell me. If it was up to me, her family would be here in a heartbeat, but there is the rest of the group to be considered. I'll have a meeting tonight when we get home, and I'll let you know what the decision is as soon as I can."

"Thank you, darling. I love you so much. I hate being apart from you. Thomas, I miss you so much!"

"I know, honey, I miss you a whole bunch too. Your love is keeping me going, along with my faith in God. He has been so good to us, Lorraine. His love is getting us through the worse time in the history of man. Stay safe. Give my girls a kiss and Harold a hug. Have to go! I'll talk to you soon."

34

Boardinghouse, April 12ᵗʰ

That night, after they got home, the men gathered around the table to start their weekly meeting. Thomas was the first to speak, "I've got an important subject to discuss tonight."

"You've got the floor, son, go ahead," James said.

"I was able to get through to Lorraine earlier today. I called her from Mark's before we went to church tonight. She has requested that we allow Christina Nelson and her three children to move up here with us. Daniel is twenty. Rachael is eighteen, and Michelle is sixteen."

Nervously, Joe rubbed his bald head and asked, "What is your opinion of letting them join us, Thomas?"

"I can vouch for Christina Nelson one hundred percent! Christina has been a close friend of ours since we were in middle school. Christina is a lovely, devoted Christian woman. She and her husband were missionaries for many years in Africa. Her husband, Dan, was the only doctor in their small village. Christina worked alongside of him as his assistant. I'm sure we could use a person with her medical experience here."

"I'll vouch for that," James said. "Christina and her husband, Dan, dedicated their lives to the mission fields of Africa. Unfortunately, that ended with Dan's death. He died of the bird flu trying to heal others."

Joe looked across the table at Sam and Albert and said, "Yes, I remember that our church helped support their mission. Do you guys remember them?"

Sam spoke up, "Yes, matter of fact, now that you mention it, I do remember them."

"I knew their kids quite well," Scott said. "Christina and Dan's family stayed at our house a few times when they had a break from the mission field. Their parents spoke at our church when they were in town. I heard that her son Daniel was going to the seminary to study to be a missionary. What I know about that family, I'd say they're all Christians."

Thomas looked around the table and asked, "So, Dad, Joe, son, what do you say? Do we open up our place of refuge to Christina's family?"

With tears in his eyes, Joe said, "How could we refuse a woman that has been so dedicated to God? I vote that her family is welcomed to join us."

Scott raised his hand and said, "I vote yes! We sure could use a doctor assistant up here."

"My vote is yes too!" James said.

Thomas smiled and said, "Then it's unanimous! She has my vote."

Albert looked at Sam as if he wanted to say something. Joe noticed and asked, "Albert, is there something you'd like to say?"

Albert stumbled around for the right words as he said, "Well, sir, after that message you brought tonight, it makes sense what you are doing here at Old Town. Sam and I were both shocked to know that we were wrong about when the rapture will occur. We knew that the peace treaty was a significant event, but we didn't realize it was the beginning of the seven-year tribulation of Revelation. It makes perfect sense now. Everything makes sense now! Even what you guys are doing up here! Sam and I have been talking, is there any chance that the two of us could stay and be part of Old Town? Seeing you have voted for another family to join you, I thought maybe you could consider us too."

Sam spoke up, "You know what kind of workers we are. You wouldn't have to pay us for any of the work we have done. We wouldn't be your employees. We'd be a part of the team!"

Joe laughed. "You don't have to sell me, boys, and I'd be thrilled to have you join us." James, Thomas and Scott agreed, and they all shook hands on the deal.

* * * * *

On April 14, the wind turbines arrived at Mark Thornton's store. Mark had agreed that Joe's mysterious delivery could be dropped off at his store. Mark was determined to respect their privacy, but his interest peaked as he saw all the huge, heavy boxes. Curiosity got the best of him. He couldn't help himself and read the shipping label. It read, Detroit Wind Turbine Company. Mark was floored! What in the world was going on? What were these guys up to? He knew that there had to be a lot more to the story than they were willing to tell.

The wind turbine company had told Joe that their order would be delivered on April fourteenth, so on that afternoon, they drove into the village of Gratiot. The five men walked into Mark's store. Mark greeted them and told them that their delivery was out back. The men were happy that that the salesman did as he promised. The windmills were there waiting for them. The others loaded the wind turbines on the wagon as James and Joe purchased the cement and equipment that they would need for the windmill's bases. Then Joe and James shook Mark's hand and thanked him for allowing their delivery to be dropped off at his store.

When they got back to Old Town, the men felt like children at Christmas morning unwrapping their presents. Each piece was laid out and studied. They worked on the windmill until it was too dark to see. They were anxious to work on the project. After all, time was running out. All too soon, the rest of the Old Town residents would be arriving.

35

Sheryl Higgin's apartment, May 29

Sheryl was lonely as she sat in front of her dressing table combing her long strawberry-blonde hair. It was her day off from work, and there was nowhere to go. Sheryl was a very attractive woman and had a fun personality. Several men asked her out since her breakup with Scott, but she only accepted a date from one. Brad, a handsome executive from Chicago, had asked her to go out on his yacht. She accepted his invitation but, at the last minute changed her mind and canceled the date. Deep down, Sheryl still felt committed to Scott. In Sheryl's mind, no man could compare to Scott.

Sheryl threw her brush at the mirror and yelled at her reflection, "You stupid idiot! Get over him! He's gone!" Her mind raced on, *What is wrong with me? Why can't I get over Scotty? Is it that cute little smirk on his face or those adorable dimples of his? No, it's not his drop-dead good looks. It is him. I have never met a more giving, loving man in my life. For that matter, probably, never will again. I have to stop this! He doesn't want me anymore! He would rather go play pioneer in the wilderness of the Upper Peninsula or be a crusader for the great*

Revelation of the Bible. He sure is caught up in all that. Although, he can be convincing at times.

Sheryl dressed and walked out of her bedroom, but her thoughts were still on Scott. She paced the floor as she remembered the last month of their relationship. *Scotty tried to convince me that there was a God, a God that loved me. He had told me that time was getting short. Soon, there would be a one-world power led by someone he called the Antichrist. Scott told me that he would actually turn into this reincarnated devil himself. Right, Scotty! I'm not sure I even believe in a God, and now you want me to believe that the leader of the world is going to magnificently changed into the devil. That's a lot for me to swallow.*

Sheryl poured herself a cup of coffee then sat down on her kitchen barstool. She began to mull over all the things that Scott had told her. *Scotty did mention that this Antichrist would come out of a ten-nation federacy. Dang! The president recently announced that there are now ten divisions of government. Who would have known a few months ago that Canada and Mexico would be part of the United States? Things have been drastically changing. Could Scott have been right? Could I have been wrong? What if I am wrong? Am I being too stubborn to believe the man that means the world to me?*

She stood up and began pacing the floor once again. *What am I going to do? I cannot live without Scotty, and I don't have a way of getting in touch with him! He has to know that I have changed my mind. I don't care what he believes or where we live. I love him, and I can't live without him!*

Then Sheryl thought of Scott's mother. She didn't know Lorraine very well, but what she knew of her, she liked. *I wonder if his sister has had her baby yet. Maybe I should call his mom. I still have her number.* With trembling fingers, Sheryl pressed in Lorraine's number. It rang a couple times. Her nerves were getting the best of her. She almost hung up when Lorraine answered. "Hello."

"Yes, ah, hi, Mrs. Perkins. This is Sheryl Higgins. I was Scotty's fiancée."

"Yes, Sheryl, good to hear from you. How are you?"

"Good, I'm doing okay. I was wondering, did Linda have her baby yet?"

"Why, yes, she did. She had a beautiful baby girl. The baby was born March 30. Brianna is just adorable!"

"I bet she is.

Do you hear anything from Scotty?"

"Well, I haven't seen him since he left for the UP, but I talk to his dad on the phone from time to time. Scott is doing well. He is really getting into farming!"

"That's great. Ah, I was wondering, is he seeing anyone now?"

"Well no, a least I don't think so. I'm sure he has been too busy up there to get involved with anyone. How about you, Sheryl? Are you dating anyone?"

"No, Mrs. Perkins, I can't seem to get your son off my mind. I really miss him." Nervously, Sheryl rattled on, "Before he left, he talked to me about God. I didn't want to talk about it then, but lately, I have been thinking a lot about it. I can't help thinking that maybe Scott was right. A lot of the prophecy he told me about seems to be coming true. The current news is full of some of the events that Scott has told me about. There's all those increasing natural disasters and epidemic of diseases. There's World War III, terrorist attacks, the economy, and world famine. And, oh yeah, dividing the world into ten nations! What's that all about? Scott said that there will be one ruler of the world, and he will be the devil reincarnated!"

"Yes, Sheryl, it is all true. The most important thing for you to know is that there is a God, and He loves you very much. He wants you to accept Him as your Savior. All you need to do is ask God to come into your heart."

"If you don't mind, Mrs. Perkins, maybe I could come visit you sometime, and we could talk more about it?"

"That would be great, Sheryl, but I only have a week before we will be moving up north."

"That soon! Who all is moving there?"

"Well, of course, there will be Linda and her family. Harold has been down here since just before the baby was born. He is staying to help us get moved. Also, my best friend Christina and her three kids are going with us."

"Oh, how nice. Are they small children?"

"Well, let's see, Michelle is sixteen. Rachael is eighteen, and Daniel is twenty."

Sheryl felt overwhelmed with jealousy when she heard that there would be young, single women living close to Scott. Were they there to take her place? Was Scott interested in one of these women? Scott was much too old for either girl, or was he? There was only six years between him and the eighteen-year-old. She had to do something quick!

"Mrs. Perkins, would you please give Scotty a message for me before you leave?"

"Sure, Sheryl. I'll leave a message for Thomas to call me. He'll give Scott the message."

"Thank you, Mrs. Perkins. My message is that I want to be with him for whatever time we have left. Please, tell him that I still love him very much. I don't care about the cold weather anymore. Just as long as I'm with him, I'll be happy. I want to be his wife so badly!"

Lorraine didn't know what to say for a couple of seconds. Her mind raced on. *I thought this woman was finally out of Scott's life! On the other hand, Scotty loved her so much. If only she would accept Christ as her Savior. Would she really be content to live up there? What if she breaks my son's heart again?*

"I don't know, Sheryl. I can't promise you anything, but I will see that Scott gets your message."

"Thank you, Mrs. Perkins, that's all I ask. Congratulations on your new grandbaby. Please, give Linda and Harold my congratulations also." With tears flowing down her cheeks, Sheryl said, "Thanks again. And please, let Scotty know how much I love him."

36

Bowling Green, Ohio High School, 1:00 p.m., June 1

Lorraine was passing out exam papers when an announcement came over the intercom. In a loud, deep voice, the principal said, "All teachers and students are required to leave their classroom immediately, and go directly to the gym in an orderly fashion."

The classroom was full of chatter and questions. What could be so important for the principal to get the whole student body in the gym during exam time? Lorraine quieted her students down as she quickly got them in an orderly line and escorted them down to the gym.

The gym was loud with students questioning why they were there, as the teachers worked hard to get them all seated and settled down. Some were happy to get away from the exam, while others just wanted to get it over. The students were confused and perplexed; they wondered what was so important that would stop a final exam.

Over the loud speaker, the principal's harsh voice yelled out, "Silence!" All eyes were on the principal, and no one spoke another word. The principal cleared his throat and started talking, "I have brought all of you in here today so you could see breaking news on the Beastavision. This news could affect all of us!"

The principal hesitated a bit and then blurred out, "There has been a devastating attack on the United States by Russia! Washington D. C. has been a target of a bomb! The White House, the Pentagon, and a good portion of Washington D. C. are now are in ashes."

The gym became loud again with questions. The principal yelled out, "Quiet! I can't answer everybody's questions at once!"

Hands started going up throughout the gym. "Yes," the principal said. "What is your question?"

The boy answered, "Is President Omidi of the newly formed One-World United still ruling over the United States? Or is there a new king in his place?"

"All I can tell you is up until to this horrifying attack, President Omidi was still king of the United States."

Pointing, the principal said, "Okay, girl in the third row. Yes, you. What's your question?"

"Was President Omidi killed?"

"At this point, I know as much as all of you do. I haven't heard if King Omidi was in Washington or in Brussels." The principal tried to answer a few more questions before he had enough. There were students crying as fear ripped through the gym in utter chaos.

The principal again grabbed the microphone and shouted, "Be quiet! That is all I know right now! That is why I brought you all in here. I wanted you to hear firsthand. As soon as I heard, I wanted to share the breaking news story with all of you. So if you will calm down and listen, I'll turn on the Beastavision."

There was no sound out of the students as the principal turned on the huge screen. Each set of eyes were wide open as they watched footage of mayhem and destruction. Cameramen riding overhead in helicopters filmed the footage. In the background was the voice of a somber journalist as he described the vast extent of the destruction.

"The United States of America's capital has been attacked today by Russia. The White House, the Capitol Building, and the Pentagon have all sustained tremendous damage and have been almost wiped out! We know that it was, in fact, several bombs that did the destruction. Thousands upon thousands have died, slaughtered by Russian bombs. Others have been badly maimed by the blasts. As yet, we do not have a confirmation if President Omidi was in the White House when it was hit or not. As soon as this journalist hears something, rest assured, I will let you know immediately."

The principal allowed the students to continue watching the news until it was time for school to be dismissed. He then turned off the screen and said, "I'm sorry to stop this. I know you are all glued to it as I am. This has been a terrible shock to all the world. I'm really not sure what will be coming next, but I am confident that our government will still be standing when the dust clears. For now, it is time for school to close for the day. Go home, and oh yes, prepare for your exams. They will be tomorrow."

Lorraine hurried home so she wouldn't miss any more of the news. When she walked through the door, she saw Linda and Harold glued to the Beastavision. Linda looked up as her mother shut the door. She asked, "Mom, have you heard about the bombing?"

"Yes, honey, I have. The whole school watched it in the gym. Isn't it awful?"

"It's scary, that's what it is! For the first time, I am looking forward to moving up to our hideaway. If they bombed Washington, what's to say they will not bomb another city? Maybe even Bowling Green! Now that I have a child, I have to think about these things."

"Quiet, Linda," Harold said. "Something else has just happened!"

Lorraine sat down in her chair as all three of them stared at the screen.

"Oh no!" said the journalist. "From our affiliate station in London, England, we just received this: Only one hour and a half from the terrifying bombing of Washington D. C, England has also been the target of our evil enemy, Russia! The British Parliament, also known as the Westminster Parliament, was hit by a bomb at two o'clock this afternoon. As in the Washington bombing, England is suffering many casualties."

The news of the two bombings continued into the evening. All other programming was interrupted. They only stopped the coverage for a station break or an advertisement.

It was going on eight o'clock when Lorraine's phone rang. To her surprise, she heard her husband's voice. "Oh, Thomas, I sure needed to hear your voice tonight. I wish I was in your arms. I sure could use one of your hugs right now."

"I just received your message tonight that was left on the fence post. Mark's note said that you called yesterday and needed to talk to me. I drove down out of the mountains until I finally got some bars on my phone. Is everything, okay?"

"No, sweetheart, nothing is okay anymore. The United States has come under attack. Russia has bombed Washington D. C., the White House, the Capitol, the Pentagon, and a good portion of the city has been blown to pieces!"

"No! You're kidding. How could something like that happen? How did they penetrate our security? What about President Omidi? Was he in Washington or Brussels?"

"So far, they don't seem to know. The report keeps talking about him, but no answers yet. They are showing so much death and destruction. But listen, honey, that's not all! In just an hour and a half after we were bombed, England was hit too! The Parliament was bombed!"

As Lorraine talked to Thomas, she had an eye on the Beastavision screen. "Wait, wait!" she cried out to her husband. "The reporter is saying that King Omidi is about to come on and speak. Can you stay on the phone, honey? I'll hold this so you can hear him."

"Yeah, sure, honey."

"Okay, here he is."

President Omidi came on the air with a somber, cold stare on his face. He was composed as he started to talk, but you could see that there was rage just under the surface, ready to jump out at anytime.

Then he began to speak, "Today, the world has witnessed the worst attack against two of the world's most powerful nations, America and Great Britain! This has been the worst disaster that America has ever witnessed on its own soil." He raised his voice and said, "America, I promise you that this cowardly, alarming event will not go without punishment! I assure you that Russia will pay for this heinous crime against humanity!"

With pain and anger in his face, the president paused for a couple seconds and then continued, "Today, you and I are left to mourn the death of some good folks. Some are important dignitaries. Some are just plain good common working people." Omidi's voice cracked as he continued, "Yes, even I have had a very personal loss today. My lovely wife, Natasha, and my two sons, Oliver and Tyron, were killed by the hands of those evil monsters."

He stopped for a moment and wiped a tear from his eye. Gaining his composure again, the president continued, "I would also like to give my deepest sympathy to our friends across the ocean in England. They too have lost many of their great leaders today. I was fortunate to be in Brussels today, but the prime minister of the United Kingdom was not so lucky. Prime Minister Hancock was killed in the bombing. My condolence goes out to his family."

A slight pause and then Omidi said, "Again, America, I want you to rest assured that we will retaliate, and Russia will be punished! As one of the leaders of the One-World United I promised to make our enemy pay, and pay they will!"

"Wow, Thomas, did you get all that?"

"Yes, honey, I did. Why don't you get things together and leave tomorrow? It's getting too dangerous down there."

"Thomas, you know I have to fulfill my obligations. I would love to leave tomorrow, but I have to wait until the end of school. There's only four days left, sweetheart, and we'll be on our way."

"Okay, but I'll feel a lot better when you are safe in my arms." Thomas thought for a moment and then asked, "By the way, honey, the bombing just happened today, right?"

"Yes, that's right, why?"

"You left a message yesterday to call."

"Oh gosh, I forgot. With all that's going on, I forgot all about it. Yes, it was important, thanks for reminding me. Sheryl Higgins called me and expressed that she wants to get back with Scott. She says that she loves him. That she would live anywhere as long as it was near Scott. She hopes they still could be married! What do we do?"

"Has she accepted Christ as her Savior yet?"

"I don't think so, but she is beginning to show an interest."

"Wow, I don't know, Lorraine. I guess I had better talk to Scott about it. I know he still loves her, but if she isn't saved? I guess if Scott does want her to come, we'll have to vote on it. Have you talked to Linda and Harold about it?"

They both agreed that whatever Scott wants, they would go along with it. I have been sitting on the fence. I don't want to see Scott's heart broken again, but whatever he wants, I'll go along with it also."

"Okay, good. I'll go back and talk to Scott, and then if he wants her to come up here, we'll vote on it."

37

Boardinghouse, June 15ᵗʰ

Thomas walked into the boardinghouse and greeted the five men who were seated around the table. He said to them, "Sorry, guys, I know it's late, but Lorraine had a lot of news to share." Thomas went on to tell them about the bombings in Washington D. C. and the Parliament in England. The men were shocked at the news as they talked about it for over an hour.

Scott stood up and stretched as he said, "I don't know about the rest of you, but I'm tired. It's going on eleven. I've got to get up early tomorrow and get the garden planted."

"Yeah," James said. "We're going to have to work hard this week to get the bathhouse done. The women will be up here by the end of the week."

Joe laughed and said, "I can't wait to see the expressions on their faces when they see the bathhouse. They will be so surprised."

James had a broad smile on his face as he said, "Marge was so concerned about how she was going to keep herself clean up here."

"Well," Joe said, "the women will have to realize that they can't take a shower every day like they do now. With only six shower stalls, we'll need to make up a schedule."

"Guys," Thomas began. "There's something else that has been on my mind. Mark Thornton hasn't said anything, but he must suspect something. With all the lumber we've been buying and all the farm equipment, he's got to be curious to what we are doing up here. I'm sure he would have seen the wind turbine company's labels when they were delivered. He's been a great friend. I don't know. Maybe we ought to let him in on what our real plans are?"

"That is a big problem," James said. "We really need to think and pray about this before we make any decisions."

The men all got up and started heading upstairs to their rooms. Thomas stopped Scott and said, "Son, I need to talk to you alone."

"Sure, Dad, what's up?"

"Your mother actually called about something else. She called about Sheryl."

"Sheryl, what about her? Is she all right?"

"Yes, son, she's fine. She called your mother a few days back and asked her to get in touch with you. Seems she has had a change of heart. The girl says she still loves you and would live up here if it meant being with you. She is still interested in marrying you."

Bewildered, Scott sunk down into a chair. He repeated his words, "Sheryl still loves me? She is willing to move up here to be with me? And she still wants to be my wife?"

"That's the message I got from your mother."

"Dad, you know how much I love her!"

"Yes, of course, I do."

"I don't know, Dad. I just don't know. Did she say anything to mom about accepting Christ as her Savior?"

"No. However, she said that Sheryl told her that she was beginning to wonder if what you told her was true. She is beginning to question if there really is a God or not."

"I've got to call her, Dad! If there's a chance that she could be saved, I want that for her! I certainly do not want her to go to hell. I love her too much. Nothing would make me happier than her being a Christian. If Sheryl was my wife, that would be a bonus!"

"Son, lets pray about it." The two men got on their knees and bowed their heads in prayer.

The next morning, Scott got up extra early, packed himself a sandwich, and was off to the farm. He had a large garden to put in, and he wanted to get it done early enough so he could go somewhere to call Sheryl. This would be her evening to work, but it was too important to wait. When he finished the planting, it was almost six. The men always tried to stop work at six thirty, giving them time to get cleaned up before starting supper. Scott hoped that he would be able to get down the mountain, call Sheryl, and get back in time to help with the meal. He jumped in the pickup and drove down the mountain. When he was able to get a signal, he stopped and punched her name on his caller list.

When Sheryl heard Scott's voice, she cried out. "Scotty, darling, is that you?"

Scott tried to keep his composure as he answered, "Yes, Sheryl, I heard you wanted me to call. What's up?"

"Scott, I love you! I was wrong! I never should have let you go. I don't care how cold it gets up there! If I'm with you, I'll be warm!"

"I love you too, Sheryl, but it's not that easy. Old Town is a retreat for Christians. Have you accepted Jesus Christ as your Savior yet?"

"I'm not sure, Scotty. I think so, but all that matters is that we love each other!"

"If you don't know, Sheryl, then I'd say you probably haven't. You would know in your heart if you were saved."

"Come on, Scotty, give me a break here. I never went to church as you did. You went to a Bible college for Pete's sake! I never heard about all of this stuff until shortly before we broke up. I didn't even know you were a Christian before that."

"You got me there, and I'm ashamed of that. What can I say, I was a backslider. I turned my back on the Lord. Thank God, He never turned His back on me. The seven-year peace treaty woke me up. I could see Bible prophecy unfolding before my eyes. I had to get back to the Lord. That's why I suddenly knew that we were living in sin, Sheryl! I had to correct the situation. That's the reason I asked you to marry me! Then I realized that that wasn't right either. The Holy Spirit spoke to my heart. I was reminded of the Bible verse that a Christian should not be unevenly yoked to a nonbeliever. Sheryl, I can't knowingly go against God's will!"

In desperation, Sheryl cried out, "I understand, but please, give me a chance! Scotty, when your mom is ready to move, please let me come along. I have seen many things that you have told me about prophecy coming true. I really believe you know what you are talking about. Scott, I have so much faith in you! If I come up there, you could teach me more about God and the tribulation. When you first told me, it was overwhelming! It was a lot to absorb all at once. I promise I will have an open mind, just give me a chance, please, Scott!"

Scott wiped the tears from his eyes and said, "I'll have to pray about it, and it's not all up to me. We are trying to keep the population of Old Town down because we're not sure if we can even support the ones we have now. Besides, the location of Old Town must be kept a secret. The less anyone knows, the better. It is really up to the others if you can come or not. We always vote on such matters."

"Please, Scotty, don't take too long. Your mother is leaving in three days."

"Yes, I'm very aware of that. Will you do me a favor, Sheryl?"

"Of course, anything!"

"Think long and hard about what I've told you. Please, will you do some real soul searching before you make your decision? There is a chance that we will never be lovers again. We may never be married. Once you have decided to come up here, there will be no turning back."

Scott hesitated for a moment then said, "Sheryl, I don't want to make you feel pressured by saying you are a Christian just so we can get married. The only way to become a Christian is to accept the Lord Jesus in your heart. You must realize that you are a sinner that deserves hell and that Jesus has paid your debt on the cross at Calvary. All you have to do is accept God's wonderful gift of salvation."

The phone call ended with both of their hearts aching for one another.

38

Old Town reunion, 2:15 p.m., June 7

Joe landed his plane at the airstrip near Gratiot after picking up James's wife and Joe's wife and sons from New York. The cargo compartment was packed as full as regulations would allow. Only the bare necessities were able to be brought along. Walk-in closets full of designer clothes and shoes were donated to the homeless shelters. They had an estate sale for both of their mansions' expensive, exquisite furniture; vintage cars; original paintings; fine jewelry; and household items. Everything had to go except for a few necessities.

In the cargo compartment was an old treadle sewing machine that Marge had bought at an antique auction. She thought it might come in handy when they were unable to buy new clothes. It brought back memories of when she was raised on the farm. She remembered how her mother sewed most of the clothes for the family. Her mother taught a sewing class for 4-H. Young Marge had made an apron with her mom's old treadle sewing machine. She won a blue ribbon for her efforts. Remembering all this, Marge thought how important it would be to have that treadle sewing machine at Old Town. It required no electricity, just perfect for their primitive new lifestyle. James was very proud of her for coming up with such a practical idea.

Also in the back of the plane were several boxes of canning jars and lids. Darlene had come up with a good idea too. She remembered a trip that Joe and she had taken a few years back. They had gone to Upper Michigan to cross the Mackinaw Bridge and to go to the famous Mackinaw Island. It was a fabulous vacation. They had stayed at the renowned Grand Hotel on the island. When they crossed back over the bridge into Mackinaw City, they noticed a sign advertising Fort Michilimackinac. The 1812 fort was intriguing to Joe, so they decided to stop. While there, they took a tour into the fort. They were both pleased that they did. It was a colonial site reconstructed from an eighteenth-century fur trading outpost. It had all the elements of days gone by including a stockade, barracks, and a guardhouse. It had an archeological excavation in progress. They also had a working colonial kitchen set up with real people, showing how they lived back in the 1800s. The day they were there, the women were canning tomatoes and peaches.

Darlene was fascinated with the canning procedure, but her life was too busy in New York, so she never got a chance to try it out. Now she would have plenty of time to learn. When she heard that they would be moving to Old Town, Darlene took a class in canning. She felt confident that she would be able to use her new knowledge. Joe was very proud that his wife had shown so much initiative and foresight by taking the class. It could be valuable for their survival in Old Town.

Soon, the anxious group was pulling up in front of the old boardinghouse. The new residents were delighted when they saw a big sign draped across the newly repaired front porch. The sign read, WELCOME HOME! in big red letters. Scott had gone into town and bought helium-filled balloons and snacks for the welcome-home party. Sam and Albert tied the balloons all around the room.

Old Town's latest residents were surprised at such a warm home-coming. Marge was the first one to walk through the door as her son-in-law and grandson were there to greet her. Thomas gave her a hefty hug. Then Scott hugged her and gave her a kiss on the check as he said, "I'm so happy to see you, Grandma!"

Through the door next was Darlene and her two teenage boys, Tim and Zachary. Thomas and Scott happily welcomed Joe's family.

Then Albert and Sam took their turns greeting the newcomers. They had met Marge and Darlene before at church but didn't know them very well.

Darlene said to Sam, "It was so sad to hear about the loss of your family. I knew your wife. Carol was a very lovely lady."

Marge added, "We will miss her. Darlene and I got to know her well from our ladies missionary meetings. I can't imagine what you are going through."

With tears in his eyes, Sam said, "Thanks, ladies. Being part of Old Town helps, but it still hurts. The hardest part is in the evening when we gather around the table to eat. My family and I always had such great times around the dinner table."

Trying to lighten the mood, James said, "Well we're all family now, and this is a welcome-home party. Soon, the rest of the family will be here. We will all be one happy family! The last report I got from Harold was that they were about three hours behind us. That was at the landing strip after we had put down and loaded up the truck. They'll be here soon, I'm sure."

Scott became more nervous as the clock slowly ticked away. The group had given their permission to allow Sheryl to join them at Old Town, but he wondered if she would have second thoughts. Was this too much to ask of Sheryl? Still a nonbeliever, would she really want to move up there? Could she have changed her mind knowing that there was no guarantee that they would be together? Maybe, thinking that they might never become man and wife, she changed he mind again.

Three hours had passed, and Scott had spent the last half hour waiting on the porch. He was impatiently waiting for the van full of friends and family to pull up. It had seemed like he had been waiting for hours. Then he saw a U-Haul truck slowly driving past the church and headed toward the boardinghouse. Lorraine's van followed. Scott yelled back though the screened double doors, "They're here!"

Thomas quickly ran out of the boardinghouse as he joined Scott to greet the awaited travelers. The vehicles pulled up to the boardinghouse. Harold was the first to get out of the truck. He went around to the passenger's side and opened the door. Linda handed him a car seat with their precious baby. Thomas helped his daughter out of the U-Haul truck. Thomas and Scott took a quick look at the latest member of their family and then hustled over to the van where Lorraine was opening up her door. Thomas gave his wife a hand as she stepped out of the van and straight into his waiting arms.

Scott went to the front passenger side where he opened the door for Christina. He gave her his hand and helped her out of the vehicle. One by one, the passengers from the backseats started to get out. Scott's heart was pounding out of control. His eyes connected with Sheryl's. All he wanted to do was to take her in his arms and passionately kiss her, but he held back. Instead, he gave her a gentle hug. Sheryl's heart sank. She had been hoping for so much more.

Next, Scott went over to Rachael and Michelle and gave each of them a hug. "Wow," he said. "You were both kids last time I saw you! Now look at you, you're both beautiful young ladies!"

"Come on, Scotty," Rachael said. "I was fourteen last time we saw each other. I had a mad crush on you! I thought it was so neat you were getting ready to go to Bible college. I thought you were so hot!"

Scott laughed. "I didn't know that. I was twenty at that time. I am sorry, but you were like a kid to me then. I must say though, you sure have grown up to be a gorgeous woman." Sheryl was seething with jealously as she listened to Scott and Rachael's reunion.

Scott turned to Daniel, and they shook hands. He gave Daniel a friendly slap on the back as he said, "Man, I'm so glad you and your family were able to join us."

Harold looked up and saw the working windmill. "Awesome, would you look at that! You guys did it! You got one of the windmills up!"

Harold was sworn to secrecy when it came to the windmills. The men didn't want the women to know until they got there. They wanted it to be a surprise to them. The women were completely surprised. Marge and Darlene were standing on the porch with their husbands when Harold drew everybody's attention to the windmills. The two women let out a squeal, and then Joe and James each got a big appreciation hug and kiss. Lorraine, along with the rest of the new residents, were all thrilled over the sight of a windmill.

"This is a wonderful surprise," Lorraine said! "I didn't think we would have any electricity up here. You guys are fabulous! How did you ever have time to build it? You've told me about all the accomplishments that you made on the houses, the farms, but this is spectacular! I know how hard you guys have been working. How did you have time to install a windmill?"

"Believe me, honey, it wasn't easy," Thomas answered his wife. "Since we got the windmills, we have been working from daylight to dark. We have another one to put in down by the farms."

"It was fairly hard mixing the cement by hand and pouring it into the forms," James added. "Then we had to rent a cherry picker to lift up the sections. Good thing that Sam and Albert are strong men. We couldn't have done it without them."

Linda gave her mother a mean look and said, "See, Mother, I told you we should bring the Beastavision along instead of that old radio."

"The radio runs either on batteries or electricity. Besides, Linda, I told you that I was quite sure that the Antichrist would probably be using the Beastavision to keep track of us!"

"Yeah, yeah, so you said."

Thomas spoke up, "Linda, don't disrespect your mother like that. She has a good point. I agree with her."

Embarrassed, Linda quickly changed the subject. She pointed and asked, "What's that building over there? That wasn't here before."

"Oh my gosh," Lorraine said. "It's a large cement-block building. What in the world is that for?"

Thomas got a big smile on his face as he said to his wife, "It's a bathhouse. We plan to put six shower stalls in there. We wanted to have them finished by the time you got here, but the windmill took longer than we thought. We should have it up and running in a couple of months."

"Halleluiah," Lorraine cried out. "I was dreading the thought of having to boil water and bathing in some kind of cramped-up tub. I have no problem with sponge baths for another month or two. Thank you so much!"

Thomas was so happy to see the joy in his wife's face. He said, "First, we have the Lord to thank for all this. He is the one providing for us. Second, we need to thank Joe and Dad for their monetary contributions, and third, we need to thank Sam and Albert for their vast electrical and mechanical skills."

James spoke up, "I'm just grateful God has blessed us so much! I know He led us to this hidden valley. Thanks to God, with the wealth Joe and I have acquired throughout the years, we should be able to survive through these troubling times."

"Praise God! It's like He is protecting us in all that we do," Thomas replied. "God definitely seems to be keeping us safe from the dangerous tribulation and the malicious Antichrist, which is soon to take over."

39

Welcome home at Old Town, June 15ᵗʰ

The twenty residents of Old Town celebrated their reunion in the boardinghouse. The new arrivals were very impressed with everything. There was the welcome sign, balloons, and even a cake that read, Welcome Home.

Later that afternoon, while everyone was enjoying the fellowship, Thomas said in a loud voice, "Please, may I have your attention? Everybody, please, gather around the table for a short meeting. I know that it will be crowded, but draw up a chair as close as you can."

When the group was settled close to the table, Thomas began, "It's getting late, so we must make a plan as to where each of us will be living for now. Then we can unpack the U-Haul and the truck. We'll unload each of your belongings in their respective places.

We had talked about giving Joe and Darlene the large house here in town. Their sons are almost adults. Tim's seventeen and Zachary fifteen. We thought they could each use a bedroom. Besides that, Joe has contributed the most with his real-estate expertise, his capital, and the use of his plane, which was vital to our endeavor. However,

Joe and Darlene have generously informed me that they would like to give this home to Christina and her family."

Joe commented, "I have talked to my wife and sons about it, and they agreed. It makes more sense that a home with three bedrooms should go to a family with two girls and a son."

Christina was overwhelmed. She raised her hand and said, "May I say something?"

"Of course, you can, Christina," Thomas said.

She looked over at Joe and Darlene and said, "That is very generous of you, but I couldn't. My family and I are grateful that you have given us the privilege of joining you here in this safe haven, far away from the rest of the world. I truly believe that God has chosen to take this small group of people away from the dangers of the coming terror of the Antichrist. It is our honor to be included. Please, just a place to sleep is all we ask."

Thomas turned to Joe with a questioning look on his face. Joe spoke up, "My offer still stands. Besides, I have another agenda for suggesting it. Everyone here will be asked to have some sort of responsibilities. Christina, we want to ask you to be our resident medical practitioner. You are the only one here with any medical training. I heard when your husband was backed up, you even did minor surgeries in his place. The larger house could be doubled as your home and a small clinic. What do you say? Will you take on this crucial responsibility?"

With her eyes full of tears, she said, "How could I say no to such an offer? I'd be happy and honored to be your resident medical practitioner."

Rachael raised her hand. Thomas said, "Yes, Rachael."

"I would like to volunteer to be mom's nurse assistant. I'll do whatever else needs to be done around here when my medical services aren't needed. I was planning on going to college to become a doctor, but that of course is impossible now. When we lived in

Africa, I volunteered to work at the hospital with Mom and Dad. I knew then that I wanted to have a medical career."

"That would be great," Thomas said. "Is there anyone that has an objection to either Christina or Rachael being our medical staff?"

There were no objections.

"Okay," Thomas said. "That settles it. Now onto the next issue. The rest of the houses with the exception of the farmhouses have two bedrooms each. The farmhouses have three bedrooms. Joe, James, and I have decided that since Scott is one of our farmers, he should live in the farmhouse on the north side of the main road. That's the farm where Scott has planted all the crops. He has been working very hard to make the ground productive. The land will require a lot more work. It will take his constant attention. Therefore, we have decided that it would be easier for him to reside at the farmhouse."

Thomas continued, "Harold will be working the other farm. That farm will be primarily our livestock farm. Therefore, it makes sense that Harold, Linda, and baby Brianna live on that that farm. Are here any objections with that?"

The group nodded in approval. Harold raised his hand and was acknowledged. "Brianna can sleep in our bedroom for now. That will leave two bedrooms. Maybe Albert and Sam would like to live out here with us."

"That's generous of you, Harold," Thomas answered. "That would work, or they can stay here in the boardinghouse."

"Whatever you men prefer, is all right with me," Harold answered.

Sam spoke up, "Thanks, Harold, that was kind of you to offer, but I believe I would like to take Thomas's offer. You guys are newlyweds with a new baby. I'm sure you would enjoy your privacy a lot more if we weren't there. I really like the thought of living in the boardinghouse."

"Yes, thanks," Sam repeated. "I have to agree with Sam. I've lived by myself for some time now. The boardinghouse would be ideal."

Thomas answered, "Good! That settles it. Sam and Albert will live in the boardinghouse."

"I've got a concern," Scott said. "I really could use a farmhand. I'm sure there will come a time when Harold could use one also. He could help between the two farms. I've got two extra bedrooms. My helper could have one of them."

"Not a bad idea. Are there any volunteers for the job?"

Christina's son, Daniel, raised his hand and said, "I'd like to volunteer. I feel I'm quite qualified for the job. In Africa, I helped establish a wheat field and a garden for the villagers. I'd love to be part of the farm crew! On top of that, Mom could use my bedroom if someone needs to be hospitalized."

"Not a bad idea," Thomas agreed. "Any objections?"

"Okay good. Now as for Lorraine and I, we will live in one of the cabins here in town. Joe, Darlene, and their boys, along with mom and dad, will live in one of the other two cabins here in town. That way, James, Joe, and myself will be close in case a big problem comes up. We'll keep on top of the world news. Good thing we've got that radio, or we wouldn't be able to know any of what's going on."

Thomas continued, "Moving on. That just leaves Sheryl. Does anyone have a suggestion about where she could live?"

Lorraine raised her hand and said, "Thomas, if it's all right with you, maybe she could stay in our extra bedroom?"

Sheryl timidly held her hand up. Thomas said, "Yes, Sheryl."

Nervously, she answered, "Well, Scott has an extra bedroom in his farmhouse. Maybe he could use another farmhand?"

Lorraine quickly raised her hand. Thomas said, "Yes, dear."

Hesitantly, she said, "Under the circumstances, I don't really think that would be the best solution."

"I'll second that," Thomas agreed.

Marge smiled sweetly and said, "Sheryl, you may stay with James and me if you want."

"Thank you, Marge and Lorraine, but what about having a room here in the boardinghouse? I'm really use to living on my own."

Thomas thought for a minute and then said, "Well, I guess it's all right with me if it's okay with everyone else. Any nays?"

Scott wanted in the worse way to say no but knew better, so he stayed quiet. Thomas looked around and saw there were no objections, so he said, "Okay, Sheryl, you can live here in the boardinghouse. Both Sam and Albert will be working on various projects in the settlement. How about you take on the responsibility of the boardinghouse's cook and general housekeeper? I'm sure we will use this place for all sorts of gatherings like dinners and parties. You can be in charge of organizing those events."

Sheryl spoke up, "I'd be happy too. I can also do Sam and Albert's laundry along with my own."

Thomas smiled and said, "Good! Now on to the next issue."

He then turned to his wife and said, "Joe, James and I have given this a great deal of thought, Lorraine. We made the decision that you would make a good domestic budget director."

Thomas looked around the table at each person and said, "We feel that Lorraine is the best qualified person here for that responsibility. For one thing, she has taught high school economics." Looking back at his wife, he said, "Plus I remember how well you took care of our bills." He looked back at the group and said, "On top of that, she was our first church's bookkeeper. Well, honey, will you take on the job? James and Joe have agreed to assist you with the money allocations."

"Well, yeah, sure. I'm not sure what all you have in mind, but whatever I can do to help, I'm all for it."

"Great," Thomas said! "Your first task will be heading up a committee to make up a grocery order for the next month. May I suggest that your committee consists of all the women in our group? We now have electricity to this part of the boardinghouse, including the kitchen. We have put in two large freezer units plus a large refrigerator. This will have to hold all our perishable food items for the entire group. You will be given an allocated amount of money, so you will need to budget very carefully. We need to get by as economically as we possibly can."

Scott raised his hand and was acknowledged. "When I'm working in the fields, it seems like I always see a lot of deer. There are plenty of rabbits and squirrels running around too, not to mention that the creek is full of fish. We can substitute many of the store's products by just hunting and fishing on our own land. In a couple months, hopefully, we can reap our own harvest. This month, we can't depend on it, but in a couple of months, we should start getting some of the vegetables we have planted."

Joe spoke up, "My boys and I love hunting and fishing. I'm sure my sons will keep us well stocked on fish."

Joe turned to Scott and Harold and asked, "Oh, by the way, are the barns and pastures ready for the animals?"

"Pretty much. We have it ready for a few animals."

"Good job, men. Mark Thornton told me about a cattle auction that's about twenty miles from here. They have an auction every Friday night. I'd like to send both of you this week. For now, you can buy a couple heifers and a bull. If they have them, it would be a good idea to pick up some baby chickens. Maybe a few laying hens and a roaster. Also, Mark said that they sell hay and straw at the auction. We'll need some bales. Mark also said that there's a feed mill right next door to the auction house. Stop in there, and ask the clerk some questions to see exactly what kind of feed you'll need for the animals."

"Great," Harold said. "I cannot wait to actually start farming!"

"Okay," Thomas said. "Next issue. I want us to all meet here in the boardinghouse at seven o'clock tomorrow morning. Ladies, if you will, maybe you could cook us up a breakfast to get the day started right."

Thomas turned to his wife and said, "After breakfast, Lorraine, I would like you to get your committee together and work on a good tangible grocery list. When you have a workable list down, you can make plans for all the ladies to go shopping."

Joe spoke up, "We will be sending you ladies to a large super-market that is about thirty miles from here. Divide up the groceries equally with each of you having your own lists. I want each of you to individually buy the groceries that you shop for. Leave the store separately. Do not acknowledge each other unless it is important. We don't want to have anyone getting suspicious."

James spoke out, "Oh by the way, Harold, there is a U-Haul rental in the same town. You can drive it there. Lorraine will follow you in and pick you up in the van. You can go shopping with Linda. That way, you will be there to help with the baby. Also, you can give the ladies a hand loading the groceries into the van. I know Marge will appreciate the help."

"Are there any questions?" Thomas asked.

No one said anything, so Thomas ended by saying, "Good! Then I believe we have all the immediate business taken care of for today. Let's go unpack!"

40

Old Town's Church, July, 4ᵗʰ

As the three elder men of the group, Thomas, James, and Joe took on leadership of their small community. However, Thomas's main role would be the valley's pastor. He had worked out a schedule to hold services three times a week. The church would also be available for their town meetings.

Lorraine was thrilled that she was going to be at Thomas's side as a pastor's wife again. She would continue her job as the domestic budget director, but she would also help Thomas with church business. It would be like old times again, just the way it was in their first church. Lorraine also would be playing the organ while the congregation sang. In addition, Thomas and Lorraine planned to offer counseling just in case there was a need.

Now after the men had worked so feverishly to restore the old church, Thomas finally had a church to preach in again. It was just in time for the Fourth of July celebration.

This first service of the rejuvenated church would be a special worship service celebrating the fourth of July. However, the reason for the celebration had a new meaning. America's freedom was gone!

It was different now. Canada and Mexico were now part of it, ruled by a king who answered to an emerging one-world power. Instead, the people of Old Town declared it to be the anniversary of discovering the forgotten valley, their safe haven. Thomas and his son had stumbled upon it exactly one year ago on the Fourth of July.

It was a wonderful church service that morning, which was full of praise and thanksgiving to the Lord. Several out of the group gave their personal testimonies. They were grateful that God had provided for them and had led them to this wonderful retreat. Sheryl listened while one after another gave their testimonies. She had never witness such a thing, and it touched her heart.

After the church service, they all gathered at the boardinghouse. Everyone was having a great time. There were games set up, and music was playing on the radio. They mingled with one another, and there was plenty of good food to eat.

Off to the side of the room, Scott and Rachael were becoming completely engrossed in stories of the fun times they had together as kids. They were laughing and recalling some of their childhood pranks that they pulled on each other. Rachael asked, "Scotty, do you remember the last time my parents stayed at your place?"

"Sure, we had a ball together. We always did."

"Yes, but do you remember when we snuck out of the house that one night when everybody was sleeping?"

Scott's mouth dropped opened as he remembered. "Yes, I do. Wow, how did we get by with that? We wanted to go somewhere quiet, where it was private. You wanted to know all about my plans about college. We snuck in the church next to the house."

"Oh my gosh, it was so dark in there. You were guiding me all around. Scotty, you made me feel so safe."

Scott chucked a little as he said, "We talked until the sun came up."

"Oh yes, I remember well." Rachael looked deep into his eyes and said, "Scott Perkins, do you know how much I wanted you to kiss me that night?"

Scott's face turned red as he nervously laughed. "I guess, I did. Do you know how hard it was not to kiss you? You looked and acted so mature for your age."

"Then why didn't you?"

"I didn't feel I had the right to! Rachael, you were only fourteen, and I was almost 19! There was no way that I was going to kiss a girl that young. I felt bad that I even had the urge. That was just not right."

"What about now?"

"Now the age doesn't seem to matter anymore. You are a mature woman."

"So now you wouldn't have any problems kissing me?"

Scott laughed her question off and quickly changed the subject. Across the room, Sheryl had been watching Scott and Rachael as they laughed and talked together. She felt completely neglected as she sat by herself in a corner. Albert looked over at Sheryl and noticed that she was wiping tears from her eyes. He walked over to her and asked, "Sheryl, is everything all right?"

"Yes, of course. I'm just a little homesick."

Albert's outgoing personality had her laughing in no time in spite of Scott and Rachael's intimate conversation. Sheryl decided that this might be a good opportunity to make Scott a little jealous. She was going to have a good time with Albert if it killed her. It worked. Scott noticed how friendly Albert was being with Sheryl. Scott wanted to go over and break them up, but he chose to ignore it instead.

Old Town business meeting, July 11

Thomas, James, and Joe sat up on the stage of the church, while the others took a place in the pews. When all were seated, Thomas stood and began the meeting. "Good evening, this will be our first town meeting since all of you have all moved up here. We will be holding a meeting each month, unless there is a need for an emergency meeting in-between. It is important that we all attend each meeting.

It has been a month and three days since we have all been reunited here at Old Town. I believe that things have been going fairly good thus far. Sure, there have been some inconveniences, like the outhouses." The group laughed. "After all," Thomas went on, "most of us have been living the 'good life.' Some of you younger ones are probably a bit bored." Everyone laughed again. With a smirk on his face, Thomas said, "Okay, maybe some of us older people are a little bored too." That brought another burst of laughter. "That has to be expected, but we should thank God every day for bringing us to this safe haven that he has provided for us. You have all been given job responsibilities. With the exception of our farmers and the men working on our construction, our jobs have been very light. But just wait! Soon, there will be so much work to be done. None of us will have a chance to get bored!

"So far, Christina and Rachael, tell me that no one has gotten sick yet! Thank God for that! And, Mom, no one has torn their clothes yet nor worn them out. Oh, and, Darlene, you won't be able to start the canning until we have a harvest. Then look out! Harvest time will keep us all busy! I know some of you are working hard already. Zach and Tim, you guys have been doing a great job supplying us with fish. Later, you'll be busier yet when you start hunting."

"Heck," Zachary said, "that's not work, that's fun!" Everyone laughed at the fifteen-year-old.

After Thomas quit laughing, he continued, "Sheryl, Albert, and Sam say that you have been doing a fantastic job keeping up the domestic chores at the boardinghouse."

Sheryl blushed and said, "Thank you. I enjoy it."

Thomas looked over at his wife and said, "Also, I would like to thank my dear wife who has been doing a great job as the budget director. More than that, it has been wonderful having you by my side once again as I pastor our little congregation. Honey, I can't tell you in words how wonderful that makes me feel! My heart goes out when I hear you play the organ once again. Your beautiful voice is such a praise to God."

Thomas turned and pointed to Joe and James as he said, "Then we can't forget our financial directors, Joe and my father-in-law. Let's give these two men a hand!" The small assembly all stood and clapped.

Joe stood and said, "Let's all give a round of applause for all of you! I'm proud of each and every one of you! You are what's making this small community work! You have given up the comforts of the world to come here and live as the pioneers did back a couple hundred years ago. I haven't heard a grumble or complaint out of any of you! Not that I'd blame you, if you did. This is going to be a hard way of life, which none of us have ever endured before. God bless you all." Joe started applauding, and the others followed.

When the group sat back down, Thomas continued, "Now I would like each of you to take turns standing up and telling us about how your job is going. Also, if you have any questions, suggestions, or concerns about anything, please feel free to express it at this time. Like Joe said, any grumbling or complaining. Well, this is the place to air them. We'll start up here with the three of us. Matter of fact, I'll go first."

Thomas stood there silently for a moment. As he tried to think of the right words to say and gaining control of his emotions, he brushed away a couple tears. His voice cracked as he said, "It's hard for me to express how wonderful it makes me feel to be the pastor of a congregation once again."

Thomas's face lighted up as he said, "Our God is a forgiving God! He has forgiven me and has allowed me to have a second chance at the calling he gave me. This is not the large church of over four hundred that I ministered to in Syracuse, but it is just as important! I know that it is even more important to me! This past month has been the happiest time of my life serving as your pastor. If anyone of you have problems or questions, feel free to talk with me or my wife. Lorraine and I have worked together many years counseling and consoling folks. No problem is ever too small or too large for you to bring to us. Sometimes, it's easier to cope with everyday problems if you are able to talk to someone about them. We love each and every one of you, and we'll be here for you if you need us.

Yes, I am worried about being in the tribulation, and I'm nervous about the Antichrist. I am concerned about how we will survive in this valley! But do you know how ignorant that is of me? All I have to do is put my life and my faith into God's capable hands. He will provide! After all, He has provided us with this beautiful valley. He has provided us with all of the resources we have needed thus far.

More important, He has provided us with good Christian people who are skillful, and willing to work. God has led us here, and He will provide!"

Looking out into the small group of people, Thomas didn't see a dry eye. He said, "Thank all of you for being such great people. I love each and every one of you!" Fighting back more tears, he said, "And now, I will turn the floor over to you, Joe."

Joe stood and said, "Thank you, Thomas." He snickered a little and said, "How does one follow something like that?" They all laughed at Joe's dry humor. He continued, "As you all know, James, Thomas, and I form the board of directors. I handle the financial distributions, and James is in charge of legal matters. And of course, Thomas is our spiritual leader and pastor. I would just like to praise the Lord at this time for blessing James and myself with the means to contribute to this secluded valley. I truly believe that God has provided it for us as our safe haven. It is not our money. It is God's! I thank him that he has entrusted us with it. Thank you."

Joe sat down, and James stood. The white-haired seventy-nine-year-old man looked out at the small group and said, "Legal matters? I guess you can see that I'm not bogged down with work."

Everyone laughed as James continued, "But if need be, I've got forty-some years behind me to deal with it." That brought laughter again.

Scott jumped to his feet and said, "Sorry, Granddad, I don't mean to interrupt you, but I just got an awesome idea." Scott looked around at the people and said, "Every town needs a mayor. I think we should name granddad the mayor of Old Town!"

Sam raised his hand and said, "I second it!"

Thomas called out, "Anyone opposed?" There were no nays. Thomas then said, "All in favor, raise your hands." Everyone with the exception of James raised their hands.

Joe looked at James and asked, "Well, James, my dear old friend, will you do us the honor of being our mayor?"

James stood on the platform, dumbfounded. He even had to wipe a couple tears from his eyes. Finally, he said in a humble voice, "It would be my honor. I feel so blessed to be here with all of you. There are no others that I would rather spend the tribulation with than you folks. There now, you did it! You got me all choked up. Who's next?"

Lorraine stood next and said, "Dad, you will make a wonderful mayor!" She cleared her throat and then began again, "As the domestic budget director, I'd like to let you know that everything is going fine. Joe has adequately supplied me with the fund allocations that I have needed. The distribution of supplies has been flowing well. Thank you, ladies, for your good job in making your food rations last. I know we are not eating as some of us are used to, but I am sure we all have plenty to eat. We need to be frugal. We don't know for sure when President Omidi will make our money obsolete. We must prepare for that time. There is a lot to be done around here yet. Zach and Tim have been supplying us with fish that has been a big help." The group applauded.

"For me, the most rewarding job I have is being a pastor's wife. I cannot tell you how fulfilled I am to be at Thomas's side again as he shepherds our little church. In spite of what my husband said, I am a little rusty on the organ. So please, be patient with me. As Thomas said, if any of you need to talk, we are here for you. You have all been so congenial and have adjusted so well thus far, but we will be in for trials and tribulations, no pun intended." The room filled with laughter. Lorraine smiled and continued, "Don't hold your fears and sorrows in. That is what Thomas and I are here for. By expressing your woes and talking them out, it will be easier for you to cope with them. Well, that's all I have for now." Lorraine wiped a tear from her eye and said, "Love you guys! Now, who's next?"

With a big smile on her face, Marge slowly stood up next. The seventy-five-year-old's hair was not beauty-salon perfect like it had always been in the past. There were even gray hairs popping out all over, which she would never allow a few months back. She began, "As you all know, before I arrived here at Old Town, I located a treadle sewing machine at an antique auction. If you are too young to know, these sewing machines were made before electricity. I learned how to sew on one when I was a girl, but I haven't done any sewing in many years. With a little practice, I'm quite sure I can do some mending or light sewing. Who knows, if I practice enough, I might be able to sew a dress or a shirt. I'm not sure about the shirt, though. They're really hard to make. We'll just have to wait and see. I'll have to practice on James." Her husband made a nasty look, and there was laughter in the church once again.

Marge was excited as she looked out over the people. She said, "I came up with a cheery thought to brighten up our days. I am going to make us some new curtains for homes and the boarding-house. I already talked to Joe, and he's all for it! Nothing fancy, but it will brighten up our houses a little. Tomorrow, I will start measuring windows. Those women that would like to can go into the city with me in a couple of days. That way, each of you can pick the color and pattern for your homes. Next week, I'll start making them." The women were especially excited about the curtains. Lorraine started another applause. Marge beamed as she said, "You're all so welcome! It is the least I can do. I'm just happy that I am able to contribute."

Michelle raised her hand, and Thomas acknowledged her. She said, "I really wasn't assigned to any particular job. I help mom and Rachael with our household chores, but I still have a lot of time on my hands. I would love to help Mrs. Patterson with making the curtains."

Marge turned to Michelle and said, "Honey, that would be grand! I would love your help. You can help me get started tomorrow measuring windows."

"Wonderful!" Thomas said. "Michelle, you have one of the most important jobs here!"

"I do? What's my job?"

"You're position is chief collaborator!"

"What's that?"

"Whenever needed, you will work with the others on any task they need you to do. You will work in every aspect of our settlement, making you a key component of our valley."

"Wow, that's pretty cool. I'll get to learn something from every job. Sounds like it will keep me busy, all right!"

"Okay," Thomas said. "Who would like to go next?"

"I will," Sam said. "Now that Harold and Scott have been assigned farming, Joe has assigned me to be in charge of construction. Of course, Albert is my assistant. This past week, we have been working on the second windmill that we will put up between the two farms. We plan on raising it up by midweek. We sure would appreciate a few extra hands when we do. The more hands we have, the less dangerous."

Scott spoke out, "Yeah, sure, Sam, just let me know. I'll help anytime you need it."

"That goes for me too," Harold said. "We're both right there. It would be no problem at all."

"Yeah, count me in too," Daniel said.

"You can count on us town men also," Joe said. "We'll be there for you."

Sam smiled and said, "Great, that's wonderful!" Then he quickly sat down.

Albert stood and said, "Yeah, thanks, guys. When you need help on the farm, in town, anything, let us know. I for one love my job.

If it weren't for the fact that we are in the tribulation and worried about that darn Antichrist, this would be my dream job! You are all a great bunch of people. I have really enjoyed fixing up this old ghost town. To me, it's like fixing up an old Western town. Don't laugh, but I feel like I am one of those pioneers from back in the 1800s. This way of life has to be very similar. I love it when I wake up in the morning, go down the stairs, and smell that delicious smell of coffee and pancakes cooking. Then walking into the kitchen and seeing the beautiful Miss Higgins cooking breakfast. She always has a warm smile every morning. What a way to start a day!"

Albert turned toward the blushing woman and said, "Sheryl, I want to thank you for all the work you do for Sam and me! You keep all the rooms tidy, our clothes washed, and good meals on the table. Thank you."

Sheryl quietly replied, "It's my job. Besides, you and Sam are a pleasure to cook and clean for. I don't know what I would do without your company. I can't wait until it is time to cook your supper each night." She giggled a little as she said, "So hurry home every night!"

Sheryl looked around the room at the others and said, "After I get the supper dishes done, the three of us always have a fun night together. If we don't play a board game, we always have interesting discussions. I'm learning a lot about the Bible from them."

Albert had a look of admiration on his face as he said, "It's my pleasure."

As Scott studied Albert's face, a tinge of jealously fell over him. It was hard to see another man yearning after his ex-fiancé.

Albert continued, "Well, back to my job. As Sam said, next week, we will be installing the second windmill. After that, Joe wants us to start restoring the blacksmith and grocery store. Hope you all are enjoying the shower house that we finally finished last week. I know I am!"

Linda spoke out, "I sure do! I have an issue about the bathhouse. I love it, but I think we should have a washer and dryer put in there too! Do you realize how much laundry a baby can produce? I was told that I had to use cloth diapers instead of disposable ones. Do you all know what a job that is? Scrubbing diapers out by hand is no easy job, especially when you have to wait for the wood stove to heat the water up." Linda held out her hands and said, "Look how red and wrinkled my hands have gotten!"

Albert spoke up, "Yeah, I'm sure all you ladies would like to have a washing machine, but there just isn't room for one."

Darlene stood and scolded, "Linda, I realize that doing washing for a baby is a lot of work, but I have two teenage boys to wash for!" As Darlene expressed her feelings, Albert quickly sat down. Darlene continued talking, "No, it's not easy, but we knew that when we moved up here! Before I moved up here, I never washed one item! My maids did it all! Now I have to scrub clothes by hand, but it doesn't help anything by complaining about it! We have to learn to live like our forefathers. They did it, and so can we!"

Darlene stopped for a couple of seconds to compose herself. She wiped a couple of tears and then shamefacedly said, "I'm sorry, Linda. I didn't mean to sound angry with you. I'm really not. I understand where you are coming from. I guess it was my frustration coming out. But you know, this is all worth it, just to be safe from the Antichrist and his persecution!"

Feeling a little ashamed too, Linda walked over to Darlene and gave her a hug. She said, "I'm sorry too. I know it's hard on all of us."

Marge added, "I know where you girls are coming from. My maid did all my chores too. Thank God I have my daughter here to help me. Lorraine and I do our laundry together. That's a big help for me. Oh by the way, when I was in that antique store, I also bought an old hot iron. It's the kind that they put on the woodstove to get hot in the old days. If anyone wants to borrow it, help yourself. I iron on Tuesdays."

"Thanks, Marge, that would be great!" Darlene said as she sat down.

Rachael was the next to stand. "Speaking of wash days, Scotty, why don't you send your washing along with my brother's? We wash Daniel's. We might as well wash yours too. I know how many hours you spend farming. When you get caught up on the farm, you are always helping others."

"Gee, Rachael, that would be awesome! I don't get a chance to do laundry as much as I would like. Thank you. I'll take you up on the offer."

Rachael laughed and said, "I've noticed! Why do you think I offered?" The room filled with laughter. Everyone got a kick out of Rachael's satire that is all but Sheryl. She was furious but tried to hold it in. Why hadn't she thought about doing Scott's laundry?

When it quieted down, Rachael continued, "Mom, stand up with me." Christina stood. "Mom and I, of course, as you all know, run the clinic. We have worked hard this past month getting all the supplies needed for a small clinic. The instruments are all now sterilized and ready to go. However, I am not telling anyone to get sick or hurt, but we are ready just in case."

"Yes," Christina spoke out. "We can handle any minor emergency such as cuts that might need stitches. I am pleased to say there have been no accidents yet. God willing, there will not be."

Christina hesitated a moment and then said, "Oh yeah, I did have my first patient a few days back. It was a checkup on baby Brianna. I gave her an excellent health report! She sure is a beautiful baby. Linda, I hope you don't mind if we all spoil her, being she is the only baby in our valley."

Linda beamed, "Of course, I don't mind."

Christina sat down, but Rachael remained standing. "Oh yes, Thomas, you said we could also give suggestions. I think it would be really good for us to have some riding horses. There's very little entertainment, so I thought it would be good for us to have horses to ride."

"Rachael, you've never been on a horse!" Christina said to her daughter.

"So? Don't you remember all the books that I read about horses? I have always loved horses, just never had a chance to ride one. Almost rode a zebra once but fell off." Everyone laughed. "Yeah, it's funny now, but not so much back then. A couple of my African playmates helped me get on his back. Only took a second to fall off. The African kids thought it was funny too. I twisted my ankle."

Joe laughed with the rest, but then he got serious. "Remember, Rachael, we can only spend money on practical things. Horses can be expensive to maintain. I don't think that it would be a very practical expense."

Scott jumped from his seat in her defense and said, "Wait a minute, Joe. Maybe riding horses would be a practical way to go. When our money is obsolete, we will still need transportation to get around the valley. A few good riding horses could be the answer."

"Scott has a good point," James said. "I do agree that we will need some riding horses."

"Yes," Joe said, "but we don't need them now."

"Maybe not," James said. "However, horses might be a factor in our young people's mental health. It would also be a good mode of transportation around the valley. It would save some on gas."

Joe gave James a disgusted look and then chuckled a little. He said, "How can I argue with that?"

There was a lot of excitement in the room. Joe's boys were thanking him. Rachael thanked him several times. All the young adults were excited. There were even joyful smiles on the older faces as well.

"Wait, wait," Joe said anxiously. "We will only start out with a couple horses. Next year, we will know better how many the farm can support. First, we have to know if the farm can support us, and then we will worry about more horses. So remember, if we do buy two riding horses, they will not belong to any one person. They will be for all of us."

Joe turned and looked over at Harold and asked, "Can you take care of a couple horses in your barn?"

"Sure, Joe, no problem!"

The group settled down, and there was a pause. Then Thomas spoke up and said, "Okay, who wants to go next?"

Darlene stood and said, "Well, I guess I haven't contributed to the community as much as the rest of you have. I have just been getting used to being a pioneer homemaker to Joe and our boys. My work will start soon when we start harvesting our vegetables. I have all the cookbooks and canning equipment ready and set to go. As soon as I get a good supply of veggies, I'll organize a group of ladies, and we will start canning!" She then sat back down.

Sheryl stood and said, "Well, first of all, I want to thank you all for welcoming me into this tight-knit family. I haven't had much of a family life. It is all so surreal to me. I am still very confused, but I feel that I have been given a very special privilege by being here. I thank you all for making me part of this loving family." Wiping away her tears, Sheryl continued, "Now about my job. I've got to be honest with you, when you gave me this job, I thought it would be really boring. I thought that I would have nothing to do all day. Boy, was I wrong! Keeping up the boardinghouse keeps me going all day. Then by night, I am exhausted. Don't get me wrong. I'm enjoying it! I love cooking and cleaning for Albert and Sam. They are so nice. They really seem to appreciate everything I do for them. Not only that, I've gained a couple of really good friends."

As Sheryl talked, Scott looked closely from her to Albert. He was trying to read their faces. Had their friendship evolved into something deeper? It bothered him more than ever. It appeared to him that they were really getting close to one another. The fact that they were living down the hall from one another didn't help either. As Sheryl went on talking, Scott thought, *I don't want her there with him! I want her to be with me! First thing, you know they are going to fall in love, if they haven't already. She does all the wifely duties for him, except...I don't want to think about that! I wish I could tell her to move out of there and marry me. We could be so happy living on the farm together. There is so little time to be together, but I can't! I know in my heart that it is not God's will.* He prayed silently, *please, Jesus, let Sheryl accept You as her Lord and Savior.*

Harold followed Sheryl. He said, "I really love it up here, but I only wish we had more time to enjoy it. I can't help think about how much Brianna would love growing up on that farm. If anybody told me a year ago that I'd be happy being a farmer, I'd ask them what have they been smoking."

Everyone laughed, and Harold went on, "Seriously, I love it here. It is really scary having to worry about the tribulation and all, but I have never been so happy! I guess, more than the place, it is because I now have the Lord Jesus in my life! I really don't know how I was able to cope with this world before I was saved. Thank you, Dad and Scott, for showing me how to open my heart to Jesus. I have a whole new outlook on life. I love all of you, my extended Christian family, and I love my beautiful wife and baby."

Harold stopped to gain his composure and continued, "The cattle barn is coming along great. As you know, we started out with two heifers and a bull. A few days back, Scott and I were able to pick up two more heifers. They will be dropping calves in the next few weeks. One of the heifers is due next week and the other about two weeks later." The group clapped their hands in excitement.

"We were also able to pick up a pasteurizer and separator from another retired farmer. We will be able to use them after they get the windmill up and running. I was told that we could expect three to five gallons of milk per cow. The farmer we bought the cows from gave me a little lesson on how to milk. It is not as easy as it looks." Laughter rang out again. "He promised that after some practice, I'd do okay. Anyway, after the milking is done, Linda and I bottle the milk. Before we moved up here, Linda and I found recipes for making butter and cottage cheese on line. Hopefully, we'll be able to produce those dairy products for all of you. When we have them ready, Daniel will deliver them to your homes. If there is any excess milk, we will feed it to the pigs. We have two of them, and they are always hungry."

Sheryl raised her hand. Thomas noticed and said, "Yes, Sheryl, do you have a question?"

"Yes, I have a question for Harold. Would it be helpful if we all saved our garbage for the pigs? Garbage can draw wild animals, so we have to dig a hole and bury it. Why not save our garbage for the pigs? We still have a lot of room in one of our coolers here in the board-inghouse. She looked over at Darlene, Marge, and Lorraine and suggested, "You ladies could bring your garbage to the boardinghouse, and we could all put our garbage into a large container and keep it in the cooler. That way, Harold could have it picked up every few days."

"That's an excellent idea, Sheryl! Scott already has been giving me his garbage. That would be great!"

Harold smiled and said, "Oh yes! One other exciting thing! My chickens are now laying eggs. Linda and I gathered over a dozen eggs this morning. We have brought in a few for each family. We'll get them out of the truck after the meeting. When the hens are all laying, we will let a couple of them sit on their nests. Hopefully, there will be a bunch of baby chicks running around soon."

Linda stood up with her husband and said, "The chickens are my job. I cannot wait until we have baby chicks. Brianna loves to go out in the chicken coop with me. She gets a kick out of me feeding the chickens. When she gets older, I'll let her feed and gather eggs with me. Today was the first time we had enough to start sharing with everyone. We have been sharing a few of the eggs with Scott and Daniel. After all, they are our closest neighbors."

"Yes, and we really enjoyed them," Scott interjected.

Linda smiled broadly and continued, "I keep really busy with the baby, but I must confess it's been kind of fun living on the farm. We get up at dawn each morning. Sometimes, I don't know which way to turn, I am so busy. It is a lot harder taking care of a baby when you don't have all the modern conveniences. I am just starting to learn to cook on that old wood stove. Harold has been really patient with me. After supper dishes are done, it is so peaceful. That's the only time we have to just have fun with our baby girl. We play with Brianna for about an hour. We are both so dead tired by then that we go right to bed. That's all I have for now."

Daniel went next. He said, "Well, I don't have much to say. Harold and Scott covered the farm chores. We really do keep busy. As I've mentioned before, I learned a lot about planting crops while I lived in Africa." He looked over at Scott and Harold and told them, "I really feel it an honor working both farms with you guys. I've learned a lot more working alongside both of you guys." Daniel chucked as he said, "It is a learning experience for all four of us. We are definitely learning as we go. I have also enjoyed living out on the farm. Scott and I both love it when Linda and Harold invite us over for dinner. Even Brianna is getting to know her uncle Daniel! I praise the Lord every day that we have this beautiful valley. Like the rest of you, I really believe that God brought us here, and He will let us survive until the end."

When Daniel sat down, Zach jumped up. He grabbed his brother by the arm and said, "Come on, Tim, we're next."

"Okay, okay," seventeen-year-old Tim said.

"We are the hunters and fishermen," Zach said.

A little shyer than his younger brother, Tim said, "Yeah, our dad will be going hunting with us soon. We have been doing a lot of fishing. My dad, Zach, and I love hunting and fishing, so there's no job we'd rather have. Of course, we will help out wherever needed. So if you need some help, we're your men!"

"Yeah, whatever you need, you can count on me," Zach said. His mood turned more serious when he said, "I am so blessed! I love hunting and fishing! We were blessed to have a dad who taught us those kinds of skills. He has taken us kids hunting and fishing since we were little. This job is the best job a guy like me could have! That's a real blessing."

After the boys sat down, Scott stood. With tears in his eyes, he said, "You all know how much I love this place! Yes, I would love to live here until I'm old, but we all know our time here will be short. But praise the Lord, when we are raptured out of this valley, we are going to an even more glorious place. Better than that, we will be in the presences of the Lord God Himself! I cannot wait to see Jesus! I don't know why he picked our little group of people to bring to this safe haven, but I will always be grateful for it. I will praise God's holy name for all eternity!"

Scott sat down, and Thomas took charge again. Wiping tears from his eyes, he said, "That was beautiful, son. You all did a great job. Seems like you are all coping with the inconveniences very well. Are there any more concerns or comments that we haven't addressed?"

No one spoke, so Thomas continued, "Wonderful! This has been a great meeting! Remember, we are all going over to the boardinghouse for a fish fry, compliments of our great fishermen." Thomas closed the meeting in prayer.

42

Old Town's first tragedy, July 18

The following week found Marge and Michelle busy going house to house in town measuring the windows for the new curtains. When they got to the clinic to measure its windows, Rachael asked, "Mrs. Patterson, could you use an extra hand on measuring the windows at the farmhouses? There are a lot more windows there, and they are so much taller than the rest. I'd love to help!"

Marge smiled and said, "Sure, honey, we'd appreciate your help. That is if your mom doesn't need you here at the clinic."

"Oh, no, everything is all set and ready to go with no patients. I am so bored."

"Well, my dear, I would say that is a good thing. We sure don't need anyone getting sick or hurt."

"Yes, of course, Mrs. Patterson," Rachael said.

After Rachael helped Michelle measure the windows in the clinic, the three women drove out to Scott's farm. Rachael couldn't wait to see Scott. She had just seen him a couple days before, but it was at a church service. That was just not enough time for Rachael. As they drove up to Scott's farm, Rachael spotted Scott out in the vegetable garden. When Marge stopped the van, Rachael jumped out of the van. She ran out in the field, calling out to Scott. He stopped hoeing to greet his guest. "Hello, Rachael, what a pleasant surprise. What are you ladies doing way out here?"

"Don't you remember, silly? We are here to measure up your windows for curtains. We are going to brighten your house up for you."

"Oh, yeah. Sure, I remember. That's nice. I've just been so busy with the farm I haven't thought of much else."

"I can imagine, Scotty, this is a huge garden, but does it really have to be so enormous?"

Scott smiled at her and said, "Yes, my dear Rachael. If we are going to make sure there is enough to feed us all winter, it has to be enormous. There are a lot of mouths to feed." He chuckled a little and said, "To tell you the truth, I don't know how much we will need or, for that matter, how much this garden will produce. I'm playing this by ear."

Frowning, Rachael and said, "Awe, that's too much work for you!"

"Your brother Daniel is a big help. Harold spends some time working on it when he gets caught up on his farm."

"That's good, but couldn't you use another hand? I sit around all day at the clinic waiting to nurse someone back to health, and no one gets sick. I need to do something to keep busy. If you would like my help, I would love to give you a hand."

"That's very generous of you, Rachael. Would your mother mind? What if she needed you in a hurry?"

"I'm sure she won't care. Mom's got a lot of spare time too. She sometimes goes over to your grandmother's and gives her a hand. Town isn't that far away. It wouldn't take long for me to get back to the clinic."

"Great! Daniel and I can use the help. Why don't you plan on coming over Thursday? I'll be helping the guys put up the windmill tomorrow."

Marge called out to Rachael, "Come on, girl, let Scotty get back to work. We've got a lot of measuring to do in the house."

"Okay, Scott, I've got to run now. I'll see you Thursday, if not before."

That next Wednesday morning, the wind-up alarm clocks at the boardinghouse went off an hour earlier than normal. Sheryl always got up an hour before the men so she could get the coffee on and breakfast started. She found out that cooking with a wood stove took much longer than on a conventional one.

It was still dark outside, so Sheryl lit the kerosene lantern beside her bed and slowly got up. She dressed and then found her way down the dark staircase. Before she could start the coffee, she had to take a trip out back. As she followed the path out to the outhouse, she was trembling. Thoughts of meeting a big black bear on the path went through her mind. She heard bushes rustling. Sheryl let out a startled yell! To her relief, it was only a deer running off.

An hour later, Albert was the first one to come down the stairs. He also headed down the path to the outhouse. Ten minutes later, he walked back into the house. The sweet smells of breakfast drew him to the kitchen. There he saw the pretty, strawberry blonde cooking. He couldn't resist himself as he walked up behind her, placing both of his hands on each side of her tiny waist and giving her a quick peck on her check.

Sheryl was startled as she said, "Why, Albert Cline, what are you up to?"

"Please, don't get mad, Sheryl, I didn't mean anything by it. You just looked so beautiful cooking on that old stove, I couldn't resist!"

Flattered, she just laughed and asked, "Where's Sam? I'm about ready to serve breakfast."

"I passed him on the path. He should be coming soon."

When Sam got back from the outhouse, the three of them sat down and enjoyed their breakfast together. Sheryl felt very close to each of them, but she felt especially close to Albert. She wasn't sure what the hug and kiss on her cheek was all about. For that matter, she wasn't sure what she felt about him doing it. All she knew was that it felt good. She was sure that she loved Scott but had her doubts if they would ever get back together again. They had never been alone since she moved to the valley. Had Scott been avoiding her? And was he enjoying Rachael's flirtation way too much?

While they were finishing up their breakfast, Albert and Sam talked about the challenging job that lay ahead of them that day. The men had an extra cup of coffee while Sheryl packed them each a couple sandwiches and an apple. She handed them each their pack lunches and said, "I feel you guys should have more than this little lunch to get you through such a big task today."

Facing Sheryl, Albert put his hands on her shoulders and said, "This is great, hon. You made us such a hardy breakfast that this lunch will be good enough. Thank you."

Sam looked at her and said, "Yes, thanks, Sheryl. We really appreciate what you do for us."

Sam and Albert each gave Sheryl a little hug, and then they were off to put up the windmill. After they left, Sheryl couldn't stop thinking about how hard all the men would be working. This was such an important project for the settlement. She then got an idea. Sheryl walked a couple houses down to Lorraine and Thomas's. She knocked on the door, and Lorraine opened it. "Sheryl, what a pleasant surprise!"

"Hello, Mrs. Perkins."

"Please, call me Lorraine."

"Okay, thanks. Well, I just came up with this great idea! The men will be working really hard all day on the windmill. I was thinking that maybe in honor of their work, we could treat them to an old-fashioned barn raising. Or in this case a windmill raising!"

"What in the world are you talking about?"

"You know a celebration! An old-fashioned windmill raising. The guys will be working really hard today putting up the windmill. Albert and Sam were saying what a big job it was going to be. So why don't we cook up some casseroles, pies, cakes, or whatever we have on hand? We can haul out the tables from the farmhouses and put the food and drinks on them. That way, when the men want a lunch break, they can have a great picnic meal. We can all celebrate the windmill raising together. What do you say, Lorraine? Do you think we could do something like that?"

Overhearing, Thomas walked into the room and said, "Yes! Sheryl, that sounds like a wonderful idea! That would really encourage the men! Joe, his boys, and I planned on going over there to give them a hand anyway."

"Okay! I agree." Lorraine said. "It would be fun! Perhaps it will make the men's work a little easier. Let's do it!"

Lorraine and Sheryl walked over to both Marge and Darlene's cabins to tell them the plan, and they were delighted to help. Then they went over to the clinic to share the news with Christina and her girls. Everyone was excited about the windmill-raising party. The women got busy and cooked up their favorite recipes.

By eleven that morning, the whole group from town had converged on the farmer's field. The men were all working hard assembling the different sections and parts of the wind turbine. Two sections laid on the ground as the men were assembling the rotors on the top. When they saw the people from town, they were happily surprised.

Scott walked over to the men and asked, "What's going on? The whole town is here?"

Thomas answered, "Sheryl had a brilliant idea. She thought we could turn this into an old-fashioned windmill raising. Sheryl and the rest of the ladies wanted you to know that they were all behind you. The women wanted you to keep up your strength, so they prepared a potluck."

Albert smiled at Sheryl and said, "Sheryl, you're an angel! I am starving. Those are nice sandwiches that you packed for Sam and me, but as hungry as I am, they'd only make a dent."

It didn't take but a short time to get the dinner set out. The men all took off an hour, and all enjoyed the fellowship and food.

Then the really hard work laid ahead of them; they had to attach four strong ropes on each side of the windmill. One rope went through a pulley on a tripod they had put up. The next three ropes would go to each side and the back. Daniel and Harold would be on the front with Joe's two boys for back up. Thomas and Joe would each take a side as Sam and Albert would hang on to the back rope. Scott would be taking the tractor and pull the windmill into place. Then Sam would bolt it to the foundation while the rest of the men held it in place. The plan seemed good; now all they had to do was execute it. A half hour later, it was a go. Slowly, the windmill began to rise at a steady pace. Minutes later, it was in place. Then Sam started bolting it down.

Thomas said, "Thank you, God, for letting us get it in place with no problems!"

Sam shouted, "Okay, I'll go up the ladder. Take those ropes down, and we'll be done."

The group was holding their breaths as Sam climbed to the top of the windmill. As Sheryl kept her eyes on Sam, Lorraine overheard her say, "Please, God, keep him safe."

Sam was working on cutting the thick ropes when Albert yelled up at him, "Hey, Sam, don't cut yourself."

Sam yelled down, "Very funny, Albert."

Minutes later, when Sam had cut through the last rope, a cheer went up from the onlookers below. With a big smile on his face, Sam started down the ladder. On the third step down, his right foot slipped off the rung of the ladder. Sam tried to hang on to the ladder but couldn't. He fell the rest of the way to the ground. He landed hard. The people standing close to where Sam landed said they felt the ground shake when he hit. Sam laid there, not moving! As everyone crowded around Sam, Christina pushed her way through to him. As she knelt down by him, she said, "Rachael, go back to the clinic and get my black bag and a neck brace. Also, get the stretcher. Someone, go with her and help."

"Yeah, I'll go," Scott said.

Christina checked him over and said, "I can tell you right now, he's got multiple fractures and a concussion. This could be very serious."

Joe nervously said, "Christina, is he going to be all right?"

"Joe, I don't know yet. He's still unconscious."

"Maybe we should rush him to the hospital!"

"No, Joe, we can't move him until I get a neck brace on him. Besides, we can't move him without a stretcher. Be patient, Rachael and Scott should be back soon."

Thomas kneeled down by Sam's side and said, "The most important thing we can do for Sam right now is to pray." The entire group kneeled around Sam as Thomas led them in prayer. Sheryl wasn't sure what she was doing, but her mind repeated each word Thomas prayed.

After the prayer, Joe began rubbing his bald head as he paced around nervously. He shouted, "I really think we should take him into the hospital!"

"Wait, Joe," James said. "Remember a couple of weeks ago, we all decided to make out our living wills?"

"Yeah, sure, James, but this is different."

"No, Joe it's not. We all put in our living wills that no matter what happened to us, we did not want to go to a hospital. We all agreed that it would be too dangerous for the entire group. Before they will treat anybody, they want all their information. We can't give them that, Joe, or our safe haven would be jeopardized. We have to keep under the radar."

Joe cried out, "But he might die, James!"

Christina put her hand on Joe's shoulder to comfort him and said, "All we can do now is put Sam in God's hands. Joe, can I ask you to put your faith in God and in me? While in Africa, Dan and I handled several emergencies like this one. Our hospital was very primitive, much like the clinic I have set up here. There's not much more that a hospital would do for him than I can do here at the clinic. Sure, they have x-ray machines and cat scans, but we can get by without them. I have put my share of casts on broken bones. As for the head trauma, we just have to keep a close eye on him. I'll hook him up intravenously. That way, we can get nutrients to his body. In addition, when he wakes up, he will be in a great deal of pain. I can administer painkillers through it. The next twenty-fours will be crucial."

43

Mark Thornton's Store in Gratiot, July 18th

"Good afternoon, George, what brings you into town today?" Mark asked.

"I have a few loose boards on some of my pens. I have this one real ornery old boar who's been trying to knock it down. Thought it was time for me to fix the dang thing. Need to pick up some nails."

"Great, always good to see you, George."

"Say, Mark, I've been doing a lot of thinking about what that fellow, what's his name? You know the one that spoke at our church several weeks back."

"Thomas Perkins?"

"Yeah, that's the name. Haven't seen him or his friends around lately. Did they finally go back to the city?"

"No, I believe they're still around."

"Must have plenty of money to be able to vacation that much."

"I don't know. Funny you should mention them. I've been thinking about them all day. I can't shake the feeling that something is wrong."

"Well, you know the spot where their hunting camp is, don't you? I can run up there and see if their still up there. If so, I can check on them and let you know if all's okay."

"Oh, no. No thanks, George. It's probably nothing. Besides, I know they like their privacy."

"Okay, but where are they camping?"

Mark shrugged his shoulder and said, "Good question."

"Well okay, I'll just go get my nails and be on my way."

* * * * *

Meanwhile, back at Old Town, Sam was brought to the clinic. He was put in the downstairs bedroom. Christina quickly hooked him up with an intravenous tube. With Rachael's help, she put a cast on his broken leg and arm.

Michelle served Lorraine and Thomas coffee as they waited for news at the clinic's kitchen table. The rest of the group waited impatiently at the boardinghouse. Sheryl put on a big pot of coffee while Scott held a prayer vigil. Everybody was in shock over their dear friend. Michelle went over to the boardinghouse occasionally to let everyone know how Sam was doing, but unfortunately, there was no change.

Then at five, Scott mentioned that they would have to get back to the farm to do the chores. "You guys can't go back hungry," Sheryl said. "I'll warm up the leftovers from the picnic. We can all eat together here in the boardinghouse."

After the meal, Scott took some food over to the clinic. Rachael met him at the door and was happy to see he brought food. "Thank you so much, Scotty. We've been so busy and worried about Sam we haven't had time to think about eating. I am really hungry now. I'm sure your mom and dad are too. Unfortunately, Sam is still lying in the bed, unconscious. I'll save some in the refrigerator for when he wakes up."

"Okay then. We have to get back to the farm. I hate to leave before I know Sam's going to be all right, but we have to do our chores. If you need me, you know where to find me."

Rachael took the food out of Scott's hands. She then reached up and gave him a quick kiss on his cheek as she whispered, "Good night, my loving friend."

The boardinghouse felt empty as Sheryl finished cleaning up after everyone left. It was just her and Albert in the big old building. They were both shaken by Sam's accident. Sheryl couldn't hold back any longer. She broke down and cried. Albert took her in his arms and comforted her. Both of their emotions were running high. He kissed her cheek a couple of times, getting closer to her lips each time. Sheryl gently pushed him away and said, "Albert, please stop. It's late, and we are both upset. We're not thinking straight tonight. Maybe we should go to our rooms before we do something we'll be sorry for."

"You're right, Sheryl. I'm sorry. Sam and I go a long ways back." Albert was fighting back tears as he said, "I don't know what I'll do if anything happens to him."

Sheryl put her arms around Albert as she tried to console him. Gaining back his composure, he gave her a quick kiss on the lips and said, "Thank you, beautiful lady. Maybe it would be best if we go to our rooms now. I'm tired, and no, I don't trust myself right now either."

Back at the clinic, Christina didn't get a lot of sleep. She sat at Sam's bedside side all night. From time to time, she nodded off, but the slightest noise woke her. At daylight, Rachael was up. She walked into the bedroom where she found her mother asleep. Christina was bent over in the chair, resting her head on the side of Sam's bed. Rachael gently put her hand on Christina's shoulder. Christina jumped. "Oh, it's you, Rachael. I must have dozed off. What time is it?"

"It's a little after six. Have there been any changes?"

Christina yawned and answered, "No, not yet. I wish he would wake up. The longer he's out, the more risky it is for him."

"Mom, I'm going to go wake up Michelle and then go make us some breakfast. After that, I want you to go get some sleep. You won't be any good to Sam if you're all tired out!"

"Okay, honey, thanks."

Before the Nelson women could finish their breakfast, they had concerned visitors. The first ones to visit were Sheryl and Albert. As Michelle opened the clinic's door, Albert could see Christina and Rachel at the kitchen table. He apologized, "Ladies, we are very sorry to interrupt your breakfast. I know it is early, but we have been so worried about Sam."

Christina stood, yawned, and said, "No, don't be sorry, I understand. I know how worried you must be about him. To tell the truth, I am worried too. I thought he would be awake by now. The longer he is out, the more dangerous his condition becomes. He needs a lot of prayers."

"Can we go in and see him?" Sheryl asked.

"Of course, dear. Sometimes, a voice of a good friend can bring a patient out of their coma. The two of you can go right in."

Tears ran down Sheryl's cheeks as she looked at their friend. He had an IV dripping fluid into his left arm and a cast was on his right leg and right arm. Sheryl said to Albert, "He looks so helpless lying there. Sam has always been such a big strong man. It is so hard to see him this way."

Albert put his arm around Sheryl and gave her a little hug and said, "Yes, I know. It hurts me to see him this way too."

Albert sat down in the chair next to Sam's bed. He started talking to him. "Hey, buddy, what do you mean taking off from work, leaving me to do it all? You know I can't do anything without your skillful guidance. You need to wake up, buddy! I get into too much trouble at the boardinghouse without you around." Albert smiled up at Sheryl and said, "Right, Sheryl?"

Sheryl knelt down by Sam's bed next to Albert. She said, "That's right, Sam, you have to hurry back to us so you can keep Albert on the straight and narrow. Matter of fact, that goes for me too!"

Sheryl turned and looked intensely into Albert's eyes. Then Albert put his arms around her, and they embraced. Out of the corner of her eye, Sheryl noticed they were not alone. Into the room walked Scott's parents. Embarrassed, Sheryl quickly pulled away from Albert as if they had been caught doing something they shouldn't.

Thomas cleared his throat and said, "Didn't mean to startle you, guys. We came over to see Sam. Christina told us to go ahead and come in."

"No, no, Thomas, it's okay," Albert nervously said. "Sheryl and I have been upset about Sam. We were just trying to console each another."

"Albert, we understand," Lorraine said. "We are all close friends. We are all in this together. The three of you have all been living together at the boardinghouse, so of course, you guys are even closer to Sam. Of course, you guys are upset. We all need to lean on somebody at times like this."

Sheryl was shaking as she said, "Oh yes, Lorraine, we miss him terribly! We are so worried about him. I think Joe was right! We should have taken him into the hospital!"

"Sheryl, Christina has assured us that at this point, she is doing everything that the hospital would do. It's just a waiting game now," Lorraine told her.

"And a time for prayers," Thomas said. "Let's pray for him now."

Thomas and Lorraine knelt beside Sam's bed. Albert and Sheryl followed suit as Thomas said a prayer for their friend. When she finished, Sheryl wondered why she was silently praying so fervent to a God she didn't know if she believed in or not.

"Okay then, I think I better get to work." Albert looked down at the comatose man as he lay motionless and said, "Good-bye for now, Sam. I will be back later. I've got to get back to the farms. There's a couple things I need to finish up on the windmill." He looked back at Thomas and said, "I'll stop by and let the others out at the farm know that there's no change."

"Yeah okay, Lorraine and I are going to get going too. I told Joe and James that we'd stop over and give them an update on Sam. After that, I'll run out to the farm with you. We don't want anyone else getting hurt."

After all the visitors left, Christina collapsed in the nearest chair. Rachael looked at her and, with her hands on her waist, said, "Oh, no, you don't, Mother, you go upstairs and go to bed! You are totally exhausted."

"Okay, okay, Rachael, but if he wakes up, be sure to come get me right away!"

"Don't worry, Mom, Rachael and I will take turns staying with him. If he wakes up, we will let you know immediately."

Rachael took the first watch. She went into the room where Sam lay motionless. She sat down next to his bed. After a couple of hours, she nodded off to sleep.

In a stupor, Sam felt himself waking up. He looked around, trying to make sense of his situation. He then realized that he was looking down at himself in the bed. He saw Rachael sitting beside him. Then he felt himself being pulled quickly away. The next thing he knew, he was standing in front of his wife and two boys. His family held out their hands to him. He cried out, "Carol, I've missed you and our boys so much! I'm so happy to be here with all of you!"

Sam's family dropped their arms to their sides as his wife said, "My darling, Sam, I love you too. Soon, we will be together again, but now you must go back."

"No, Carol, I don't ever want to be apart from you again."

"Sam, you have a lot of work to do yet. You have people that count on you and that love you. Don't be afraid, my darling, to give your love, for later on, we will be together for all eternity."

"No, Carol, please, don't send me back!"

As Carol and his sons began to fade away, Sam saw a great light. Out of the light walked Jesus. His powerful voice said to him. "Sam, you must go back for a short time. Your job on earth is not over yet."

"Please, Jesus, let me stay, I don't want to go back! Please."

Sam felt a harsh jolt as he reentered his body. Now it felt as if his whole body was on fire with pain! Rachael woke up with a start when she heard Sam moaning. By that time, he was twisting and turning in pain. Rachael was trying to hold him down as she screamed to her sister. Michelle jumped up from the couch and ran into Sam's room. "I'm sorry, sis, why didn't you call soon. Oh my gosh! He's awake!"

"Yes, Michelle! Just run and get Mom!"

After a few hours of solid sleep, Christina was awakened by Michelle screaming up the staircase, "Mom, Mom, wake up. Rachael said to come quick. Sam is awake!"

Minutes later, Christina was at Sam's side as he thrashed around in the bed. Sam cried out, "Carol, I can't move! It hurts! Please, Carol, help me!"

"Sam, Sam, can you hear me! It's all right, Sam. It's me, Christina! You need to lay still. You might hurt yourself more! Can you show me where you are hurting?"

Sam wrinkled up his face and nodded his head. "All over! It hurts so badly!"

Christina shouted to Rachael, "Increase his pain meds to the next level."

As the medicine started to ease Sam's pain, he cried out, "I can't move my right leg or my right arm!"

Christina gently held his left hand and said, "Sam, do you remember falling from the windmill?"

"No, but I remember my wife and boys. I want to go back there. I want to be with my family. It was so beautiful there. I can't describe it, but it was so beautiful and peaceful. Then I saw Jesus. I was so happy, but then I heard him say that I had to go back, that he had work for me to do yet. I was begging him to let me stay, that's when I woke up. I'm in so much pain. I can't move my one side. Am I paralyzed?"

"No, Sam, you're not paralyzed. When you fell, you fractured your right leg and arm. You have casts on them, so you will not be able to move them."

Sam cried out, "No, it can't be! I can't be laid up! The others are all counting on me. I have to get up and help. There's a lot of work that needs to be done on the windmill yet. Albert and I have to get the lines laid to put in electricity!" Sam thrashed around and cried out, "Get these darn casts off me, woman!"

"Now you just settle down, mister. I'm not taking these casts off from you! You would never be of any use to the others if those bones didn't heal right!"

As Sam began to calm down a bit, Christina softened her voice, "Sam, I know you are good at what you do, and the men will miss your help, but they will manage without you for a while. Albert is already working on the windmill. If he needs help, anyone of the men will be eager to help him. When you are strong enough, you can supervise them from a chair. When your leg and arm are healed, you'll be good as new."

"How long will that take?"

"It depends how fast they heal. I would say it will take ten to twenty-four weeks."

Sam's eyes opened wide as he repeated what she said. "Ten to twenty-four weeks! I can't take off that much time!"

"Sam, that time will go fast."

"So after you determine my leg and arm is healed up, then I can go back to work, right?"

"Not exactly. You will need physical therapy."

"How the heck long will that take?"

"That will depend on you." Christina laughed a little as she said, "I'm sure it will be in record time, as much as you want to get back to work."

It took some time for Christina to get Sam settled down. Michelle fixed breakfast, and Sam was able to eat a little. After the breakfast, Christina asked Michelle to go next door to let Joe and Darlene know that Sam had come out of his coma so they could spread the good news.

Joe and Darlene went over to tell James and Marge. They were so excited. "Let's get in the truck and let everybody know," James said. "We'll stop at the boardinghouse first and let Sheryl and Albert know. Then Lorraine and Thomas! Then we can run out to the farms!"

Marge told her husband, "I believe that Lorraine and Thomas are at the church this morning. Lorraine said something about wanting to extend the backyard of the church."

"Okay, thanks, honey."

44

Old Town's grave yard, July 19th

Thomas and Lorraine were behind the church trying to get it cleared out so they could have a nice backyard for church outings. They were digging up small trees and tearing down bushes and weeds. When the truck pulled up to the church, Thomas immediately thought of Sam. He quickly asked, "Is there any news about Sam?"

"Yes," Joe eagerly answered. "That's why we are here! Sam is out of his coma!"

"Praise the Lord!" Lorraine shouted.

"Yes! That's the best news I've heard in a long time," Thomas said. "Does Sheryl and Albert know yet?"

"Yes, we just came from the boardinghouse. They are thrilled! They were on their way to the clinic when I left."

"All right," Thomas said. "I think that Lorraine and I will visit Sam later today. I know that you guys will want to visit him. We'll wait until later today to go see him."

"Yeah," Lorraine agreed. "We haven't been able to get a lot done around here. We couldn't get our hearts into it. We were so afraid that he might not make it. Now with this good news, there's hope.

That gives me the enthusiasm I needed! Maybe now I'll have the heart to get this yardwork done!"

"Okay then," James said. "We're on our way to the farms to let everyone down there know. We'll stop in and visit Sam when we get back."

After their visitors left, Thomas said, "Come on, Lorraine, let's get down on our knees right here on the ground and give God the praise and glory for bringing Sam out of the coma."

The rest of the morning, Lorraine and Thomas spent clearing the land out back of the church. Now that they knew Sam was out of the coma and had a fighting chance, they were actually enjoying the yard work. They worked hard as they tore into the bushes, knocking them down. Finally, at five o'clock, they were done for the day. They were tired, worn out, and hungry. They had only stopped around noon to have a sandwich that Lorraine had packed for them. Putting down his shovel, Thomas said, "Honey, we'd better call it a day. It's almost time to get supper started, and we still need to go see Sam."

"Yes, honey, you're right, but please, just a couple more minutes. We have almost made our goal. We have almost cleared enough to have a nice backyard for the congregation. This will make a wonderful spot for our church picnics."

"Okay, another half an hour."

The couple worked with more vigor than ever, trying to accomplish as much as they could. Then all of a sudden, Thomas heard a clanging sound as his shovel hit against something. "What the heck? What is this?"

Lorraine rushed over to where her husband was working. She asked, "What, Thomas, what did you find?"

"I'm not sure! Help me clear away these weeds."

Thomas and Lorraine worked hard until they were able to see an old wrought-iron fence. They kept clearing the weeds from it until they came to what appeared to be the fence's gate. They worked enthusiastically, tearing all the growth away from a broken down gate. It was getting late, but neither of them wanted to stop cutting and digging their way through the underbrush.

"What do you suppose is behind this gate, Thomas?"

"I'm not sure. It must have something to do with the church."

As Lorraine was cutting down weeds, she tripped over something and fell to the ground. Thomas ran to her. "Honey, are you all right?"

Lorraine brushed off the leaves and debris from herself as Thomas helped her up. "Yes, I'm fine! A little shook up, but I'm okay."

"What did you do? Get tangled in some weeds?"

"No, I don't think so. It was hard. A stone or something."

They both knelt down looking to see what it was that tripped her. "Here it is, Thomas. It's not round like a stone. It has a straight edge."

"Let's see, honey." Thomas started pulling away weeds, which were covering the object. "It's definitely cement."

Lorraine watched him as he ripped the weeds away. Finally, to her amazement, she saw carved writing on the piece of cement. She gasped and said, "It's a broken tombstone! Thomas, this is an old graveyard!"

"By gosh, you are right! In the old days, people put their grave-yards out behind their churches."

"Come on, Thomas, help me get it cleaned off. Maybe this old cemetery can give us some answers to what happened to the people from this settlement."

Within the next twenty minutes, the old fallen-down tombstone laid uncovered. It was hard to read the inscription on it, but Thomas and Lorraine were determined that the name on it was Elizabeth Roberts. She was born 1834 and died 1865. "That's so sad," Lorraine said. "She was so young."

"Honey, it was a hard life for people back then. They grew old fast and died young. I wish her stone had more information on it."

"Yes, Thomas, but at least we know that there were people that lived here in 1865."

"Yes, that's true. I hope we will find more stones. Once we get this area cleared, we might. Then maybe that will give us more clues. We might even be able to solve some of this lost valley's mysteries."

"Yes, my darling, but we aren't going to do it tonight. It's getting late. If I am going to make you any supper, we had better go. The graves have been here all these years. I am sure they will wait for us one more day."

45

Linda and Harold's farm, July 20th

Daniel had his farm chores caught up for the day, so he decided to take the rest of day off to go fishing with Zach and Tim. They were fishing on the bank of the river near the bridge. Between the three young men, they had caught a good mess of fish. They were about ready to stop for the day when they heard a strange, chilling sound far off. They all looked in the direction of the noise and saw something in the distance.

"What the heck was that?" Zach asked. "It looked like something being chased."

"My guess is coyotes or wolves," Daniel answered.

"Yeah, but It was something bigger than a coyote. Almost looked like a bear on his hind legs," Tim suggested.

Zack gave his brother a nasty look and said, "That's just stupid! A bear can't run standing up!"

Tim laughed and said, "Maybe it was Big Foot!" They all got a big laugh over that.

When the laughter subsided, Daniel said, "Hey, guys, on a serious note, we really need to get over to the farms and warn Scott and

Harold. All the cows and the horses are out grazing. A large animal like that could easily harm or even kill one of the herd. Come on, let's get going."

* * * * *

The following morning, both Harold and Linda had a very busy day ahead of them. After breakfast, Harold went to the barn to feed and milk the cows. Linda washed the breakfast dishes. Next, she fed and bathed Brianna. She laid her down in her crib and went to the living room to take a break. As she was enjoying her midmorning break, she heard her husband at the door. She knew that he would have both hands full, carrying in the two pails of milk. She jumped up quickly and opened the door for her him.

"I've got two full buckets from those girls today," Harold proudly said.

Linda reached for one, "Here, I'll help you carry them back to the kitchen." In the kitchen, they poured the milk into the pasteurizer.

Harold had a wide grin on his face as he said, "Thank God, Albert got us hooked up with electricity yesterday. This will be a lot easier than heating the milk on the wood stove. This way, we know the milk has reached its correct temperature to ensure the germs are killed."

Next, Harold separated some of the cream so Linda could make butter and attempt to make cottage cheese.

Then the rest of the milk was put in glass jars that Linda had sterilized while she was cooking breakfast. The milk that had the heavy cream separated out was labeled Skim Milk; the rest was marked Whole Milk. They added these bottles to the rest of the bottles of milk that were in their small refrigerator. Soon there would be enough to share with the others. They were grateful that they no longer needed to keep the refrigerator full of ice to keep the milk cool. They now had electricity.

Linda took the cream and set it on the table to be churned into cottage cheese and butter. Next, she filled two pails of water and put them on the stove to heat because it was laundry day—the day of the week she dreaded the most.

Linda was busily separating the laundry when baby Brianna woke up crying. When she picked her up, her cotton diaper was a soaked mess. She changed her, but Brianna still fussed. Linda cuddled and rocked her baby in her arms as she repeated. "It's okay. It's okay. Don't cry. Mommy will get you a bottle warmed up as soon as she can." Linda took the baby with her into the kitchen. She opened up the refrigerator and took out a prepared baby bottle. Then, she filled a small pan with water and put it on the wooden cooking stove. Brianna began to cry harder. She wanted her bottle! Linda tried soothing her as she nervously said, "Yes, baby, Mama knows you are hungry, but this darn old stove doesn't work that fast. If Daddy hadn't dragged us up to this God forsaken place, Mama could have your bottle warmed in seconds."

Then a sudden pang of guilt hit her heart. Her mind raced on, *This place is not Godforsaken at all. God led us here. God is with us, each part of our journey. What is the matter with me? How could I have doubted that God exists?*

With Brianna in her arms and still crying, Linda knelt down on the kitchen floor and prayed, *Please, God, please, forgive me for doubting your presences in my life. You have proved repeatedly that you are in control. I am so sorry that I doubted you! I got so caught up in the world's pleasures I blocked you out of my life. I was so frightened, I won't let myself even believe in you anymore! How could I have done that? You are my Savior, my Lord! Dear God, please forgive all my sins. Please, forgive my rejection of you.*

Linda stood up and wiped away her tears. Brianna's bottle was doing a little dance in the hot pan as the water boiled rapidly around it. She quickly grabbed it out of the boiling water, nearly dropping it. It was hot enough to burn her fingers. She grabbed a kitchen towel and shook the bottle a few times to cool it down. Then she tested it on her arm. Linda yelled out, "Ouch!" She dumped out the boiling water, set the bottle back in the pan, and pumped some cold water into it. Brianna was really screaming up a storm. Linda tested the milk one more time. Now it was cool enough for the baby. While cradling Brianna in her arms, Linda put the nipple in her little mouth. Brianna's tiny little hands grasp hold of the bottle as she sucked on the nipple as if she was starving. Soon, Brianna was a contented baby, and at last, Linda's heart was contented, as well.

After the bottle and another change of diaper, Linda said, "Okay, Brianna, our laundry water is hot. Let's go out to the barn and see if we can get Daddy to help us lift it off the stove."

Harold was cleaning out the cow stalls when his wife and baby came into the barn. Harold called out, "Hi, how are my sweethearts?" With excitement in her step and Brianna on her hip, Linda hurried up to her husband. She threw her free arm around him and gave him a big kiss.

"What's that all about?" surprised Harold asked.

"What? Do I have to have an excuse to kiss my own husband?"

Harold laughed and said, "Of course not, but something is up. I haven't seen you this happy in months."

"Well, yes, you might say so! All of a sudden, it all became clear to me. How could I be so stupid to turn my back on my Savior! He is everything to me. Harold, I asked Jesus to forgive me. I know He has forgiven me for all my sins. I feel like a huge weight has been lifted off me. We have little time left on this earth. At least as we know it. I don't want to spend one more moment without living for my God!"

Harold put both of his arms around his wife and baby as he gave them each a hug. "I am so happy, Linda! Does that mean that you aren't mad at me anymore for becoming a Christian?"

Linda was laughing and crying all at the same time. "Of course! I am so happy that in spite of me, you still were able to be saved. Now I have the Christian family that I wanted before I rejected God. I couldn't be happier."

When they got back in the house, Harold reminded Linda that it was already afternoon, and he was getting quite hungry. "Oh, Harold, I'm sorry. I have been so busy time got away from me. I'll fix us a quick sandwich. Will that be okay with you?"

"Of course, darling. That would be great!"

After lunch, Harold grabbed the large, heavy boiling pail of water off the stove. He carried it over to the entry room off the kitchen. He dumped them into two old laundry tubs. Linda put Brianna in a playpen next to the tubs. She then began scrubbing the clothes with an old laundry scrub board. The laundry tubs and the scrub board were left in the farmhouse when they moved in.

After hand scrubbing the piles of laundry, Linda was exhausted. She still had the job of hanging them out on the line. She moved the playpen from the laundry area to outside. It was hard for her to carry the baby and drag the playpen out, so she got it just outside the door. The clothesline was a distance from Brianna, but she was able to keep an eye on her. It was getting late, and Linda was hurrying to get the clothes up. It was a windy day, and Linda was involved with hanging up a bed sheet, which is not the simplest thing to do.

From the baby's direction, she heard a strange muffled sound. Linda thought it was Brianna fussing about something. As she wrestled with the flipping sheet, she yelled out, "Just a minute, Brianna. Mama has to get this hung up so it doesn't drag on the ground and get all dirty." She hoped to calm her down just long enough to get that monstrous sheet hung. "Hush, baby, be good. Mama has to get this sheet hung up."

At that moment, Linda's mind was on getting her laundry done. It was getting late, and they were going to the Friday night fish fry at the boardinghouse. She needed to hurry and get done so she could help Harold finish his chores so they could get out of there in time. On top of that, she had to get the baby ready for the evening out. Linda felt overwhelmed. Finally, she had fought the wind and had won. The sheet was evenly hung on the line. She hurried over to her baby to see what all her fussing was about. Walking toward Breanna, Linda shouted out, "What's the matter? Is Mama's baby tired?"

When Linda got to the playpen, Brianna was cooing and playing with her toy. Linda still heard the sound. It was a whimpering sound coming from behind the playpen. About six feet away lay a large bloody animal down flat on the ground, watching Brianna. Linda grabbed her baby out of the playpen and frantically ran toward the barn. She yelled out, "Harold, Harold, come quickly!"

Hearing his wife's screams, Harold dropped his pitchfork and went running toward her and Brianna. Concerned, he yelled back to her, "What happened? What's wrong?"

Out of breath, Linda managed to say, "There's a big wolf, or maybe it's a large dog! I don't know, but he's all tore up and bloody! Harold, he is really hurt bad."

That made Harold remember what Daniel and the Wydeck boys had told him yesterday. The boys had told him about a large animal that appeared to be chasing something. He hadn't mention it to Linda because he didn't want to alarm her. He had only thought about keeping a closer eye on the cattle. He didn't think whatever it was would come close to the house.

Harold yelled, "Take the baby into the barn, and keep the doors closed. I'm going to the house to get the gun."

As Linda watched her husband run to the house, her mind raced, *He is going to shoot that poor creature! I can't let him shoot a wounded animal. Maybe it was trying to get me to help it. The poor thing didn't even growl at me. It was whimpering. It wanted me to help.*

It was trying to get help. Now he is going to get shot! That is just not right!
I have to stop Harold!

With the baby still in her arms, Linda ran back to the playpen.
The poor creature was in the same place. She sat Brianna back in the
playpen. Linda slowly inched her way toward the wounded animal,
talking to it as she slowly moved toward him. Harold came running
out of the house just as Linda was approaching the wounded animal.
He yelled out to her. "Linda, get away from that animal before he
bites you!"

Linda ignored her husband's warnings as she kept creeping
closer to the wounded animal.

Harold ran up behind his wife yelling at the animal, "Get! Get
out of here you mangy mutt!"

The wounded animal made an effort to get up but to no avail. It
stiffly fell back down. With the most pathetic eyes, the animal looked
directly into Linda's eyes. She could see the pain and pleading in his
eyes.

"Linda, get out of the way. I've got to put it out of its misery!"

"No! Don't shoot him! Please, Harold, he wants me to help
him. He came to me for help. We can get him help. He must be
starving. Please, honey, let me help this poor dog."

"Linda, we don't know if he even is a dog! He might be a coyote
or a wolf. He could be dangerous. Daniel stopped over yesterday and
told me that there was some huge animal chasing after something
yesterday."

"Maybe it was chasing him," Linda reasoned. "Maybe this poor
animal was able to get away before whatever it was killed him."

"That's why I have to put him out of his misery now, Linda. He
is suffering. It's the humane thing to do!"

"But there might be a chance we can save him." Linda took
a few steps closer and was now at arm's length away. Slowly, Linda
stretched out her hand toward the animal.

Harold yelled out, "No, Linda, don't touch him. He might bite you! He might have rabies!" It was too late. Linda had already reached out her hand and held it in front of the shaking animal. The creature looked at her with big brown eyes as he slowly tried to lick her hand.

Harold stood there looking at Linda in shock. "He could have hurt you! You're lucky he acts friendly. But, honey, he really looks messed up. I still think the humane thing to do here is to put him down."

Linda's eyes filled with tears. "No, Harold, you can't! We've got to give him a chance!"

"Linda, you live on a farm now. You need to learn how to cope with things like this. There will be times when it's necessary to put down animals."

"But he looked at me with pleading eyes. I know he wants me to help him. At least let me go get him some water."

Harold watched as his wife gently petted the animal's blood-drenched fur. He thought to himself, *There's no way this animal is going to make it, but how can I say no to her? She'd never forgive me if I didn't at least give it a chance. Maybe it will help her accept its death better if I give it a chance.*

"Okay, go get some water."

Linda ran to the house and pumped a bowl full of water. She hurried back to the ailing animal as fast as she could. She set the bowl down by his nose and said, "Hi, fellow, are you thirsty?" He did not react. "Come on, boy, you've got to drink something," Linda said as tears began to fill her eyes.

He laid there with his head flat on the ground and his tongue hanging out. Linda sprinkled a little water on his tongue. She then set the bowl next to his mouth. The animal slowly raised his head just enough to lap up the water a couple of times. His head then fell back down. Excitedly, Linda cried out, "Good boy, good boy." She looked up at Harold and said, "See, honey, he's going to be okay."

"Linda, be realistic! Just because he drank a couple sips of water doesn't mean he's going to make it."

"It means he has a chance, Harold. Go get Christina. If anyone can help, she can!"

"I'm not going to haul her away from Sam right now. Sam is much more important than some wild animal."

"Okay, but how about Rachael? She knows a lot about things like this. Please, go get her, Harold! Please?"

"She's not a veterinarian! She mends people, not animals!"

"Please, honey! Go see if she will help."

"All right, but everybody in the settlement will say I'm crazy for wasting my time on a stray animal that's almost dead. I'll leave you my gun in case he turns on you."

A half hour later, Rachael opened the door of the clinic. She was surprised to see Harold standing there. He seemed to be a bit hesitant to speak, so Rachael said, "Come in, Harold. What brings you to town? Is the baby all right?"

"Oh, sure, she's great."

"Good, good. Then you're here to visit with Sam?"

"Well, I have been wanting to come visit him, but I've been so busy at the farm. Rachael, the reason I'm here is to ask you a favor."

"Sure, Harold, you know I'd help you and Scotty with anything that needs to be done."

"Yes, I know, you've been very helpful on the farms. But no, this is a favor for Linda."

"Sure, I imagine she has her hands full with the baby and all. I know it is a big chore just keeping up with household duties here, let alone with a baby and farm chores."

"Yeah, Linda works very hard, but that's not it. You see, Linda is an animal lover. Some almost dead mutt wandered into the yard today. Linda thinks it can be saved. I wanted to put it down, but she got so upset I couldn't. She wanted me to come get you to help. Next to your mom, you have the most knowledge in that sort of thing."

"Thank you, Harold, for having faith in me. I'm not sure if I can do anything. I have only worked with people, not animals. Does it show any signs of rabies?"

"No, matter of fact, contrary to yelling at her to stay away from the wounded critter, she went and reached out to him. He licked her hand. Linda brought him some water. He was barely able to drink. He doesn't appear to be ferocious. I left the gun in case."

"Okay, I'll go ask Mom if it's all right with her if I go. Come along, she's in with Sam. You can say hi to him while I ask her."

Rachael and Harold walked into Sam's room. Harold visited with Sam a couple minutes, letting him know how sorry he was about his accident. Then Rachael asked her mother, "May I speak with you for a moment?"

"Sure, honey. Let's go over to the window to talk, and let Sam and Harold visit."

Rachael told her mother about the wounded animal that was close to death at Harold and Linda's farm. She told her that Harold was there asking for help to heal it. Christina gave Rachael a puzzling look as she said, "I don't know if you can help that poor animal or not, but I'm a little apprehensive about you working on a wounded animal by yourself."

Overhearing, some of the women's conversation, Sam suggested, "Christina, why don't you go with Rachael? You have been at my side day and night. You need a break from me." In a kidding way, he said, "To tell the truth, I need a break from you women."

Sam looked back at Harold and said, "These women are always hovering around me."

Christina went over to him and asked, "Sam, are you sure?" She touched his forehead and said, "No fever."

"There! See, I'm fine! Now, you ladies get out of here!"

"I don't feel right leaving you. What would you do if you needed something?"

"Michelle's around the house somewhere, isn't she?"

"Yes, but—"

"No buts about it! I'll be fine! Go, go!"

"Okay, but I'll be back as soon as possible," Christina said as she grabbed her medical bag. She let Michelle know and they both left with Harold.

When Harold got back to the farm, Linda was sitting on the ground, holding Brianna on her lap. Right beside them was the badly hurt animal. Linda was holding on to her baby while gently petting the animal with her free hand.

Harold was angry with Linda as he yelled out to her, "Linda get the baby away from that animal right now!"

Hearing the anger in her husband's voice, she jumped up. "Okay, okay!"

Linda looked over at Christina and Rachael and said, "Thank you, ladies, for coming! I'm sure you can do something for him, can't you?"

Christina looked down at the critter and said, "He doesn't look all that good, Linda, but we will try our best."

"That's all I ask."

Christina and Rachael were touched by the love Linda was showing the hurting animal. Christina then examined the canine. "Let's move him to the barn. Harold, would you please fix a bed of straw for him? Also, Linda, see if you can find an old blanket we can move him on."

Harold and Linda did as Christina had instructed, and soon, the wounded animal was being carried to the barn.

Old Town's fish fry, July 23rd

Over the next few days, Sam was beginning to regain his strength. With the exception of going out to the farm to nurse a torn up animal, Christina only left his side to eat and sleep. Rachael and Michelle took over all the household chores so their mother could care for Sam.

Christina and Sam enjoyed each other's company as their friendship was growing. They seemed to have a lot in common. Shedding a few tears together, they each talked about the grief of losing their spouses. Christina reminisced about her life in Africa with Dan. Sam talked about the many happy times he had shared with his late wife and boys. Sam even shared his out-of-body experience with her. He told her about the vision of being with his wife and boys and talking with Jesus. Christina assured him that what he had seen was probably a near-death experience. Years before, she had done a study on the subject and was convinced that God actually gives some people a glimpse of heaven when they are near death.

* * * * *

Behind the church, Thomas, Lorraine and the Wydeck boys were busy finding and uncovering gravestones. This had become a serious mission for Thomas and Lorraine. If for no other reason, it was to honor those who were buried there. Second of all, they wanted to gather information as to what really happened to this settlement over a century ago. Lorraine had brought along a pen and tablet and was recording everything they found on each tombstone. Thus far, they had uncovered six stones, and the information was beginning to mount up.

Thomas had asked Zach and Tim to help them work on the yard that day because Lorraine could only work on it until three o'clock. She would have to leave early to help with the fish fry. The Friday night fish fry was the favorite entertainment of the week, so she wanted to make sure everything was just right.

The day before, Zach, Tim, and Daniel caught a large mess of fish. They cleaned all the fish and had them ready so the ladies could have them in the frying pan by five thirty, just in time for everyone to gather.

That evening, even Sam was able to attend. Albert had helped him into a wheelchair and pushed him over to the boardinghouse. Tables were put together to make one big table so all the members of the small community could sit together.

When all were seated and the voices quieted down, Thomas began the blessing, "Our almighty Lord and Savior, we humbly come to you in thanksgiving. You have truly blessed our little group. We want to give thanks especially for our dear friend Sam and for his quick recovery. We are so blessed that with your healing hand, he will be good as new in a few weeks. We thank you for the abundance of fish you have graced us with. We thank you for the skillful fishermen that caught them and the loving hands that prepared them. Most of all, Lord, we want to praise you! Again, thank you for leading us to this bountiful forgotten valley. May we continue to do your will. We ask You to forgive us for our shortcomings and sins. For we know that in Romans 3:23, KJV it says, 'For all have sinned, and come short of the glory of God. You also tell us in Romans 6:23, KJV, 'For the wages of sin is death; but the gift of God is eternal life through Jesus Christ our Lord.' Even though the Holy Spirit lives in our hearts, we are still flesh, so please, forgive our weaknesses. Amen."

Sheryl sat with her head still bowed as she wondered why she was feeling so emotional. She wiped a tear from her eye and nervously looked at Scott sitting across the table from her.

Once again, as they passed around the fish and the various dishes, they had a fun and wonderful fellowship with their friends and family. The three young men shared their adventure while fishing a couple days earlier. They told of the mysterious large animal that was chasing something through the field.

Joe then asked Harold, "Hear you and Linda had some excitement out at your farm today?"

With a disgusted look on his face, Harold answered, "More of a nuisance! Some wild, half-dead animal came into the yard, and Linda wanted to save it."

"Was it a wolf or coyote?" Scott asked.

"Yeah, I guess it's something like that," Harold answered.

Linda spoke up, "I'm sure it's a dog. I know he has to have some German shepherd in him. Must be a mixed breed. I suppose he could be half wolf. Thanks to Christina and Rachael, they came over and patched him up."

Joe looked at Christina and laughed. "Is that so? Looks like our community has a veterinarian too."

Christina smiled and said, "I guess so. By the way, Linda, how is our patient doing?"

"Doesn't seem to be much of a change. I got him to take a few more drinks of water, but he's not interested in eating yet."

"That's because he is too weak to eat, Linda. As I told you before, I'm not sure if we can save him or not."

"At least you've done all you could. Now the rest is up to God," Linda said with a sad smile on her face.

When Lorraine and Thomas heard that, they both looked at each with big grins on their faces. Lorraine asked, "Excuse me, Linda, did I hear you say you were leaving it up to God?"

"Yes, Mother, I did!" Then tears began to fall from Linda's eyes as she blurted out, "Earlier today, the Holy Spirit spoke to my heart. I have been so wrong! I am so ashamed that I denied God. After all He has done for me! He died on the cross so I could have eternal life forever with Him. I let my selfish desires rule my life! Dad, what's that verse in the Bible that says the devil roams the earth devouring whomever?"

"Yes, honey, it's in 1 Peter 5:8, KJV. It says, 'Be sober, be vigilant; because your adversary the devil, as a roaring lion, walketh about seeking whom he may devour.'"

"Yes, that's the verse! Thanks, Dad. Thank God, the devil did not devour me! I let my God down, but he pulled me back to him again."

Thomas looked at his daughter and said, "That's God's assurance. He picked up his Bible and started thumbing through the pages. "God gave us that assurance in Ephesians 1:10–4, KJV. Here it is. I'll read it to you. 'That in the dispensation of the fullness of times he might gather together in one all things in Christ, both which are in heaven, and which are on earth; even in him: In whom also we have obtained an inheritance, being predestinated according to the purpose of him who worketh all things after the counsel of his own will. That we should be to the praise of his glory, who first, trusted in Christ. In whom ye also trusted, after that ye heard the word of truth, the gospel of your salvation in whom also after that ye believed, ye were sealed with that Holy Spirit of promise, which is the earnest of our inheritance until the redemption of the purchased possession, unto purchased possession, unto the praise of his glory.'"

Thomas closed his Bible and said to Linda, "So you see, my sweet daughter, once you have been saved, you are God's purchased possession. Jesus paid that debt on the cross. You can lose fellowship with the Lord, but you will always be His. You have His promise!" You could hear an Amen or two while they sat around the table. Then a reverent quietness filled the room.

After a bit, James looked over at Sam and said, "Sam, I can't tell you how happy I am to see you at the table tonight. How are you feeling, buddy? Any weakness?"

"Thanks, James, I'm thrilled to be here too! Even though I have had very good care from three lovely ladies, it really feels good to be getting out.

I'm a little weak yet, but don't worry." He smiled over at Christina and said, "The doc has given me strict orders. If I feel any dizziness or fatigue, I'm to let her know, pronto."

Then Marge looked from Thomas to Lorraine and asked, "How are things going at the old cemetery behind the church?"

"It's going great, Mom!" Lorraine responded. "Finding those old graves was a very exciting discovery! It is really neat! There is a wrought-iron fence completely surrounding its entire perimeter with a gate. It needs a lot of work, but the fence is all there. We found most of it lying on the ground covered in brushes and weeds."

"Yeah, it was a big find and a big job," Thomas said. "Lorraine and I have been working on it nonstop for several days. Zach and Tim gave us a hand today."

"How many graves did you find, Dad?"

"I'm not sure, Scott. Mom's got a list of them. How many were there, honey?"

"We were able to uncover eighteen headstones. They were all lying on the ground. Some we could not make out because they were too weather beaten, but we could read a few of them. I recorded what was on those stones. I haven't had time to study all the data I received from them yet. When I get some clue, I will let you all know. There is one thing I found out, though. The oldest tombstone we could read said that this man was buried in 1831. Therefore, that tells us that this village was started at least back in 1831. When we have all the headstones cleaned, we'll be able to have an estimated guess as to when this settlement ended."

After the meal, the women started cleaning up while the men sat around, drinking coffee and talking about their plans for the next day.

"Oh by the way," Joe said, "I wanted to let you know there is a cattle auction coming up Thursday afternoon. I thought Scott, Daniel, and Harold might want to go to it. Maybe you can find us a couple of good riding horses that we talked about." The men happily agreed.

Then Scott said, "I'm fairly caught up on the fields and the vegetable garden right now. I was thinking tomorrow would be an excellent time to take a hike. Maybe, taking another stab at locating the old copper mine. Anyone interested in going with me?"

"Hey, that sounds like a heck of an idea," James said. "I'm in, Scott!"

"Awesome, Granddad! How about the rest of you guys? Would you like to come?"

"I'd love to go, son!" Thomas said. "I need a break from that graveyard."

"That sounds like fun," Joe answered.

"I guess you better count me out," Harold said. "I have too many chores with the milking. On top of that, I don't want to leave Linda alone with that wild animal."

"About tomorrow," James said, "remember, guys, the old gent said it was only rumored that there was a mine on this land, but one way or the other, I want to find out!"

"Can Tim and I go too, Dad?" Zach asked his dad.

"Yeah, sure. I don't have a problem with my boys going. It'll be fun. Bring your guns along in case we run across a bear or deer. We could use the meat."

"Harold, I feel bad that you can't go," Scott said.

"Yeah, but I can't. There is too much to do around my farm. Those heifers have to be milked twice a day, every day! Then I've got to keep an eye on that mutt Linda adopted. I am afraid if it gets its strength back, it might turn on her. You can't trust wild animals."

"Hey, Harold, go ahead, and I'll look after the farm," Daniel said.

"Thanks, Daniel, but I know you want to go, right?"

Daniel smiled and said, "Yeah, but I know you've wanted to find the mine a lot longer than I have."

"Thanks, buddy, but no thanks. I better stay home. I've got a system with all the chores." Harold then chuckled and said, "I'd like to think this farm couldn't run without me."

"Okay," Daniel said. "If Harold doesn't change his mind, you guys can count me in!"

"How about you, Albert?" Thomas asked. "Do you want to go exploring with us guys?"

"Thanks, but I can't. I have a lot of work around here to do. I need to run into Gratiot to get some nails. Joe asked me to build some shelves here in the boardinghouse. He said that the women are going to need more room for their canning when the harvest is in."

"Albert, that can wait a day. Why don't you join us?" Joe asked.

"Thanks, Joe, but I don't want to get behind. I want to make sure those shelves are ready when all those vegetables start rolling in."

Sheryl and Rachael were wiping off the table while listening to the men's conversation. When Sheryl heard what Albert said, she walked up to him and put her hand on his shoulder. She smiled at him and said, "What's this I hear? You're going to be working in the boardinghouse a couple days?"

Albert got a big smile on his face as he answered her, "You heard right! I'm going to be under your feet for a couple days."

She patted his back a couple of times and said, "Cool!"

Scott's face flushed with jealousy as he heard them talking. He was not that happy about her staying at the boardinghouse alone with Albert, but he knew he had no right to say anything.

On the other hand, Rachael was delighted to see the flirtatious exchange between Sheryl and Albert. She went over to Scott with a playful grin on her face and said, "Scotty, you are going to teach me how to ride, aren't you? Why don't I go with you guys Thursday? I could help you pick out the horses."

Her mother overheard. "I don't think that going with the guys to the cattle sale would be a good idea, Rachael. There is enough work around the clinic to do. You don't need to help the guys pick out the horses! I'm sure they are capable of picking out the right horses on their own."

"Okay, Mom, sure." Rachael's heart sank. The idea of spending the day with Scott would have been a dream come true.

Sheryl chuckled inside and thought, *That is what you get for wanting to horn in on my man!* Her mood changed as she asked herself, *Your man? Come on, Sheryl, get a grip. He is not your man anymore. He barely speaks to you. I wonder what really is going on with him and Rachael.*

The rest of the women joined the men around the table as they all continued making plans. Marge spoke up and said, "You know, I believe tomorrow would be a good day for us ladies to go to town and buy the material for our curtains. The men will probably be gone most of the day exploring. That will give us plenty of time to shop."

"Good idea, honey," James told his wife. Joe thought it was a terrific idea also.

"So, who all is going shopping with me?" Marge asked.

"I really would like to, Marge, but I have responsibility here," Christina said. "If anybody should need me, I'll be here. However, my girls could go. They have good taste. I know they will pick out some nice material for the clinic."

Still a little angry about her mother's refusal to let her go with Scott, Rachael sarcastically answered, "No, thanks! There is too much work around here. Michelle, you can go pick out the clinic's material. I'm sure Mother has faith in your judgment."

"All right, I'd love to go!" Michelle said with a broad smile on her face.

Rachael bit her lip, thinking that she should have kept her mouth shut but felt she had made a point to her mother.

Linda got a big frown on her face as she said, "I'd love to go with you, Grandma, but there's too much work around the farm, plus there's the baby."

"The baby! My land, Linda, bring Brianna along. She would enjoy an outing."

"Yeah, I guess, I could take Brianna, but I need to help Harold process the milk in the morning and at night."

"That's no problem," Scott spoke up. "Daniel and I can stop and help Harold with the morning milk processing before we leave to find the mine. If you ladies leave early, you could get back by the evening's milking, couldn't you?"

"Yes, of course. I'll make a point of it. Good thinking, grandson! What do you think Harold and Linda, would that work?"

"I don't know," Linda said with a little hesitation in her voice. "There is still that poor wounded animal in the barn. He will die if

I cannot get him to eat. He only drinks when I put his nose in the water. I couldn't leave him unattended."

"For heaven's sake, Linda, go with your grandmother. I'll watch over the mutt."

"Really, Harold? I thought you didn't want anything to do with him?"

"I came into town and picked up the doc, didn't I?"

"Yes, honey! Thank you so much! Yes, Grandma, Brianna and I can go."

"Now you, dear," Marge said as she turned to Sheryl. "I know Darlene is going. We have been talking about it for days. That only leaves you. Are you onboard?"

"You know what, I'd really enjoy going with you ladies. It would have really been fun picking out the pattern for the boardinghouse, but I feel I would be more helpful here. Albert will need some help holding boards. I'm happy to do whatever I can to make his work easier. I think I will stay here and help Albert, if you don't mind, Marge."

"No, dear, that is very nice of you to stay and give Albert a hand. I'm sure he will appreciate it. I know how you were looking forward to the shopping trip."

Hearing the conversation, Scott was not happy about Sheryl's decision, but Albert was elated.

47

Heartfelt stroll down Old Town's dusty road, late July 23rd

Later that evening, all the guest at the boardinghouse had gone home except for Scott and Daniel. Scott made a point to stick around until everyone else had gone. He had something on his mind, and he wanted to talk to Sheryl alone. Scott mustered up the courage and walked over to her and asked, "Would you take a walk with me?"

Sheryl's mind was racing. *Is this the night that Scotty is going to tell me that we are definitely through? That Rachael is more compatible for him, and he is falling in love with her?*

Hesitantly, she answered, "Yeah, sure, Scott, let's go."

As Sheryl and Scott walked out the door, Albert sat down next to Daniel and asked, "What's that all about?"

"What? Oh, you mean Scott asking Sheryl for a walk?"

"Yeah!"

"I don't know, but you do know that Scott had a history with her, right?"

"Of course, I did, but he's barely given her the time of day since she arrived. I thought he had a thing going with your sister."

"Rachael? Come on, Albert, my sisters and I have known Scott and Linda since we've been kids. Scott's dad was pastor at one of the churches that sponsored our family's mission. We stayed at their home during those times."

"Excuse me, Daniel, but Rachael acts like more than just a friend of Scott's. If you ask me, it really looks like she is in love with him."

"Well, I can't deny that she has always had a big crush on him. She has been hanging around the farm a lot lately."

"What about Scott? Has he ever had a crush on her?"

"Why all these questions? Have you got something going on with Sheryl?"

"Me? No, heck no! She is still hung up on Scott. I just thought that maybe he was ending it with her tonight. Maybe he is telling her right now that it's over between the two of them."

"And if it is? Would you pursue her?"

"I can't lie to you, Daniel. Yes, I would! I can't deny that I have feelings for Sheryl. I just hope Scott is getting off the fence and making a decision if he wants her or not. If he doesn't, then I'll be here for her!"

Meanwhile, Scott and Sheryl walked for a while down the dirt road without saying a word. Sheryl finally broke the silence. "So, Scotty, was there something on your mind, or did you think it was just a nice night for a walk?"

That lifted the tense mood between them, and both had a little chuckle. Then Scott got serious again. "Sheryl, is there something going on between you and Albert?"

"Why? What do you care? You have been treating me like a stranger ever since I moved up here!"

Scott stopped walking and put both hands on her shoulders as he looked her straight in the eyes. "Sheryl, I'm sorry if I made you feel that way. It has been very difficult for me because I still love you very much! I still want to be with you. Don't you know how hard it has been, keeping my distance from you?"

"Scott, that doesn't make any sense if you really love me!"

"Sheryl, we have been all through this! I can't be with you unless we are married, and I can't marry you if you are not a Christian!"

"Scott, you knew I was undecided about it when you said I could come up here."

"I know, I know! I keep hoping that the Holy Spirit would put a conviction on your heart. It gets me so frustrated when I see Albert putting moves on you! I really want you as my wife!"

"Let me get this straight. I don't believe what you believe, then there's no chance that I will be your wife? So how about Miss perfect Rachael? She seems to be a staunch believer, and it is evident that she is out to get you with all her charms!"

"Oh come on, Sheryl, we're just good friends. Maybe, Rachael does have a little crush on me. I don't know, but I don't look at her that way."

"Do you want me to lie and say I'm a Christian? I could put on an act if that's what it will take!"

"No! Of course not. You're no hypocrite!"

"Scotty, I'm just not sure! There are times when I hear your dad preach that I do believe in God, but the next day, I'm not sure again. This end-time stuff is hard for me to swallow. Tonight, when Linda testified, I felt something in my heart. Maybe I'm saved and don't know it."

"Sheryl, do you believe without a shadow of a doubt that what the Bible says is true?"

"I'm not sure."

"The Holy Bible is God's word! If you believe in God, you must also accept His Holy Bible as the truth. Everything written in the Bible is inspired by God Himself. Sheryl, unless you accept in your heart that Jesus Christ died on the cross to save you from your sins, you are not saved! Salvation is a gift from God. It's that simple! Either you accept that gift or not. When the Holy Spirit saves you, you will know it in your heart."

"Yes, I understand, but are you telling me that in the meantime, I have to sit around and watch you and Rachael get closer and closer?"

"Do you think it's easy for me to see the way you and Albert interact with each other? I have to live by myself while you and Albert live together in the boardinghouse alone! It's like you're playing house together."

"Playing house! What is that supposed to mean? It is not my fault that Sam fell and has to stay at the clinic!"

"No, Sheryl, but I can't help noticing the way the two of you look at each other. I can sense the chemistry between you guys. You almost act like a married couple."

"Have you forgotten the chemistry we used to share? Why should you even care? You don't love me anymore."

"But that's it! I do love you! And no, I have not forgotten the chemistry! That is why I have to keep my distance from you. Don't you think that I'd love to take you in my arms right now and never let go! You are such a temptation to me! I cannot help it, Sheryl, it really bothers me that you and Albert are here alone! You do everything for him like a wife would do. You cook for him, wash his clothes, and clean up after him. It's no secret you enjoy each other's company."

"Hold it right there, Scott! That is my job! And yes, we do have a good time together. He even helps me with supper dishes. I tell him he doesn't have to, but he insists. He says that way we will have more time to relax and have some fun. I need that, Scott! We talk a lot and sometimes play board games together. Albert has such a kind heart. Lately, I have been missing my mother and siblings a lot. I've really been worried about my mother. You remember she has a drinking problem, and who knows what else. Albert is a good listener and lets me cry on his shoulders. I know he has feelings for me, but we're just friends right now. Once he did kiss me, but only that one time. It was right after Sam's accident. All we had at that moment was each other. We just needed someone to lean on. We were both so vulnerable then."

"See what I mean! So how much did you lean on him? You act like a married couple."

"I bet he would accept me just like I am! I bet he would marry me no matter what I believed. It wouldn't matter to him, as long as I was a good wife!" Sheryl was so annoyed with him she ran back to the boardinghouse with tears flowing from her eyes. She burst through the door of the boardinghouse and went over to Daniel. "Scott's ready to go! He's waiting for you outside."

When Daniel walked out the door, Albert grabbed Sheryl by the shoulders and asked, "What did Scott say that's got you so upset?"

"I don't want to talk about it tonight," she said as she tore out of his grip. "I just want to go to my room! I'll see you in the morning."

Scott was sitting on the porch when Daniel walked up to him. He asked, "What is going on?"

Scott said in a gruff voice, "Get in the truck."

The two men got in the truck and headed back to the farm. Daniel couldn't keep silent. "Scott, why are you so angry and uptight? Why was Sheryl crying when she came in? Do you want to talk about it?"

"No, I don't want to talk about it."

"Okay, man, that's cool, but we've been friends for a long time. Scott, I'm sorry, but I need to get something off my chest."

"If you have to, go for it. What?"

"What is going on with you and my sister? I can see you are both flirtatious around each other. It is obvious that there are some serious feelings there. I know for a fact that Rachael is falling hard for you. Rachael told Michelle that she wants to marry you. Michelle told me. I don't want my sister to get hurt over all this. I'm sure it's just a matter of time, and Sheryl will see the truth and accept Jesus as her savior. Where will that leave my sister, then? I hope you aren't using Rachael to make Sheryl jealous!"

"Do you want to know what my intentions are toward your sister?" Scott laughed a little and said, "Okay. I guess that is your job as her big brother. I assure you, I will do nothing to hurt your sister. I love her too. I love her as a very close friend. I can't lie, sometimes I think about her as my wife. She would make a very good wife, but right now, I don't love her that way. However, I still don't want to give up our friendship. I've tried to tell her that, but I do realize that she has special feelings for me. If I could get over Sheryl, maybe then there would be a chance for us."

"I guess, I can't fault you for that. Sheryl is a very desirable woman. To tell you the truth, if I wasn't so close to you and your family, I'd make a move on her myself. I really can't blame Albert either!"

"But she's not saved!"

"Scott, there is still a good chance that she will be. Okay, that's all I've got to say. If there's anything you want to talk about, anytime, just let me know. I'm done talking about this tonight!"

"Yeah, sure, buddy, okay."

When Scott got home, he went straight to his room and fell to his knees beside the bed and prayed aloud.

"Dear God, am I wrong with the way I'm treating Sheryl? Am I wrong for not wanting to marry her because she's not a Christian? I know in your Holy Scriptures it says not to be unequally yoked together with unbelievers, but we have lived together! When I repented and was back in fellowship with you, I broke up with her. Oh, dear Lord, I am so confused! You also say in the Bible that when two are joined together, they are of one body and shall be of one flesh. Oh, God, I have been such a sinner! Before Sheryl, there were many others. I know I have asked your forgiveness, and you have forgiven me, but it's hard to forgive myself. Sheryl was different from all the others. I loved her and was committed to her. We even were going to get married, but then I felt convicted about being unequally yoked, so I left her. Dear God, please, help me to do the right thing. My dad is the spiritual leader of our community, and I have a seminary background. The people look up to my dad and me to be examples! What do I do? Please, dear Jesus, guide me. In Jesus Christ's name, Amen."

48

The town's mine, July 24ᵗʰ

The next morning, Scott had made up his mind that he was going to put Sheryl out of his thoughts for the day. He had convinced himself that this would be a much needed day of fun and relaxation shared with his dad, granddad, and friends.

After breakfast, Scott and Daniel met up with their fellow explorers in town. Joe and his boys each brought along their guns in case of a bear or any other aggressive creature. Scott and Daniel brought flashlights for everyone. Thomas had a knapsack full of sandwiches that Lorraine had made for the explorers. Darlene sent along a couple of thermoses of coffee, and Marge had made some cookies for them to take along as well.

Scott led the way as the small group of men started their day's journey. Daniel and the Wydeck boys followed close behind Scott while the older men trailed behind. Periodically, the younger men had to stop, letting the older men catch up. James was struggling hard to keep up the pace but tried not to let it show.

The men followed the winding trail, which was leading slowly up the mountainside. They had taken the same path several months ago. At that time, they had discovered a cave. At first, the men thought that it could be the mine. However, Thomas had surmised that it didn't look like a mine, that it looked more like just a plain cave. He guessed that it could be home for a bear. Back then, they decided not to go into the cave. It was getting late, and they didn't have flashlights or guns with them at that time.

After a thirty-five-minute hike up the side of the mountain, Scott spotted the cave that they had discovered months earlier. Next to him was Zach and Tim, who were just as excited as Scott. They stopped in front of the cave opening, waiting for the three older men to catch up. James was the last one to arrive. He looked for the closest rock and collapsed on it.

"Gramps, it looks like you are tired out." Scott looked concerned at his granddad and asked, "Why don't you sit here while we check out the cave? After that, we can call it a day if you are too tired."

"Oh hogwash," James said. "I'm a little slower than you youngsters are, but I can make it! I want to find that mine as bad as the rest of you, but if I'm holding you up?"

"No! No, Gramps. I can slow our pace down a bit. I'm sorry, I should have been more thoughtful of you. You are going to be eighty next month! It was just that I was so excited about finding the cave I wasn't thinking."

Joe's face showed concern. "James, old buddy, you do look a bit chalky, and you're wet with sweat, are you sure you are all right?"

"I'll be fine, Joe. I'll rest here for a bit while you guys go in and check out the cave."

Thomas was also concerned about his father-in-law but tried not to let it show. He told the rest, "Okay you guys go check out the cave. I'm going to wait here with Dad. I could use the rest myself."

"Good idea, Dad. If there's anything worth seeing, we'll let you know."

With flashlight in hand, Joe and Scott were the first to go into the cave. They had to bend down to get through the entrance. Zach, Tim, and Daniel followed behind them. After carefully making their way into the cave about twelve feet, they shined their lights up and saw that the ceiling of the cave was getting higher. Another three feet, and they were able to stand. Scott and Joe shined their lights from side to side and realized that they were in a good-sized chamber. The men walked around the edge of the cave's walls and determined that the cave ended there. Scott said, "Well, it looks like Dad was right. It's only a cave."

Zack flashed his light around on the dirt floor. "No doubt bears use it in the winter to hibernate. Look over there at the tracks," Zach said.

"Yeah, I believe you're right, son." Joe confirmed.

In its own right, the cave was an astounding discovery, but the mine was still the overshadowing criteria of their day's journey. After hearing the report from the men, James decided that he didn't need to see the cave. The rest seemed more important to him. Thomas, however, thought it was worth seeing, so Scotty guided his dad back into the cave. Thomas was also awe-inspired to see a bear's den out in the wild. Just a quick look satisfied him, and he was ready to pursue their journey of finding the mine.

An hour later, the men decided to stop and take another break. Joe looked over at James. He noticed that James was not looking well. He suggested, "Why don't us older guys go back home and let these young bucks search for the mine?"

"Oh come on, Joe, you might be sixty-one, but you are as fit as any of those youngsters. You are just worried about me! I'm all right now! We've had a few stops. I'm rested enough. I just want to find that darn mine."

"Are you sure, Gramps?" Scott asked as he gave his granddad a suspicious look.

"Sure, I'm sure, Scott! Now let's stop all this talk and go find that darn mine!"

"Okay, but we're going to slow the pace down some. Every twenty minutes, we'll take a break unless you need to stop sooner, Granddad. Will you promise me that you will tell someone if you need to stop?" Scott asked.

"Yeah, sure, Scott. I'll let you know." James chuckled a little.

Scott and the small group continued on, following the path. It led them over a small knoll and around a sharp curve. To their amazement, there it was! Right in front of them was the mine!

Scott was smiling from ear to ear. He looked at his dad and said, "How about it, Dad? It looks just like the entrance of the mines we went into while sightseeing. There's still some of the old iron rail tracks coming out from under the door."

"Yeah, Scott, and this entry is incased with the same crude framework and door that was on some of the ones we saw." Thomas's eyes followed the broken tracks to mounds of dirt. "Yeah, Scott, and there's where they dumped out the muck. There is no doubt, gentlemen, we have found the mine!"

There was a lot of growth covering the door. Daniel and Scott worked feverishly to free it. They tugged on the old door until it finally cracked opened a bit. The excitement grew tense as Scott held down the handle and pushed the creaking door open, just enough to get inside. It was pitch-dark inside when the men squeezed their way through the door. Each man had his own flashlight, so they were able to see somewhat.

"Did anyone think about bringing matches?" Scott asked as he saw a lantern hanging on a nail near the door.

"Yeah, I did," James answered. "I always keep a handful of stick matches with me to light Marge's cookstove."

"Awesome, Granddad. You're our hero!" Everyone looked as Scott held his light on the lantern. "Now if there is any oil in it after all these years, it'll be a miracle."

"Heck, even if there is some gas left in it, it would be a bigger miracle if it still works after all these years," Zach said as he laughed.

"Well, let's take a look," Daniel said as he reached out and grabbed the lantern. He shook it and said, "Praise the Lord, there is oil in it!"

Daniel took off the chimney and turned the knob on the lantern so the wick could be raised to light. James took a match out of his pocket, struck the match on the side of the wood frame, and then lit the wick. The lantern came to life and lit up the small entryway. Daniel and the others were shaking their heads in amazement that the lantern still worked as they continued to walk further into the mine.

Thomas noticed a row of aged, worn jackets and hard hats hanging on nails. Next to them were picks and shovels.

"Come here you guys!" Zach said as he and his brother noticed the cars sitting on the old track.

Tim yelled out, "This mine even has cars! There are two of them!"

The other men joined the excited brothers as they looked over the old cars.

"Let's follow along the track and see where it takes us," Scott suggested.

As the men walked next to the track, the passageway began to widen. Soon, it opened into a larger chamber.

"Looks like this area is about twenty-feet wide by fifteen," Joe said as he moved his lantern in a couple directions. "Let's walk around the walls and see if there's another passageway."

Just ahead of them was a big pile of rock and dirt. A couple of feet later, they found a smaller pile of rock.

"If I did my homework right, I believe we have stumbled on the old miner's last copper find," Joe said as he picked up a piece of the rock and examined it. He took his knife out of his pocket and scraped the dusty rock, and a little a copper color appeared. The men were excited but reverent over their discovery.

"And this was probably the pick that they last used to extract the copper from the rock," James said as he grabbed a pick that was leaning against the wall of the rock. He wiped a tear from his eyes. Each of the men hung their heads in deep respect and admiration to the men who had worked this small mine many years ago.

Scott led the men along the side of the chamber's wall until he came to another narrow passageway. It was about six feet wide. They all followed down its long and curving trail until James stopped and gasped for breath and then fell to his knees. Thomas was right behind him and was the first to reach him. He fell to his knees in front of James. In a loud voice, he cried out to him, "Dad, Dad, what's the matter?"

James forced out the words, "My chest, it hurts."

Scott cried out as he hurried to his granddad's side. "Granddad, what's wrong?"

Thomas answered his son, "It's his heart, son." Then the rest of the guys gathered around the aging man as he laid on the ground moaning with his hand to his chest.

"Quick, someone go get one of those cars!" Scott yelled.

Joe yelled at his sons, "Zach and Tim, you guys run back as fast as you can to town and get Christina!"

49

Boardinghouse, July 25th

Earlier that Saturday morning, Sheryl had made a hearty breakfast for her and Albert. As always, Albert was full of compliments about her cooking. Sheryl was quieter than usual while they ate their breakfast. Albert had wanted to bring up what happened between Scott and her but thought better of it. He finished his breakfast, stretched, and then went to gather the boards and supplies that he would need for making the new shelves.

Sheryl was happy that he would be there all day, working. She needed his company more than ever. Their friendship had been steadily growing, and she really needed a friend this morning more than ever. Sheryl hurried and did the breakfast dishes so she would be ready to help Albert with the task of building the large shelving area. The morning went quickly for both Sheryl and Albert. It was way past noon as Albert's stomach let out a loud growl. He apologized and said, "Must be that delicious breakfast you made me is wearing off."

"Oh, I'm so sorry, I didn't realize it was so late! You must be starving. It's way past lunch time."

"Don't be sorry! You have been working right alongside of me, but if you are getting hungry, maybe we should stop and get a bite."

The two of them enjoyed a sandwich together while laughing and discussing the morning's work. Albert suddenly stopped and romantically looked into Sheryl's eyes as he said, "Sheryl, I've never had so much fun working before! Thank you so much for helping me today. We make a good team! I know you were looking forward to that shopping trip to the city. You probably should have gone, but I'm glad you didn't."

"Me too, Al. I haven't had this much fun in a long time. I love your company, work or play. I just really enjoy doing things with you."

"Al! I haven't been called that since I was a kid!"

"I'm sorry, it just came out."

"No, no, I like the way you say it. Please, call me that from now on. It makes me feel like I'm...you know, special to you."

"And you are! You are one of the best friends I've ever had!"

"Sheryl, you know that you are very special to me too, don't you?"

"Yes, I believe so."

Then Albert blurted out, "Sheryl, I'm in love with you!"

"My dear, Al. I love you too but as a close friend. You know that I'm still in love with Scotty, right?"

"Yes, I know you have told me that, but he has really hurt you. I would never do that! You came in last night with tears running down your cheeks. What did he say to upset you so much?"

"Well, for one thing, he accused me of something going on between us. He's one to talk. Rachael is always flirting with him, and he doesn't seem to mind a bit! He says he still loves me, but he is not willing to be with me unless I'm a Christian. I couldn't tell him if I was a Christian or not. I don't know! With all that talk about an

Antichrist that wants to kill Christians, why would I want to become one?"

Albert answered her, "So you could be with the Lord for all eternity instead of burning in hell."

A chill ran up Sheryl's spine as she said, "Well, that would be true, if I bought into it. I did give up my family and lifestyle to follow Scott up here! You would think that would mean something to him."

"Yeah, and he should be able to see the change in you. You are the sweetest, loveliest woman I have ever met. I'm sure in no time you will be able to understand it all and be saved."

"Yes, you are probably right! I never went to church before. When Scotty and I were first together, he never even mentioned God. I didn't know that he went to a Bible college until we broke up. He told me that he had went to college, but he didn't say it was a Bible college. Then all of a sudden, Scotty tells me that he was a backslider. He said that he was going to change his ways and obey the Lord. I guess that included breaking up with me. I'm not really sure why he let me move up here. Maybe I should go home."

"No, Sheryl, don't do that! Please, stay here with me. I'm not like Scott. You don't have to prove yourself to me. I'd marry you in a heartbeat!"

Sheryl was touched by Albert's words as she gave him a loving smile. He took her in his arms and kissed her check a few times. He was about to kiss her lips. Sheryl's lips were willing until she glanced out the window. She noticed that Zach and Tim were franticly running toward the clinic.

Suddenly, Sheryl pulled away from Albert's arms. "Al, there's something wrong! I just saw the Wydeck brothers running into the clinic. They should be out looking for the mine with the others. Something is really wrong."

Both Sheryl and Albert ran across the street to the clinic. When they got to the door, Christina and the boys were already coming out. Zach was carrying the stretcher, and Tim had Christina's medical bag.

"Christina, what's happened?" Albert yelled out.

"It's James! Sounds like he had a heart attack while exploring the mine. Sheryl and Albert, can the two of you stay here with Sam while I go check on James?"

"Of course, Christina!"

"Are you sure you don't want me to go along and help?" Albert asked.

"No, it would be better if you stay here in case anything else happens. Rachael's out back hanging up clothes. She can help you if anything else changes."

Back at the mine, the men had just loaded James into one of the mining cars. James sputtered about it, but he too was concerned about the nagging pain in his chest. The car was small and uncomfortable for a six-foot man, but James wanted to get out of that old mine as soon as he could. It was hard for him to breathe in there. He wouldn't let on, but he was scared. He knew it was his heart. He worried about his wife. How could she survive without him?

Going back through the mine's passageways seemed to take much longer than it did coming in. When they came in, they had been all excited about exploring the mine, but now, their thoughts and concerns were focused on James. Finally, they reached the opening of the mine and saw daylight. With the help of adrenalin kicking in, Joe pushed the old heavy door to the mine wide open. Scott and Daniel carefully lifted James up out of the car. They carried him outside where they laid him down on a grassy area. Scott sat down beside him and held his grandfather's head and shoulders on his lap.

It seemed like hours before Christina arrived. As soon as she got there, Thomas filled her in to what had happened. Then Christina fell to her knees next to the dazed man and, in a loud voice, said, "James, James, can you hear me?"

"Yes," he muttered.

"Good! I want you to try to talk to me. Can you do that?"

"Yes, Christina."

"Okay, good! James, do you have any pain right now?"

"Yes, I do."

"Can you show me where it hurts?"

James pointed to his chest. He indicated that the pain was coming just left of the middle.

Christina ordered, "Quick hand me the medical bag!" Quickly, she opened her bag and pulled out a small bottle of nitro pills.

"Okay, James, I want you to open your mouth so I can put this nitroglycerin pill under your tongue."

James did as she had instructed. The pill melted under James's tongue. Soon after, James told her, "The pain is letting up, Christina." He touched his head with his hand and said, "I'm getting an awful headache."

"That's good, James. That means the nitro is working. Here, let me take your arm so I can check your blood pressure."

Scott wiped a tear from his eye and asked, "Is Granddad going to be all right, Christina?"

"Scott, it's too soon to know. Hopefully, the nitro will keep the pain away. It will also help his blood flow better. We'll wait here for another fifteen minutes, and if his pain is still gone, then we'll transport him back to the clinic."

After ten minutes had passed, James started sitting up. "I'm okay now. Let's get going!"

"Okay." Christina chuckled. "But you are going to have a ride back."

James looked at the stretcher that was being brought over to him. He grumbled, "No, no! That's not necessary. The boys had to carry me out of the mine. I'm not going to make them carry me all the way back to the town!"

"Now, James, I'm the doc here, not you! I say you are going to ride back. That's final!"

"Come on, Granddad," Scott said. "You won't be too heavy for us big strapping boys!"

"That's right, Dad," Thomas said. "Joe and I can take turns with Scott and Daniel."

"Yeah," Zach said. "Tim and I can help too."

They managed to get the grumbling elderly man on the stretcher. He wouldn't admit it to the others, but he really appreciated the ride. He was feeling weak, but he did not want to let it show.

50

Late afternoon, same day

Sheryl and Albert had been waiting impatiently for information about James for over two hours. Then they saw the van pull up to the Patterson's home. Sheryl cried out, "Oh my gosh, Marge and the others are back from the town. How are we going to tell Marge what happened to James?"

Albert answered, "I don't know, but we better get over to her home. We have to prepare her." He called out to Michelle, "Will you watch over Sam? The women are home from shopping. Marge has to be told about James!"

Albert quickly grabbed Sheryl by the hand and said, "We better hurry before they get back with James." Albert desperately prayed out loud, "Oh, dear God, please let James be all right!"

Sheryl looked up at the sky and prayed, "Yes, God, if you are out there, please save our dear friend."

Albert gave Sheryl a quick smile and said, "He's there all right, but it's in His hands now."

Sheryl and Albert ran out the door. They ran over to the van where the women were unloading all the new colorful material. They had had a wonderful time shopping, and they were all smiling and laughing as they were unloading the van. Linda looked up and saw Sheryl and Albert approaching and asked, "What's with the long faces?"

Albert quietly told her, "Linda, it's your granddad. We don't know the details, but the Wydeck boys came to get Christina to help. We need to talk to your grandmother."

Overhearing that there was something going on, Marge asked, "What's all the fuss?"

Sheryl put her arms around Marge and said, "We have some bad news for you." Marge almost went down, but Sheryl held her up.

"It's my James! Isn't it?" Marge's tears began to flow. "Is he all right? Please tell me my husband is all right!"

Albert could see that Sheryl was having a difficult time holding the grieving woman up. He stepped in and put his arms around her as he kindly said, "Marge, come on in the house and sit down. I'll tell you everything we know."

Albert led the grieving woman to a chair in her home. He sat down beside her and took her hand in his as he said to her, "Marge, the men found the mine, and while they were exploring it, James got tired out. Apparently, he had some discomfort in his chest."

"Oh no! No, Lord, not my James! Did he have a heart attack?"

"Marge, try not to worry, Christina is with him," he said, trying to assure her. "We don't really know anything yet, but he's in capable hands."

Knowing that something was wrong, Lorraine had followed Albert and Marge into the house. She listened to what he told her mother. Stepped in grief herself, she must put up a good front for her mother. She put her arms around her mother. They both held each other tight, trying to comfort each other. Then Lorraine said, "Mom, we need to get down on our knees and pray for Dad!"

"Will you please help me get on my knees?" Marge asked Albert.

When Marge and Lorraine were on their knees, the rest of the women joined them on their knees before God. Lorraine led them all in prayer, asking God to let James live and have a fast recovery. Then Linda tried to pray, but her sobs got in the way. It was difficult for anyone to understand her prayer because she was sobbing so hard, only God could hear her prayer. Brianna put her tiny arms around her mother's neck and whimpered. She knew that her mommy was unhappy.

Darlene was the next to pray for her dear friend James. Then Michelle said a short prayer. Albert finished the prayer circle. In Sheryl's heart, she felt like she wanted to say a prayer for James but she didn't feel she had the right. After all, she still didn't know if she believed in God or not. Besides, she didn't want to appear as a hypocrite. For some reason, perhaps out of desperation, she caught herself silently praying for James's recovery.

Scott and Daniel were carrying James on the stretcher when they got into town. As they started to pass by Marge and James's home, Christina could hear someone praying.

"Stop!" Christina ordered. "Do you hear the praying? It's coming from his cabin. I'm sure God's Holy Spirit is in that house today! God is the best physician. Let's take him home."

Christina opened up the door while Scott and Daniel carried James in on the stretcher. Everyone got out of the way so they could take James to his wife. Albert helped Marge up from her knees.

"James! James, are you all right?" Marge called out as she burst into tears. Then between the sobs, she looked up at Christina and asked, "He is all right, isn't he?"

"Of course, I'm all right," he grumbled as he tried to sit up. "I just need to get off this darn stretcher and walk around a bit. I'll be all right."

"Not so quick, mister," Christina demanded. "Thomas and Joe are going to take you over to the clinic and give you a little bed rest first."

Sheryl told Christina, "While we were waiting for you to get home, Albert brought over a single bed from the boardinghouse. He set it up next to Sam's bed. Then I put clean linen on it, so it's ready for him." Christina was grateful for their help.

Christina got James all settled into the clinic. Marge was right by his side.

James smiled and gave his wife a wink as he said, "See, I'm doing just fine. Everybody has just been making a big fuss over nothing."

"You old fool," Marge said with a big frown. "I told you that running off and looking for that mine was not for an old goat like yourself. Darn it, James, you are going to be eighty next month! Act your age. You can't go running off with the youngsters, acting like a kid! You can't die and leave me here to face the Antichrist without you!"

James glanced around the room and saw concerned faces all around him. He joked, "Oh come on now, Marge. With all this family and friends around ready to support you, you would do just fine without me." He chuckled.

"James," Marge scolded, "you know that it wouldn't be the same without you! Would you want to go through this without me?"

"Of course not, honey, but it's not up to me or even you. It is up to the Lord! I think that God just gave us a little scare, that's all."

Marge looked up at Christina and said, "Be straight with me, Christina, did he have a heart attack?"

"Maybe we should go in the other room, Marge," Christina said with a little hesitation.

"Oh no, you don't, Doc," James said as he looked up and gave Christina a dirty look. "If you have anything to say about my condition, I want to know! You can be straight with me."

"He's right," Marge said. "James is strong. He can handle it. Our strength comes first from God and then from our love. Go ahead, tell us."

"Okay. First of all, after the examination and according to the symptoms, it is my opinion that James has suffered a heart attack. I feel that it was a mild one, but I can't be sure without more tests."

"Well, by all means, do them!" Marge ordered.

"Marge, I would if I could, but this clinic is not setup with the equipment that I would need. Those types of tests can only be carried out in a hospital lab."

"Okay, come on! Let's get him to the hospital," Marge frantically cried out.

"Marge, honey, calm down," James told his wife. "I am not going to the hospital! You know that we all pledged that we would never go to a hospital."

"Yes, James, I know that, but this is different! You might die if you don't go."

"Honey, if it's God's will; We have to accept it."

"Maybe, Marge is right, James," Christina said. "You might need a procedure or perhaps even open-heart surgery."

"My dear Christina, I'm touched by your concern, but we all agreed that we would never use a hospital. It would be too dangerous for all of us. I might have to go home to see the Lord a couple years before the rest of you, that's all."

Christina folded her arms and said, "All right, but you better follow all my orders, James Patterson!"

"Yes, ma'am."

"Actually, I'm as equipped in this clinic as we were in our hospital in Africa. We had heart attack patients there as well. I cannot do anything more for James here then what we could have done for them there. The most important medicine that we had there was prayer. When someone was down with a serious illness, all the village gathered together and prayed for them. I have already seen that here as well. So now as James said, it is up to the Lord.

Now I know you all want to be with him, but he needs his rest. I suggest that Marge should be the only one with him until she needs a break. Lorraine, you and your family can take turns. One at a time! As for you, Mr. Patterson, I want you to rest! "

Distress at Old Town's settlement, July 27ᵗʰ

Worried about her husband's heart attack, Marge stayed at the clinic with Christina. When she couldn't hold up anymore on the chair, there was a bed made for her in the mammoth living room. Knowing that James was in good hands, the rest of the group decided to wait for news at the boardinghouse. After all, they were just across the street in case James's condition changed. The men all gathered around to talk while Sheryl and Darlene started preparing their meal.

"Gentlemen," Joe said as he nervously rubbed his forehead. "This is not the best time to address this issue, but it has been on my mind ever since I was in town the other day. I've been waiting for the right time to bring it up. Not that this is a good time, but it simply can't wait any longer!"

"Joe, what is it! What news did you hear?" Thomas anxiously asked.

"Mark has informed me that after September first, all transactions will be done with a one-world money system. He thought we should know so we could transfer what money we have left into the new currencies. James and I each have a large amount of money left in the New York Bank. Mark told me that a lot of businesses are only accepting the new money system now! It will be getting harder each day we delay! We need to move on this as soon as possible," Joe said as his voice got louder. "I just don't know what we are going to do! To retrieve or exchange money, all parties on the loan must be present at the bank. Both our wives' names are on the loans. I didn't want our wives to go because New York is too dangerous. Now James has suffered a heart attack. I just don't know what we are going to do, but we needed to go get our money. We can't survive without it!"

"Granddad is in no shape to travel!" Scott shouted. "We don't even know if he will survive this heart attack or not!"

In a desperate voice, Joe said, "I know, I know, Scott! That's what has me so distressed. I'm worried about my old buddy! On the other hand, I'm concerned about our money! I'm not sure we can survive without that extra money. There is so much we need yet!"

"Maybe we should turn on the radio, see if there's any news about it," Thomas said with deep sadness.

Scott turned the radio on as a swift-talking journalist was bringing a special bulletin.

The broadcaster nervously announced, "This is Eric Swanson from CNN News. I'm interrupting this program with breaking news, which is unfolding as I speak!"

Overhearing the broadcast, the women also gathered around the radio.

The news reporter cleared his throat and continued, "I'm here at Brussels, Belgium, just outside the Temple, the One-World United headquarters. The press has been here since early morning as President Hamarat started releasing information to the press. We have watched leaders and diplomats from all ten nations, including President Omidi, entering the Temple all day.

Just a few days ago, we brought you the breaking news that Russia has taken responsibility for the Washington D. C. and England bombings that happened several months ago. We also reported that intelligence tells us that Russia has plans in the works to bomb Paris, Berlin, and Tokyo. The intelligence department of the One-World United Army has squashed those efforts.

One can only speculate what the reason for today's collection of top dignitaries of the world are here for. Could it be that all these heads of the nations are here to discuss the consequences that are rightly due Russia?"

"Go, One-World United!" Sheryl cheered. "With our nation in total lawlessness, we are lucky to have a powerful army like that."

"Lucky, really?" Scott asked as he gave Sheryl a disgusting look. "The One-World United is our enemy. The OWU organization now controls our world, but soon, the Antichrist will be in control of it."

"Well, thank goodness for the OWU Army," Sheryl snapped back. "It is the only army we have."

"Of course, I know," Scott said. "That's my point. Their army is already policing most of the world. There's the militia, but unfortunately, you can't tell what ones are the radical ones or not. Besides, they are illegal now."

Thomas scolded, "Shall we just listen now? You guys can discuss that later."

"Yes, sure, Dad. I'm sorry."

"I'm sorry too, Thomas," Sheryl said.

The journalist went on filling up air space with facts and figures until more news could come trickling in. "We've been here outside the site of the Temple now for hours," the reporter said. "During this time, we have brought you some exciting news, but the kings of the world are still all locked together behind closed doors. You can rest assured that this journalist will stay here until all the news is reported. Wait! There's something about to go down. The meeting has just been dismissed. Leaders are filing back into the hall. No! Wait! Wait a minute. I just got word that the OWU press secretary is going to give a statement in the meeting hall."

Then the secretary walked up to the podium. "People of the world, as you know, our world has been in a turmoil of late because of wars and terrorism. As you can see from current events, this is not being tolerated! When there are crimes committed against our newly formed united world, we will retaliate! We will crush our enemies! The only way that we can do this is to unite as a one-world power.

Recently, as you all know, the European Union and the United Nations have united, making this union the most powerful government in the world! Now it is my pleasure to report that all of the ten nations have agreed here today to become a united world power! Even the Russians and the Middle East countries have surrendered to the One-Word United government! Both regions took our nuclear threats seriously! This is the only way to have peace in the world. After several hours of deliberation, the new One-World United has nominated a king to rule over the whole world!"

There was cheering and applause all over the large auditorium. Then with sheer excitement, the secretary announced, "I'd like to introduce to you the king of the newly formed One-World Union! It is my pleasure to introduce to you our new king." The applause grew louder and louder.

"Darn," Scott said. "I didn't catch his name. Did any of you?"

"No," Joe said in a rough voice. "There's too much clapping and cheering. Must be the world is happy with their decision."

"Listen," Scott said. "They're going to repeat it."

Everyone was glued to the radio in anticipation! They all wondered who it would be! There were some guesses, some very good possibilities, but no one knew exactly who he would be! There was one thing that this small group was sure of: he would not only be the world's king, but also, he would also be the diabolical Antichrist—the one who would be bringing deadly chaos to the Jews and Christians alike!

The reporter was about to repeat the name again when the radio became full of static. The station started to spit and sputtered as the volume became full of static.

"Oh shoot," Darlene said. "Just when we were about to hear the name of the Antichrist, the radio goes haywire! Scott, see if you can get another station in."

Scott tried, but all the stations were full of static.

"Well," Thomas said. "It really doesn't matter who it is! The first horseman of Revelation from chapter six has been released. He is the white horse of the apocalypse, the Antichrist. We only have about two and a half years before the Antichrist reveals his diabolical side."

"There's not much we can do for James. I don't know if he will live or die," Thomas continued with tears in his eye. "We're not sure if we can get our finances or if we are safe here from the Antichrist. All we know is that God led us here to this valley. Whatever happens to us, it will be His will."

About the Author

Judy's interest in writing began when God inspired her to write a book about a young woman and her two teenage children. Lorraine and her teen's everyday decisions allegedly lead all three to the fiery gates of hell. From her novel *Journey to the Great White Throne Judgment*, Judy has written this spin off end-time thriller filled with romance, *Prophecy of Wrath*.

A graduate from Baker College, Judy has a bachelor of arts degree, with a dual major in business and marketing. She pursued a career in both marketing and education. As an educator, she taught business at a community college, preschool, and worked as a substitute teacher. She also worked in retail management and held a position as a marketing representative. Fortunately, now that she has retired, she can fulfill the passion that God gave her for writing.

CPSIA information can be obtained
at www.ICGtesting.com
Printed in the USA
FFOW02n0349291116
29750FF